More Praise for

TO SANCTIFY THE WORLD

"Anyone interested in a bold yet authentic interpretation of Vatican II should read this book, in which George Weigel persuasively demonstrates that the Council—the Holy Spirit's greatest gift to Catholicism in the twentieth century—was not so much about reinventing and 'modernizing' the Church as Christifying and converting the world."

—Robert Barron, Bishop of Winona-Rochester and
founder, Word on Fire Catholic Ministries

"All of Weigel's best qualities are displayed here—penetrating intelligence, erudition, clarity, breadth of vision, remarkable range of insider's knowledge. I doubt that Vatican II—still bitterly contested in some quarters sixty years after the event—will ever be more interestingly or more accurately understood than in this deeply moving book."

—Lance Morrow, author of
God and Mammon

"In a time of widespread Christological amnesia and even denial, Weigel's new book offers a bracing remedy. He provides a magisterial recovery of the Christological vision and commitment that permeate the documents of the Second Vatican Council and that illuminate the Church's way forward. It is the way toward the sanctification of the world through living and sharing faith in Jesus Christ, who is the true joy of the Gospel."

—Robert Imbelli, author of
Rekindling the Christic Imagination

TO SANCTIFY
THE WORLD

ALSO BY GEORGE WEIGEL

*The Final Revolution: The Resistance Church
and the Collapse of Communism*

Letters to a Young Catholic

*The Cube and the Cathedral: Europe, America,
and Politics Without God*

Evangelical Catholicism: Deep Reform in the 21st-Century Church

Roman Pilgrimage: The Station Churches

The Fragility of Order: Catholic Reflections on Turbulent Times

*The Irony of Modern Catholic History: How the Church
Rediscovered Itself and Challenged the Modern World to Reform*

The Next Pope: The Office of Peter and a Church in Mission

THE JOHN PAUL II TRILOGY

Witness to Hope: The Biography of Pope John Paul II

*The End and the Beginning: Pope John Paul II—The Victory of
Freedom, the Last Years, the Legacy*

Lessons in Hope: My Unexpected Life with St. John Paul II

TO SANCTIFY
THE WORLD

The Vital Legacy of Vatican II

GEORGE WEIGEL

BASIC BOOKS
NEW YORK

Basic Books
Hachette Book Group
1290 Avenue of the Americas, New York, NY 10104
www.basicbooks.com

Printed in the United States of America
First Edition: October 2022

Published by Basic Books, an imprint of Perseus Books, LLC, a subsidiary of
Hachette Book Group, Inc. The Basic Books name and logo is a trademark
of the Hachette Book Group.

The Hachette Speakers Bureau provides a wide range of authors for speaking
events. To find out more, go to www.hachettespeakersbureau.com or call
(866) 376-6591.

The publisher is not responsible for websites (or their content) that are not
owned by the publisher.

Print book interior design by Linda Mark.

Library of Congress Cataloging-in-Publication Data
Names: Weigel, George, 1951- author.
Title: To sanctify the world : the vital legacy of Vatican II / George Weigel.
Description: First edition. | New York : Basic Books, 2022. | Includes
    bibliographical references and index.
Identifiers: LCCN 2022012426 | ISBN 9780465094318 (hardcover) |
    ISBN 9780465094325 (epub)
Subjects: LCSH: Vatican Council (2nd : 1962-1965 : Basilica di San Pietro in
    Vaticano) | Catholic Church—Doctrines.
Classification: LCC BX830 1962 .W385 2022 | DDC 262/.52—dc23/eng/20220627
LC record available at https://lccn.loc.gov/2022012426

ISBNs: 9780465094318 (hardcover), 9780465094325 (ebook)

LSC-C

Printing 1, 2022

For God sent the Son into the world, not to condemn the world, but that the world might be saved through him.

John 3.17

Jesus Christ is . . . the great hidden key to human history and the part we play in it.

Pope Paul VI, Homily in Manila,
November 29, 1970

For John

and in memory of Linda (1953–2020)

Contents

Contents

PART III
THE KEYS TO VATICAN II

The Documents of the Second Vatican Council

Gravissimum Educationis
> The Declaration on Christian Education

Inter Mirifica
> The Decree on the Means of Social Communication

Lumen Gentium
> The Dogmatic Constitution on the Church

Nostra Aetate
> The Declaration on the Relationship of the
> Church to Non-Christian Religions

Optatam Totius
> The Decree on Priestly Formation

Orientalium Ecclesiarum
> The Decree on the Eastern Catholic Churches

Perfectae Caritatis
> The Decree on the Appropriate Renewal of
> Religious Life

Presbyterorum Ordinis
> The Decree on the Ministry and Life of Priests

Sacrosanctum Concilium
> The Constitution on the Sacred Liturgy

Unitatis Redintegratio
> The Decree on Ecumenism

Introduction:
Reimagining Vatican II

THE SECOND ECUMENICAL COUNCIL OF THE VATICAN—
"Vatican II," in the familiar shorthand—was the most important event in the history of Catholicism since the Council of Trent responded to the various Protestant Reformations of the sixteenth century. The world shook the Catholic Church severely in the next four hundred years: the various European Enlightenments, the French Revolution, the nineteenth-century assault on the papacy and the Church by secular powers, three totalitarianisms, two world wars, the Cold War, and decolonization all had profound effects. Yet viewed from inside the household of faith, no Catholic event since the Council of Trent had so dramatic an impact on world Catholicism as the Second Vatican Council.

And virtually none has been so contentious.

Sixty years after it solemnly opened on October 11, 1962, the meaning of Vatican II remained controverted, and sometimes bitterly controverted, throughout the world Church. Some contemporary Catholic voices—no longer limited to the disaffected elderly but now including deeply committed young Catholics—claim that the Council was a fatal concession to the modern world that should be repudiated or quietly buried. Much of the German-speaking Catholic world seems to think that "the spirit of Vatican II" was an invitation to reinvent Catholicism as another liberal Protestant denomination. In Germany and elsewhere, prominent Catholic academics regard the Council as an unfortunate compromise that failed to achieve its great promise. In contrast, the new and vibrant local churches of sub-Saharan Africa consider Vatican II a great blessing, the Magna Carta for their tremendous growth.

These are arguments at the macro level; beneath them are the practical issues of daily Catholic life with which the people of the Church regularly contend. How should Catholics celebrate Mass, so that their worship enriches their lives and empowers them for mission? What does Catholicism have to say to the sexual revolution and the erosion of the family throughout the West? How is the faith to be transmitted to future generations—and what, precisely, is to be handed on? What, if anything, estranges a Catholic from the Church? What is Catholicism's response to contested issues of society, culture, and public life—and who speaks for the Church in these fields? How does the Church recover from the plague of clerical sexual abuse, reform itself, and bring healing and justice to the victims of these grave sins and crimes?

To many, including most of the cardinal-electors at the conclave of 2013, the pontificates of John Paul II (1978–2005) and Benedict XVI (2005–2013) settled the debate over what Vatican II taught and how that teaching should be embodied in the Church's pastoral practice. Many of the old questions and controversies about the Council burst back to the surface of Catholic life during the pontificate of Pope Francis, however. Relitigating those arguments has raised the temperature of Catholic debate beyond the boiling point on more than one occasion since the newly elected Argentine and Jesuit pope stepped out onto the Vatican basilica's Loggia of Blessings and greeted the crowds in St. Peter's Square on the evening of March 13, 2013.

This is not healthy. A Catholic Church endlessly debating what Vatican II meant is a Church disempowered in its proclamation of the Gospel of Jesus Christ and disengaged from its service to an ever more fractious postmodern world. A reimagining of the Council's purpose, and a fresh encounter with its teaching, is in order.

W hat, precisely, was "Vatican II"?

Vatican II, the actual conciliar assembly, met in four formal sessions (technically known as "periods") in the autumn months of 1962, 1963, 1964, and 1965. The pre-conciliar preparatory process was also a part of "Vatican II," however, and so was the work done on behalf of the Council during the months between its formal periods. And given the ongoing post-conciliar debates over its purpose and meaning, it seems fair to say that the *event* of Vatican II continues six decades after the Council opened.

It all began on January 25, 1959, when John XXIII, a newly elected pope chosen as an elderly placeholder, attended a service at the Basilica of St. Paul Outside the Walls during an octave of prayer for Christian unity. There, the genial, octogenarian pontiff stunned the Church and the world by announcing that he would summon an ecumenical council: a deliberative assembly of all the world's Catholic bishops. The shock came in part because some Catholic thinkers imagined that this venerable form of ecclesiastical gathering had been consigned to the dustbin of history in 1870 by the First Vatican Council's definition of the pope's infallible teaching authority. Others imagined that the unprecedented centralization of Church authority in Rome since Vatican I had rendered ecumenical councils irrelevant. Still others wondered why a seemingly rock-solid and self-confident religious institution should conduct a rigorous self-examination.

John XXIII, whose affability could conceal a penetrating insight into the Church's mid-twentieth-century situation, thought differently.

The event of Vatican II continued through a multiyear preparatory process, including an extensive consultation with bishops, superiors of religious orders of men, and pontifical faculties in Catholic universities around the world during what was known as the Council's "antepreparatory" period. The results of those consultations were then sifted through various pre-conciliar committees dominated by officials of the Roman Curia, the Church's central administrative bureaucracy. In this "preparatory" phase, the committees wrote draft texts for a council that members of the Curia and many of the world's bishops imagined would finish its work in a few months.

Yet within days of the Council's formal opening in October 1962, those expectations were falsified by events and it became clear that the Council would continue for some time. John XXIII died on June 3, 1963, between Vatican II's first and second periods. The conclave that elected his successor, Pope Paul VI, should be considered another moment in the event of Vatican II, as the question of whether the Council would continue—and if so, to what ends—was part of a rather bruising electoral process.[1]

More than a conclave happened between the end of Vatican II's first period on December 8, 1962, and the opening of its second period on September 29, 1963, however: during the months that conciliar historians call an "intersession." Conciliar commissions drafted documents to replace those that had been found inadequate during the Council's first period. Bishops and their theological advisers held consequential conversations about the proper way forward. And the new pope took steps to ensure that the Council would continue its work in an orderly fashion. This pattern, of conciliar commissions continuing to draft and redraft documents and groups of bishops consulting with each other on the issues, repeated itself during the 1963–1964 and 1964–1965 intersessions, with important consequences for the Second Vatican Council's substantive product, its sixteen documents.

From the narrowest of viewpoints, that of its formal periods, the Second Vatican Council thus began on October 11, 1962, when John XXIII solemnly opened the proceedings with an address of great consequence, and concluded on December 8, 1965, when Paul VI formally declared the Council closed at the end of its fourth period. A more accurate view of Vatican II as a historical event would mark it as beginning with John XXIII's announcement of his intention to summon a Council on January 25, 1959; note that the Council-as-event included its antepreparatory and preparatory phases (1959–1962), its formal periods (in the autumn months of 1962–1965), and the intersessions of 1963, 1964, and 1965; and mark its conclusion as December 8, 1965, when, after the closing ceremonies, some 2,400 bishops poured out of the Vatican basilica, then left Rome and returned to their dioceses. Even that widening of the historical lens is insufficient, though.

For Vatican II, the event, continues in the mid-twenty-first century as a Church of some 1.3 billion adherents strives to receive the Council's teaching and put it into practice in a vast array of diverse cultural, social, and political contexts. Moreover, different receptions of the Council define the fault lines in Catholicism throughout the world. And the sharpest of those fault lines are jagged indeed.

Some twenty-first-century partisans of the view that the Second Ecumenical Council of the Vatican was a terrible mistake have had their voices magnified by two phenomena no one saw coming at the time of Council—social media and the Internet—and the more fevered of these voices imagine the Council to have been the result of wicked conspiracies involving treasonous Catholics allied with malignant worldly powers.[2] Other voices claim that the Council began the Catholic Church anew: that what took place in Rome in the first half of the 1960s initiated a paradigm shift in Catholic self-understanding similar to the Copernican revolution in cosmology.[3] There is a striking similarity, however, between the voices claiming that the Council was a catastrophic mistake and those insisting that it ushered in a Brave New Catholicism. Both seem largely ignorant of the reasons why John XXIII thought an ecumenical council necessary, just as they seem unfamiliar with what Vatican II actually taught.

Then there are the vibrant parts of the world Church, which have embraced the Council as a summons to new evangelical and missionary energy. These Catholics are bringing Vatican II alive in parishes, dioceses, religious orders, renewal movements, evangelization initiatives, educational institutions, social service agencies, and medical facilities. And while many of the living parts of the Church have been inspired by the interpretation of the Council offered by Popes John Paul II and Benedict XVI, even these conciliar Catholics can be less than well informed about the deeper reasons behind the Council: why an essentially conservative and traditional pope, John XXIII, believed that the Catholic Church needed a new Pentecostal experience of the Holy Spirit as the third millennium of Christian history drew near.

In sum, few of those most involved in the ongoing Catholic debate over the continuing event of Vatican II have read the Council through the prism of its original intention. Doing so, however, offers the possibility of re-ballasting the Church so that successor generations of Catholics might realize John XXIII's great hope: that Vatican II would launch a new era of Christ-centered and evangelical Catholic vitality.

Although Catholicism regards the teaching of ecumenical councils as having unique solemnity and binding force, it has typically taken considerable lengths of time for those teachings to work their way into the rhythms of Catholic life. It took at least a century, for example, for the Church to really begin living the teaching of the Council of Trent, the Catholic "answer" to the Protestant Reformations. Any notion that Trent spoke, and the Church then snapped to attention and quickly implemented its reforms, is a fantasy.[4] The same difficult process of conciliar reception, at the level of ideas, and conciliar implementation, at the pastoral level, can be found in the history of the councils of the first millennium. That the decades between the formal conclusion of the Second Vatican Council in 1965 and the first decades of the twenty-first century have been turbulent and contentious would not have been a surprise to such giants of conciliar history as St. Athanasius and those who continued to battle the heresy of Arianism after the first ecumenical council, held in Nicaea in Asia Minor in 325; or to Pope St. Leo the Great, whose intervention in 451 determined the Council of Chalcedon's doctrinal course but failed to resolve the divisions in the Church over the relationship between divinity and humanity in Jesus Christ; or to St. Charles Borromeo, the heroic archbishop of Milan, whose attempts to implement the Council of Trent led one aggrieved man, furious at the archbishop's reform of a corrupt and wealthy religious order, to shoot him while he was celebrating Vespers in the chapel of his residence.[5] The bitterness displayed in many post–Vatican II contentions would have saddened John XXIII. But those contentions would not have altogether surprised him, for his special interest as a Church historian was Charles Borromeo.

Any proper consideration of the Second Ecumenical Council of the Vatican must look back before looking at the present and the future. That is, we must look closely at John XXIII's original intention for the Council and why he and others thought such an exercise necessary. Then we must look at the actual teaching of the Council. That teaching is found in Vatican II's sixteen texts, which must be read closely and in the proper order, such that the most doctrinally authoritative of them shape our understanding of how the Council addressed specific pastoral issues in the life of the Church.

The Council's sixteen texts were not self-interpreting, however, and the Council itself did not define their interrelationships. It took two men of the Council, Karol Wojtyła and Joseph Ratzinger, to offer the Church authoritative keys to Vatican II's proper inter-pretation: an epic project undertaken during their reigns as Pope John Paul II and Pope Benedict XVI, respectively. Those keys must be grasped, and the question of whether there is a "master key" to unlocking the deep meaning of Vatican II must be answered. Only then can any serious Catholic or sympathetic observer of Catholic affairs begin to assess the difficulties Catholicism has experienced in the post–Vatican II years and appreciate the Council's enduring, vital legacy.

This examination of Vatican II will follow that trajectory, addressing several large questions in the proper sequence: Was Vatican II necessary, and if so, why? What exactly did Vatican II teach, and how do those teachings reflect the Council's purposes in renewing the Church and sanctifying the world? What keys unlock the full meaning of the Council's teaching and define its legacy for the future?

PART I

WHY VATICAN II WAS NECESSARY

1

Crisis? What Crisis?

AS THE CATHOLIC CHURCH RECKONS THESE THINGS, THERE have been twenty-one ecumenical councils in two millennia of Christian history. Few were placid affairs. Little wonder, then, that St. Gregory of Nazianzus (a man later honored with the title "Doctor of the Church") should have declined an invitation to a meeting of bishops in 382 aimed at sorting out the work of the First Council of Constantinople: "To tell the truth, I am convinced that every assembly of bishops is to be avoided, for I have never experienced a happy ending to any such council; not even the abolition of abuses . . . but only ambition or wrangling about what was taking place."[1]

The first assembly of Church authorities to settle disputed questions dividing the Christian community was the apostolic council in Jerusalem described in Acts 15.1–30, thought to have been held c. AD 48. Although not numbered among the twenty-one ecumenical councils, that meeting, called to resolve the question of whether Gentile converts to Christianity would be required to undergo circumcision in order to enjoy the salvation won by Jesus Christ, set the pattern for the councils to follow: a dispute, often sharp-edged; debates over resolving the dispute; a resolution that could command an overwhelming consensus, even if some refused to join the consensus and continued straining the Church's unity afterward.

The first ecumenical council, strictly speaking, was the First Council of Nicaea, in 325. Nicaea I was summoned by the emperor Constantine to end the bitter, Church-dividing quarrel associated with the teaching of the Alexandrian theologian Arius, which was roiling both the Church and the Roman Empire. According to Arius, there was a time when "the Son was not"; that is, he whom Christian orthodoxy believed to be the Second Person of the Trinity—the Son who was "begotten" by the Father and who became incarnate in history as Jesus of Nazareth—was not God, but a divinized creation of God. The occasional bitterness of the debate at Nicaea I is illustrated by the story that the bishop Nicholas of Myra, who had been tortured during the pre-Constantinian persecution of the Church, and whose reputation for charity later became the inspiration for "jolly old St. Nicholas," took a most un-Santa-Claus-like punch at Arius during the Council's deliberations; the tale is almost certainly apocryphal, but nonetheless instructive as to the temper of the times. The orthodox view prevailed at Nicaea, and the Nicene Creed (still recited today) was written to confirm that Jesus Christ was "Light from Light, true God from true God, begotten not made, consubstantial with the Father." Yet Arianism and related heresies continued to disrupt the Church for decades, even centuries, and variants of Arianism have reappeared in different guises until the present.

With the question of Jesus's relationship to God the Father seemingly resolved, Church controversy focused on the question of the relationship between Christ's humanity and divinity. Was Jesus truly God and truly man, or was he God in a kind of human disguise, as the theologians known as "Monophysites" taught? Was it legitimate for the Church to honor Mary, Jesus's mother, with the title "Mother of God," or was that formula unacceptable? Nestorius, patriarch of Constantinople, took the latter position, which was condemned at the Council of Ephesus in 431, where Mary's title as *Theotokos*, or "God-bearer," was affirmed, and Christ's divinity thereby reaffirmed. In 451, the Council of

Chalcedon (influenced by an epistolary intervention from Pope Leo I) declared that there was both a divine nature and a fully human nature in the one person of Jesus Christ. As at Nicaea, the bishops of those councils, held under imperial authority, may have imagined that they had settled the questions at issue. Yet contrary to the decisions of Ephesus and Chalcedon, "Nestorianism" and "Monophysitism" continue today, to one degree or another, in several Eastern Christian Churches.

Such delicately calibrated theological arguments, conducted via metaphysical concepts and a technical vocabulary unfamiliar today, may seem arcane. Yet they were in fact Church-dividing in an era when "orthodoxy" was thought to be something worth fighting about, even dying for. Perhaps easier to grasp was the Church-dividing controversy over those masterpieces of Byzantine art—icons—that drove Eastern Christianity into warring camps for the better part of a century and a quarter. At issue was whether the veneration of icons violated the Second Commandment's proscription on making "images" of God (Exodus 20.4), and whether their use violated the Church's understanding of Christ's divine nature. In 726, the Byzantine emperor Leo III banned the use of icons, ordered their destruction, and persecuted those who refused to obey his decree; monks were eventually martyred in defense of their icons. Subsequent emperors got involved and the controversy raged on until, under the influence of the icon-revering dowager empress Irene, the Second Council of Nicaea in 787 affirmed the veneration of icons and allowed them to be publicly displayed. The controversy did not end there, however; imperial politics exacerbated it further, until the Iconoclast Controversy eventually burned itself out in the Christian East with the death in 842 of the iconoclast emperor Theophilus. Even then, bishops elsewhere in the world Church refused to accept Nicaea II, such that the Iconoclast Controversy in Western Christianity finally ended in the tenth century—only to be revived by the radical Reformations of the sixteenth century in their destruction of representational Christian artworks.[2]

Ecumenical councils in the first half of the second Christian millennium attempted to resolve a wide variety of Church-dividing disputes, with varying degrees of success. One of the more successful was the Council of Constance (1414–1417), which ended the scandalous "Great Schism" in the West, during which three rival claimants to the papacy split the Church asunder; yet Constance also created a centuries-long controversy over the relationship between councils and popes. Far less successful was the Fifth Lateran Council (1512–1517), so called because it met in the Papal Archbasilica of St. John Lateran in Rome: a failed attempt at identifying and then implementing essential reforms in the late medieval Church.[3]

Historians dispute whether Lateran V's failures of analysis and prescription were primary causes of the various sixteenth-century Reformations; whatever the outcome of that debate, Lateran V certainly failed to resolve the grave questions of ecclesiastical corruption that were one reason for the Protestants' break with Rome.[4] The Council of Trent, held over eighteen years in three stages (1545–1547, 1551–1552, and 1562–1563), thus had to deal with the ecclesiastical results of the splintering of Western Christendom. One might have thought that the greatest Christian crisis since the Muslim destruction of much of North African Christianity in the seventh and eighth centuries would have tempered controversies within the Council of Trent. But like so many of its predecessors, Trent was a difficult affair, given both theological controversies and the resistance of some clergy and political leaders to essential reforms. Trent eventually gave Catholicism a well-articulated doctrine and a solid basis for spiritual reform and growth. But it took decades for those "Tridentine" reforms to be implemented, and at least a century for the teachings of Trent to become the common self-understanding of the Catholic Church.

As these examples illustrate, ecumenical councils typically sought to address, and, if possible, to heal, divisions within the Church caused by doctrinal disputes and contradictory practices that led to the breakdown of ecclesial unity, or, in the technical term, ecclesial communion. Ecumenical councils, in short, were last-resort responses to Church-dividing crises when no other remedies had been found. It might be argued that the First Vatican Council, held in 1869–1870, was not such a last resort. But Vatican I certainly dealt with two Church-threatening crises: the profound challenge to Christian faith posed by Enlightenment rationalism, and the (not unrelated) attempts by various forms of political modernity to bring the Church to heel by fostering national Churches subordinate to the state. By affirming the reality of the supernatural order and the possibility of knowing the existence of God through reason, and by defining the pope's universal jurisdiction within the Catholic Church, Vatican I met at least some aspects of the crisis that had disturbed the Church since the French Revolution—indeed, since the revolution's intellectual antecedents in Voltaire and those other Enlightenment thinkers and publicists determined to, as Voltaire put it, *écrasez l'infâme*: "crush the infamy," the Catholic Church.

If ecumenical councils are responses to profound threats to the Church's unity or its very life, what was the crisis that necessitated the Second Ecumenical Council of the Vatican?

That question was asked immediately after John XXIII announced his intention to summon Vatican II. It was asked during the Council itself, especially by those dismayed by the Council's theological direction. And it continues to be asked today. So persistent a question deserves an answer.

The answer was given a century and a half ago by one of Catholicism's greatest modern minds and spirits, the nineteenth-century theologian John Henry Newman, whom the Catholic Church now recognizes as a saint.

On October 2, 1873, Newman, a founder of the reforming Oxford Movement within the Church of England whose historical studies eventually led him into full communion with the Catholic Church, was asked to preach the sermon at the opening of a new English seminary, St. Bernard's in Olton. It was a moment of great satisfaction for those who had long suffered under Great Britain's anti-Catholic penal laws. Newman, however, chose to describe in the sharpest terms the challenges that would be faced by the future priests being trained at St. Bernard's:

> I know that all times are perilous, and that in every time serious and anxious minds, alive to the honour of God and the needs of man, are apt to consider no times so perilous as their own. . . . [S]till I think that the trials which lay before us are such as would appal and make dizzy even such courageous hearts as St. Athanasius, St. Gregory I, or St. Gregory VII. And they would confess that dark as the prospect of their own day was to them severally, ours has a darkness different in kind from any that has been before it. . . . [For] *Christianity has never yet had experience of a world simply irreligious.*[5]

For almost 1,900 years, Catholicism had contended with false gods, superstitions, and heresies. Now, Newman claimed, it was challenged by something new, different, and ominous—a world closed in upon itself, yet confident of its own powers to facilitate personal happiness and a just society; a world of spiritual emptiness that, as another English Catholic would later protest, had "no end beyond its own satisfaction."[6] This "epidemic," as Newman called it, was widespread in "the educated world, scientific, literary, political, professional, artistic." It had infected those who defined society's mores and aspirations: the "thinking, speaking and acting England." That it would spill out into all of society from the cultural elite, Newman did not doubt.[7]

In such a claustrophobic world, what would happen to modernity's quest for a mature, liberated humanity, living freedom in justice and prosperity? If a society can only be as great as its spiritual aspirations, what would happen if there were no such aspirations—if the world should become, so to speak, ultramundane?

Eighty-six years before Pope John XXIII announced his intention to summon the Second Ecumenical Council of the Vatican, John Henry Newman identified the crisis that such an assembly of Catholic leaders would have to address: the challenge of proclaiming the Gospel of Jesus Christ amid the civilizational crisis of a modernity that had cut itself loose from some of its deepest cultural roots.

Understanding that crisis and its impacts on the course of history between Newman's prescient diagnosis and John XXIII's bold initiative is thus essential to understanding the necessity of Vatican II.

2

Modernity as Ideology

THE CHALLENGE TO CATHOLICISM POSED BY THE MODERN world was fundamentally a challenge in the order of ideas and culture. There was, of course, a political dimension to the challenge, the gravity of which sometimes masked the depth and seriousness of the cultural challenge—as did the often wooden-headed approach to new ideas of certain nineteenth-century churchmen. To recognize the severity of the challenge that modernity posed to Catholicism, however, and to grasp what was at stake in that confrontation, means recognizing that "modernity" ought not be understood as merely "the ways things are." Much more was afoot, according to conciliar historian John W. O'Malley, SJ:

> Modernity is a handy catchword for summing up what was at stake. The thinkers of the Enlightenment turned their backs on the past, turned their faces resolutely to the future, and looked forward to ever better things to come. Among those things was a new era of liberty, equality, and fraternity. Religion and monarchy would no longer shackle the human spirit. Freedom of expression and freedom of the press were rights that could not be denied. No more religious dogma, for Reason was the only god to be adored. . . . Modernity had become an ideology, perhaps several ideologies, all of them antagonistic in some measure to Catholicism.[1]

"Modernity" was not just the way things happened to be in the modern world. Modernity's expressions in social, cultural, and political life were carriers of an implicit (and sometimes explicit) anthropology: a concept of the human person.[2]

One root of the spiritual emptiness and self-absorption that threatened to shut modern humanity up within a dungeon of its own making could be found in the philosophical work of René Descartes, the inaugurator of the "turn to the subject" in Western philosophy. Descartes was a brilliant man who made significant contributions to mathematics and science. His most enduring cultural impact, however, was the result of his attempt to ground philosophy in the self-conscious subject. In a world in which everything could be doubted, the one thing Descartes could not doubt was that he was doubting—and doubting was a form of thought. And so Descartes devised his famous formula, "*Cogito ergo sum*" (I think, therefore I am), by which he intended to relaunch the entire Western philosophical enterprise from the self-reflective subject. Epistemology (thinking about thinking) subsequently displaced metaphysics (thinking about reality, and the deep truths embedded in reality) as the center of philosophy. And ideas, as ever, had consequences.

Over time, thinking about thinking would become thinking about thinking about thinking, and Western philosophy found itself caught in what the late twentieth-century Polish philosopher Wojciech Chudy once called the "trap of reflection."[3] Immanuel Kant's *Critique of Pure Reason* seemed to drive a stake through the heart of classical metaphysics and its claim to have identified the deep structures of reality. Post-Kantian Western thought thus found itself with no secure grasp on the permanent truth of things—no brake on the sloping path to a profound skepticism. That slippage became an avalanche when G.W.F. Hegel taught the West that history was everything. The flow of history

19

judged the past—including what centuries of Christians had understood to be divine revelation—rather than history being judged by permanent (even divinely warranted) standards of truth and falsehood, nobility and baseness that human beings could actually *know*.

Ideas begotten in the seventeenth and eighteenth centuries came to full flower in the ideology of modernity in the nineteenth: the century of what the French theologian Henri de Lubac, SJ, would later dub "the drama of atheistic humanism."[4] Building on the Enlightenment critique of Christianity that had eventually led to the enthronement of a Goddess of Reason in Paris's Notre-Dame Cathedral, that intellectual and cultural drama reversed Western high culture's relationship to biblical religion.

Through the People of Israel and later through Christianity, the God of the Bible entered the civilizational story of the West as a liberator. Unlike the fierce Canaanite gods who demanded and got human sacrifice, and unlike the gods of Olympus for whom even supremely powerful Greeks—think of Achilles—were ultimately playthings on a cosmic game board, the God of the Bible was neither bloodthirsty nor wantonly, whimsically cruel. The God of Israel did not demand the sacrifice of children; the God of Israel and the prophets who spoke in his name passionately decried such savagery. The God of Israel and the God of Christians did not play with humanity; that God entered the human story, first in his revelation of himself to Israel, and later in the person of his Son, to ennoble and redeem humanity by inviting men and women into communion with divinity.

According to de Lubac, the "atheistic humanists" of the nineteenth century taught precisely the opposite: that the God of the Bible, rather than being one of the inspirations of the Western humanistic tradition, was the enemy of human maturation and liberation. Various points in this indictment can be quickly noted from among the many thinkers de Lubac analyzed. Auguste Comte taught the nineteenth century that the only certain knowledge was empirically verifiable knowledge, and that natural science offered the only secure paradigm for understanding the world and the human condition: which rather read the God of the Bible out of the story. Ludwig Feuerbach went a step further and taught that "God" was a mythological projection of humanity's noblest aspirations. Karl Marx took Hegel beyond Hegel and taught that history was merely the exhaust fumes of impersonal economic processes, the "means of production." And Friedrich Nietzsche, drawing what seemed the appropriate conclusions from all this, stressed that the will to power, not the quest for truth, goodness, and beauty, was the driver of the human condition.

European high culture was deeply influenced by these men and by another towering figure in nineteenth-century European thought, Charles Darwin. *On the Origin of Species* and *The Descent of Man* certainly challenged traditional views of human origins. But more thoughtful Christians, recognizing that Genesis was not a history book as moderns understand "history," knew that the "descent" of *Homo sapiens* from more primitive life forms could be squared with the biblical account of humanity by stressing the unique, divine creation of the human soul. The more immediate, and lethal, problem with Darwinian evolutionary theory came from its translation into "social Darwinism," which in turn fueled a host of cultural pathologies, including eugenics and radical theories of racial superiority and inferiority.[5] Combined with nationalist passions and the Nietzschean will to power, these ideas not only challenged Catholic orthodoxy but also helped create a political tinderbox in Europe. Then, on June 28, 1914, the spark of the bullets from Gavrilo Princip's FN Browning M1910 set the European world aflame.

3

The New Thirty Years War

IN THE PREFACE TO HIS STUDY OF THE ATHEISTIC HUMANISTS, Henri de Lubac noted that, whatever their other differences, their common rejection of the God of the Bible ineluctably led to "the annihilation of the human person." That rejection of the biblical view of humanity, its origins, and its destiny had the gravest historical consequences: "It is not true, as is sometimes said, that man cannot organize the world without God. What is true is that, without God, he can only organize it against man. Exclusive humanism is inhuman humanism."[1] Modernity-as-ideology thus led to a New Thirty Years War, which shattered Western civilization between 1914 and 1945, leaving in its wake a Cold War that threatened the survival of the human race.

In the retrospect of more than a century, the "Great War," World War I, seems an exercise in civilizational suicide. Europe had experienced wars for millennia, but Europe had never experienced anything like this: as the historian Philipp Blom put it, "an overwhelming dystopia of technology run amok, leaving in its wake a trail of mangled corpses."[2] Europe went to war in 1914 with many of its traditional concepts of chivalrous military service intact. Those ideas, Blom recounted, were destroyed by a tsunami of artillery shells, especially in the trench warfare of the Western Front:

> Soldiers on both sides of the conflict experienced this mechanical apocalypse as a deep betrayal of their bravery and their will to sacrifice themselves for a just cause. Their courage was no match for industrialized slaughter; their very bodies were transformed into a raw material of death, almost indistinguishable from the grayish-brown mud around them, pounded and churned up so often by shells and grenades that it became transformed into an omnipresent slime reeking of corpses and human excrement, and swallowing boots and whole bodies like a putrid swamp.[3]

In his 1983 Templeton Prize Lecture, Aleksandr Solzhenitsyn described the Great War in terms of civilizational self-destruction and made the appropriate connection to the drama of atheistic humanism:

> The failings of human consciousness, deprived of its divine dimension, have been a determining factor in all the major crimes of this century. The first of these was World War I, and much of our present predicament can be traced back to it. That war . . . took place when Europe, bursting with health and abundance, fell into a rage of self-mutilation that could not but sap its strength for a century or more, and perhaps forever. The only possible explanation for this is a mental eclipse among the leaders of Europe due to their lost awareness of a Supreme Power above them.[4]

Solzhenitsyn's analysis is even more persuasive when the question turns from "Why did World War I begin?" to "Why did World War I continue?" When the guns of August 1914 first shattered the peace of Europe, everyone expected a short, brisk war, like

23

the Franco-Prussian War of 1870–1871. As things turned out, the more accurate model was the American Civil War of 1861–1865, and that became clear sooner rather than later. By early 1915 at the latest, it was obvious that the war was stalemated, both on the Western Front, where impenetrable trenches ran from the English Channel to the Swiss border, and on the Eastern Front, where neither Russia nor Germany and its ally Austria-Hungary could land a decisive, war-winning blow. Why, then, did no one have the authority to say "Stop!"—to pull the emergency brake that would keep the train of Western civilization from careening off a broken bridge into a chasm of destruction that would eventually leave behind the debris of four empires and three historic monarchies?

Some measure of responsibility for this must be charged to the moral account of Christian leaders. Pope Pius X died shortly after the German invasion of Belgium in August 1914. At the conclave to elect his successor, Cardinal Felix von Hartmann of Germany said, rather haughtily, to his Belgian colleague, Cardinal Désiré-Joseph Mercier, "I hope that we shall not speak of war"—to which Mercier replied, in something less than a fraternal spirit, "And I hope that we shall not speak of peace." Throughout the warring countries, clergy displayed a striking susceptibility to the hypernationalism fueled by social Darwinism, eugenics, and the crackpot racial theories that were by-products of atheistic humanism. Many seemed blind to what the Great Powers had set in motion. One German army chaplain preached to his troops, in perfervid terms, "Rage, over Germany, you great holy war of freedom. Tear down all that is rotten and sick, heal the wounds on the body of our German people and let a breed grow, a new breed, full of reverence for God, faithfulness to duty, and brotherly love." The Catholic bishop of the Austrian diocese of Seckau seemed to be looking at history through the wrong end of a telescope as he celebrated the beginning of the war as "the end of culture without God, without Christ, [and of] high politics without religion." Yet another German pastor preached that German troops would become "wonderful evangelists for idealism," while the Anglican bishop of London urged his countrymen to "kill Germans; kill them, not for the sake of killing, but to save the world. . . . [K]ill the good as well as the bad," because it was a "war for purity."[5]

Pope Benedict XV, a veteran diplomat elected to the papacy just weeks after the war broke out, tried to stem the tide of slaughter and refused to join the ranks of those who, from various, contradictory national perspectives, proclaimed the struggle a holy war. His inaugural encyclical on being called to the Apostolic See, *Ad Beatissimi Apostolorum,** included an extended plea for peace and identified two of the conflict's causes: a secularism detached from moral truths, and new forms of racism. Throughout the war, Pope Benedict urged a negotiated settlement and offered the services of the Holy See as a mediator between the two warring alliances. Italian anticlericalism, written into the agreement that brought Italy into the war on the side of Great Britain, Russia, and France, helped frustrate those efforts. Benedict's efforts at humanitarian relief during the Great War virtually bankrupted the Vatican, but none of his various peace plans got a serious hearing.[6]

Thus the carnage continued until the European belligerents had exhausted themselves morally, demographically, and economically, to the point where the Bolshevik Revolution in Russia and U.S. intervention on the Western Front tipped the balance against Germany and its allies and brought the war to a halt with the Armistice of November 11, 1918.

---

* The titles of papal and conciliar documents are taken from the first Latin words of a given text, known as the *incipit*. An *incipit* is sometimes pro forma, as here, or it can provide a succinct summary of a text's key point (as in the Dogmatic Constitution on the Church, *Lumen Gentium*, which anchors the Council's teaching on the Church in the conviction that Christ is the "Light of the Nations"). The *incipit* of a text is either explained or translated below when doing so helps clarify the content and purpose of the document.

A lethal cataclysm of the magnitude of World War I inevitably had profound cultural effects, especially given the optimism about the human future that was characteristic of European culture at the turn of the twentieth century. Tutored by science and unshackled from such traditional constraints as biblical religion, humanity was destined for sustainable, even limitless, progress. Or so it seemed in 1900. That confidence, a critical feature of the ideology of modernity, was shattered between August 1914 and November 1918. Postwar developments in science contributed to the cultural vertigo that followed.

In 1923, astronomer Edwin Hubble demonstrated that our galaxy was but one of an incalculable array of such galaxies in an expanding cosmos—a discovery that eroded what was left of humanity's sense of its central place in the universal scheme of things.[7] Werner Heisenberg upended what were long thought to be the certainties of the physical world with his quantum physics, which suggested that statistical probabilities, not the fixed laws that Isaac Newton and other founders of modern science thought governed the universe, were nature's bottom line at the basic, subatomic level.[8] And so the war that had shattered humanity's naïve confidence in its capabilities and falsified its certainties about progress was followed in short order by scientific discoveries that further diminished humanity's sense of itself in the vastness of the cosmos, and by a radical dismantling of certainty in the most prestigious of hard sciences, physics. The cultural uncertainties created by the Great War seemed underwritten by the authority of science.

The arts soon gave expression to a postwar cultural atmosphere of disdain for the old truths and values, anticipated in the antiwar poetry of men such as England's Wilfred Owen, writing of "The old Lie: *Dulce et decorum est, / Pro patria mori.*"[9] If the novels of Erich Maria Remarque (*All Quiet on the Western Front*) and Ernest Hemingway (*A Farewell to Arms*) embodied a generation's disillusionment with the greatness of the so-called Great War, Franz Kafka's work took on the vertigo of living in a world without moorings—a post-metaphysical world in which there were no fixed points of reference, no reliable moral truths.[10] If the conventional wisdom had led to the slaughters of Verdun and the depersonalization found in the nearby Douaumont Ossuary, with its piles of anonymous skeletal remains, then why take convention seriously in any form of human endeavor, including the arts? Jazz was a musical response to postwar culture's disdain for convention; so, one might argue, were the atonal compositions of Arnold Schoenberg and others. Dada was a self-consciously irrational, or perhaps better, anti-rational, postwar form of poetry, painting, design, and performance art. And while Dada and its cousin, Surrealism, could, by some accounts, trace their artistic pedigrees to early Modernist movements such as Post-Impressionism and Fauvism, the nonsense art of the Dadaists and the work of the Surrealists were as far removed from the art of Cézanne, van Gogh, Matisse, and Braque as those artists were from Rembrandt and Vermeer. That gulf, in both sensibility and artistic expression, was a cultural by-product of the First World War.[11]

Politics being downstream from culture, the deracination of European politics followed the deracination of European culture in the wake of the Great War. Indeed, that process of political decay began during the last phase of the war itself, when Lenin's Bolsheviks hijacked the Russian people's revolution in November 1917 and launched the world's first totalitarian state. Italian Fascism and German National Socialism followed in due course. Their rise to power was fueled in part by a lack of confidence in political liberalism, greatly exacerbated by the economic catastrophe of the Great Depression—which, in the German context, was crucial in undermining the Weimar Republic's experiment in democracy and bringing Adolf Hitler and the Nazis to power.[12]

Yet something else was involved in the rise of the totalitarian powers: an ultramundane quest for community in response to the atomization of society that often characterized modernity. Analyzing the tensions between *Gemeinschaft*—organic, traditional communities—and *Gesellschaft*—the rational, often impersonal associations that form the infrastructure of modern societies—had helped birth the discipline of sociology, and so the conundrums of modern social cohesion were not unknown before the Great War. But the war and the Great Depression accelerated the breakdown of traditional communities and fed the hunger for something to fill the void. The ersatz forms of *Gemeinschaft* promoted by the totalitarian powers promised to address that emptiness. That was an utterly false pledge, of course, as demonstrated by the fate of those who did not fit within the new community of class (such as the Ukrainians starved to death by Stalin in the Holodomor, the Terror Famine of 1932–1933) or race (European Jewry, slaughtered in its millions in the Holocaust, and all those others deemed unfit by Nazi eugenic and racial ideology).[13]

Viewed politically, totalitarianism was a by-product of the Great War. Viewed culturally, however, totalitarianism was an especially lethal product of modernity-as-ideology, and of the distorted view of the human person that had worked its way into the texture of European political life under the influence of atheistic humanism. Arthur Koestler chillingly captured that distortion in its communist form (of which there were echoes in fascism and Nazism) in *Darkness at Noon*, a fictional recreation of Stalin's show trials. In the novel, a condemned old Bolshevik, Rubashov, begins to doubt that his had been a well-lived life: "Looking back, it seemed that he had spent forty years in a mad frenzy. . . . Perhaps it wasn't healthy . . . to cut off the old ties, to disengage the brakes of 'thou shalt not.'"[14]

The rise of the totalitarian powers and their incompatible ideologies confirmed French marshal Ferdinand Foch's description of the Treaty of Versailles: "This is not Peace. It is an Armistice for twenty years."[15] So the New Thirty Years War continued with the even greater catastrophe of the Second World War.

Asked by President Franklin Roosevelt what the new global conflagration should be called, British prime minister Winston Churchill quickly replied, "The Unnecessary War."[16] Wiser policies by the victors in the Great War, Churchill insisted, could have prevented what ultimately became known as World War II. And there was surely much to criticize in the punitive actions taken by the Allies at Versailles, as there was in the lax response by the Western democracies to the first totalitarian aggressions in Abyssinia (Ethiopia), Austria, Albania, and Czechoslovakia, which did not appease, but only emboldened, Benito Mussolini and Hitler.[17] Yet if the totalitarian powers that launched Churchill's "Unnecessary War" were in fact the political expressions of a modernity unhinged—and unhinged precisely at the level of its dominant ideas about the nature of the human person and human community—then perhaps there were elements of inevitability to World War II. Hitler's racial theories, for example, could not indefinitely coexist with a Slavic great power occupying what the Nazi dictator regarded as Germany's *Lebensraum*, even if Stalin's USSR displayed many of the same totalitarian political characteristics as the Third Reich.

The causes of World War II will be contested for centuries. What is incontestable is that the second phase of modernity's New Thirty Years War was orders of magnitude greater in lethality. Estimates of World War I's military and civilian fatalities range from 15 million to 20 million dead. World War II killed three or four times as many human beings, soldiers and civilians alike, with noncombatants suffering the greater slaughter. More than 25 million died in the Soviet Union alone, and perhaps 15 million in China. Six million Poles, one-fifth of the country's prewar population in 1939, were dead by 1945, and Yugoslavia experienced somewhere between 1.5 million and 2 million deaths. Germany lost 4 million and Japan 2 million. Historian Gerhard Weinberg reckoned the total global death count at 60 million, one-tenth of whom were murdered Jews.[18]

Small wonder, then, that one of the great captains of the war, General of the Army Dwight D. Eisenhower, could write of World War II, decades later, that "the loss of lives that might have been creatively lived scars the mind of the modern world."[19]

And, he might have added, the soul.

4

The End of Christendom

T HE NEW THIRTY YEARS WAR OFFICIALLY ENDED ON SEP-
tember 2, 1945, when representatives of the Imperial Japanese Government signed the instruments of surrender on board
the battleship USS *Missouri* in Tokyo Bay. Like its predecessor,
however, the second global war of the twentieth century did not
settle the question of humanity's political future. A Cold War followed, featuring nuclear-armed powers holding each other hos-
tage and endangering the entire planet. During the Cold War, the
colonial empires that had been assembled in Africa and Asia since
the days of the Council of Trent were dismantled and dozens of
new states came onto the historical stage. And while the transformation of culture that had followed the Great War was not
replicated in quite so dramatic a fashion after World War II, urgent questions of human self-understanding had been sharpened
by the war, and new, perhaps even more urgent, questions had
been posed. Among them was the question of whether a shrinking
and globalized world, in which previously subject peoples were
claiming their independence in free states, could find a common
understanding of the human condition and a common ethic to
guide human affairs—and do so in an age of intense ideological
conflict down to first principles.

For the most alert Catholic minds of the mid-twentieth century,
the meaning of all this was clear: the Church was now living in

the situation John Henry Newman had presciently described in his Olton sermon in 1873. The Church was confronted by "a darkness different in kind from any that has been before it." The Church was living in "a world simply irreligious"—and particularly irreligious in Christianity's historical center of gravity, Europe.

To live in a world "simply irreligious" did not mean a world devoid of religious believers, of whom there were hundreds of millions. It meant a world in which the biblical view of the human person, the human community, human origins, and human destiny no longer had significant public traction among those whose decisions shaped the human future. It meant a world in which religion was increasingly considered a personal lifestyle choice rather than a matter of life-defining convictions and practices with eternal consequences. It meant a world that had passed through a moral and cultural trapgate from which there was no return to the past: hereafter, religious faith would be a conscious decision. It meant a world in which Catholicism would cease to be an ethnic, national, or cultural inheritance.

In a word, "Christendom" was over.

What was left of Christendom after the cataclysm of the French Revolution shattered the old order in Europe had been deconstructed culturally by the atheistic humanists, by Darwin, by the historical-critical method of reading ancient texts, by advances in physics and astronomy that reconfigured humanity's sense of its place in the cosmos, and by various schools of psychiatry, notably Freudianism. What was left of political Christendom after the French Revolution had been largely dismantled by various forms of anticlerical secularism in Europe in the nineteenth century; then the Great War administered the coup de grâce. The Catholic Church now faced the challenge of proclaiming the Gospel of Jesus Christ in a world after Passchendaele and Verdun; after the Gulag and the Holodomor; after Auschwitz and Treblinka and Ravensbrück; after the Rape of Nanking and the bombings of Rotterdam, London, Dresden, Tokyo, Hiroshima,

and Nagasaki. Humanity had not matured, as the secular prophets of nineteenth-century high culture had confidently predicted.
Civilization had come perilously close to self-immolation—and
still might do so in a nuclear war to end, not only all wars, but
humanity itself.

Christendom was over.

In its European heartland, Catholicism (and, more broadly,
Christianity) had lost the allegiance of both the intellectuals and
the working classes. That process had begun in the nineteenth century, if not earlier.[1] The disasters of the New Thirty Years War had
not driven the religiously disaffected back to the Church, however;
the disaffection had hardened and metastasized. Elements of the
old nineteenth-century anticlerical hostility remained in some intellectual and political quarters, and the Church was under severe
persecution by communist regimes after World War II. In Western
Europe, however, where Christianity and Catholicism had long
seemed most firmly anchored, the problem by the mid-twentieth
century was less one of overt animosity than of religious and spiritual boredom.

The *anima naturaliter Christiana*, the soul once naturally in-
clined to the God of the Bible and Christianity, seemed to have
withered; how might that human instinct for the transcendent,
for contact with a reality greater and nobler than we are, be re-
kindled? Or had that instinct been snuffed out for vast numbers
of people by the historical disasters of the New Thirty Years War?
How did men and women hear the voice of God in a world after
Auschwitz? How could those who claimed that they heard such
a word of revelation credibly share that conviction with others?
Those questions pressed hard on mid-twentieth-century Catholic leaders and thinkers who grasped the nature of the cataclysm
through which humanity had just passed.

Christendom was over.

Catholicism had not disappeared; in some parts of a shattered
Europe, and especially in a North America physically unscarred

by the world wars, Catholicism seemed to be flourishing. That flourishing now looks to have been the last flickering of the light of an exhausted Christendom. The candle would shortly be extinguished, and keener minds sensed that coming in the 1950s, perhaps even earlier. They saw that the symbiotic relationship of the Church to political power, which had begun with the Roman emperor Constantine, was breaking down, even if it was still maintained in one form or another in intensely Catholic venues such as Québec, Ireland, Spain, Portugal, and Bavaria. They understood that postwar social mores would, over time, no longer help transmit the Church's faith, but would undercut its teaching about righteous living. The cultural air, already full of toxins, would become ever more hostile to the God of the Bible and the biblical view of the human person; those who had received Catholicism as an ethnic or national identity, but who had not experienced a personal conversion to Christ and the Church, risked being hollowed out spiritually.

One of the first to sound the death knell of Christendom was a thirty-four-year-old Bavarian theologian who had just completed the "habilitation" degree that qualified him for a university professorship. His name was Joseph Ratzinger. In October 1958, the month Pope Pius XII died and left behind a Church that many still perceived as stable, vigorous, unshaken, and indeed unshakeable, Father Ratzinger published an article in *Hochland*, a German journal of ideas. His description of the end of Christendom and its impact on Catholicism was unsparing:

According to religious statistics, old Europe is still a part of the Earth that is almost completely Christian. But there is hardly another case in which everyone knows as well as they do here that the statistic is false: This so-called Christian Europe . . . has become the birthplace of a new paganism, which is growing steadily in the heart of the Church, and threatens to undermine her from within. The outward shape of the modern Church is determined essentially by the fact that, in a totally new way, she has become the Church of pagans, and is constantly becoming even more so. She is no longer, as she once was, a Church composed of pagans who have become Christians, but a Church of pagans who still call themselves Christians, but actually have become pagans.[2]

Ratzinger's stringent analysis of the spiritual condition of postwar Catholicism in its European heartland was not unique.[3] He put the matter more sharply than most, but similar concerns had been raised for decades. In response to those concerns about the end of Christendom and what that portended for the future of Catholicism, fresh approaches to proclaiming ancient truths had been explored by creative Catholic thinkers in the last half of the nineteenth century and the first six decades of the twentieth. That renewal of the Catholic mind was awaiting its historical moment. For its mid-twentieth-century protagonists believed that, given the opportunity, Catholicism's engagement with modernity could be reshaped, the Church given new vitality in the post-Christendom world, and effective pastoral responses devised to help repair the damage wrought by modernity-as-ideology and the New Thirty Years War.

5

The Renewal of the Catholic Mind

THE RESPONSE OF THE CATHOLIC CHURCH'S HIGHEST
teaching authority—the papacy—to the cultural, social, and
political challenges posed by modernity was, in the main, decidedly negative throughout the early and middle decades of the nineteenth century. During the Napoleonic era, Pope Pius VII first tried
to reach a rapprochement with the violent forces set loose by the
French Revolution (his predecessor, Pius VI, had died in exile after being kidnapped by French troops). But Napoleon's bullying,
which led to Pius VII's virtual imprisonment at Fontainebleau for
years, soured that project.[1] The status-quo-minded Congress of
Vienna in 1814–1815 restored Pius to power in the Papal States,
and the popes who succeeded him took an increasingly critical,
even acerbic, line on the modern project in all its forms, especially
after the revolutions of 1848 seemed to threaten the European
social order with anarchy.[2]

The apogee of this papal critique of modernity-as-ideology
was the *Syllabus of Errors*, issued by Pope Pius IX in 1864
as an appendix to an encyclical deploring various contemporary
errors, *Quanta Cura*.[3] Among the eighty false propositions it
condemned were claims that no serious Christian could possibly
accept. The *Syllabus* rejected the ideas that God did not exist,

that God did not act in history, that Jesus was a mythical figure, that the prophecies and miracles recorded in the Old and New Testaments were fictions, and that religious faith was ultimately irrational (devout Jews would reject many of those claims as well). Mirroring the concerns of Alexis de Tocqueville, and indeed anyone serious about the role of civil society in a democracy, the *Syllabus* condemned the notions that the Church only functioned in society with the permission of the state, that local Churches could publish letters from the pope only when the state agreed to their dissemination, and that the Church had no right to own property. And whatever the ideologues of the French Revolution may have thought, the American Founders and Framers would have agreed with Pius IX when he blasted the notion that "the state, being the origin and source of all rights, is endowed with a certain right not circumscribed by any limit"—a claim that could (and, as history eventually showed, did) lead to totalitarianism and the abrogation of civil and political rights.

Thus the *Syllabus of Errors* was not altogether a reactionary rejection of all things modern. Read with a degree of sympathy and an understanding of its intellectual context, parts of the *Syllabus* seem a prescient warning against the erosion of Western civilization's conviction—first articulated by classic Greek philosophy—that human beings could grasp the truth of things, including the moral truth of things, and thereby know their responsibilities and duties. Its last condemned proposition—that "the Roman Pontiff can and should reconcile himself with progress, liberalism, and modern civilization"—was a serious mistake, however. Such catch-all bluster seemed mindless and confirmed suspicions that Catholicism could never find its way in the world as it had become. The format of the *Syllabus* also obscured the appositeness of its critique of themes within the ideologies of modernity that deserved serious critique. At a moment in European cultural history when there was still some space open for debate, to condemn flatly and comprehensively rather than to argue and persuade was often taken to mean that the Catholic Church had no serious arguments to make, and that it relied exclusively on an authority that had long been called into question to support its truth claims.

Pius IX continued to address the challenges modernity posed to the Church in the First Vatican Council. Vatican I is primarily remembered for teaching that, under certain carefully defined circumstances, the pope could teach infallibly on faith and morals: a claim that many theologians had long held to be true but which had never been formally defined as such. The Council's definition of papal infallibility was, however, quickly and erroneously taken to mean that Catholics could not be reliable citizens, the argument being that the pope's claims on Catholics' loyalties would always trump the state's. William Ewart Gladstone tried to press this argument in Great Britain but was successfully refuted by John Henry Newman, who explained that the teaching authority of the pope as defined by Vatican I did not bind Catholics in their voting or their views on public policy.[4] German chancellor Otto von Bismarck used the definition of infallibility as one excuse for his Kulturkampf against the Catholic Church.[5] These post-conciliar political maneuvers illustrated the importance of another accomplishment of the First Vatican Council that is too little remarked.

Vatican I was in many respects the apogee of the "ultramontanism"—the extreme view of papal authority—that began among Catholics sympathetic to some aspects of modernity, but that migrated over time to the more stringently conservative sectors of Catholic thought.[6] The conservative ultramontanists were instrumental in achieving a definition of papal infallibility at the Council, although its language was far more constrained than they would have liked. But in their determination to concentrate authority in the papacy, the conservative ultramontanists, perhaps inadvertently, struck a blow for religious freedom and the liberty of the Church.

From the eighteenth-century "Enlightened Despotism" of the Habsburg emperor Joseph II through the French Revolution's "Civil

Constitution of the Clergy," and on to the Swiss Articles of Baden, the Italian Risorgimento, and the Bismarckian Kulturkampf, political modernity had sought to subjugate the Catholic Church, in part by separating local Catholic communities from the Church's Roman center and turning them into national Churches—pillars of the new nationalism then rising throughout Europe. Vatican I threw down the gauntlet to this state interference with the Church's internal affairs, which had festered for centuries but had become far more acute under political modernity. It did so in *Pastor Aeternus*, the Council's dogmatic constitution on the church. In addition to defining papal infallibility, *Pastor Aeternus* declared that the Bishop of Rome, the pope, exercised a universal jurisdiction throughout the world Church—an authority that could not be mediated through monarchs, prime ministers, presidents, or other supreme state authorities, particularly in such crucial matters as the appointment of bishops. Philosopher Russell Hittinger explained the implications of this assertion when he wrote that Vatican I

> solved a problem that had been simmering since the [early medieval] investiture controversy. To whom do bishops belong? Regalists would have said, "to the crown"; moderate regalists would have said, "to the apostolic college as supervised by the external bishopric of the crown"; the revolutionaries of 1789 said, "to the people constituted as a nation." The Council of 1870 said that they belong to the whole Church in which the pope exercises universal jurisdiction. . . .
>
> . . . *Pastor Aeternus* guaranteed that in whatever ways church-state relations might evolve, there would not be a restoration [of the old altar-and-throne arrangements].[7]

Thus Vatican I, rather than being the antithesis of Vatican II, in fact opened one of the paths that would lead to Vatican II's teachings on the Church's relationship to secular power and political modernity.

Despite the dominantly negative attitude in Rome toward virtually all aspects of modernity during the middle decades of the nineteenth century, the Catholic mind was not entombed in intellectual amber in those years.

Johann Adam Möhler (1796–1838), a German theologian and historian, worked to bring the first millennium's Fathers of the Church back into Catholic theology, from which they had largely been exiled for centuries. Through his retrieval of a great intellectual and spiritual patrimony, he developed an ecclesiology, a theology of the Church, that was more sacramental, spiritual, and organic than the prevailing Roman legal-juridical model, which, influenced by Catholicism's long entanglement with worldly power, conceived the Church as the *societas perfecta*, the "perfect society." Möhler's conviction that the Holy Spirit enlivened the Church throughout history also led him to a proto-ecumenism in which Catholicism engaged Protestantism rather than merely conducting polemics against other Christian communities.

Antonio Rosmini-Serbati (1797–1855), Italian Catholicism's most creative nineteenth-century mind, mounted a formidable challenge to both ecclesiastical intransigents (who rejected modernity root and branch) and secular liberals (for whom the past was an unmitigated horror). He was as concerned about the culturally corrosive effects of Enlightenment rationalism as more conservative Catholic thinkers were. Rather than just condemning rationalism, however, his philosophical studies explained the development of knowledge in all fields not through the workings of a Hegelian "World Spirit" but through growth that proceeded from fundamental principles that could be known with surety. Rosmini was also a Church reformer who understood that a Catholicism capable of making the case for the God of the Bible and the Gospel of Jesus Christ had to have a far better-educated clergy and laity; moreover, it could not be a Church that put state power behind its proposals. At the same time, he resisted political theories and practices that attempted to corral the Church within the confines of a putatively omnicompetent state.

Some of his contemporaries considered Matthias Joseph Scheeben (1835–1888) the greatest German theological talent since the sixteenth-century Reformations. Like Möhler, Scheeben worked to retrieve the insights of the great theologians of the first millennium, although, in his case, the emphasis was on the Eastern or Greek-speaking Fathers of the Church, including Athanasius, Cyril of Alexandria, and Gregory of Nyssa. Another of Scheeben's key themes—the spousal nature of God's supernatural love for humanity—prefigured major developments in twentieth-century Catholic thought. So did his insistence that Jesus Christ must always be at the center of the Church's proclamation and theology. In stressing divine love rather than divine judgment, Scheeben taught that the Son of God had become incarnate in history not only to repair the mess human beings had been making since Adam and Eve, but to fulfill God's purposes in creation and to make men and women "partakers of the divine life." Scheeben also sought a path beyond the ecclesiology of the "perfect society" and thought it lay in the concept of the Church as the "Mystical Body" of Christ in the world—the continuation of Christ's salvific mission over time. That image would become one of the intellectual pivots toward the Second Vatican Council via the teaching of Pope Pius XII.[8]

Creative Catholic thinking in the mid-nineteenth century did not neglect the challenges posed by political and economic modernity, the demise of the old monarchies, and the Industrial Revolution. Foremost among Catholicism's nineteenth-century social, political, and economic thinkers was the German bishop Wilhelm Emmanuel von Ketteler (1811–1877), a lawyer and Prussian civil servant before becoming a churchman. Ketteler laid much of the intellectual groundwork for twentieth-century Catholic social doctrine, drawing on the political theory of St. Thomas Aquinas to chart a path for modernizing societies that affirmed both the freedom of the individual and the imperative of using that freedom in service to the common good. Bishop Ketteler insisted that the Church rethink the problems of the new urban working class, which he said could not be ameliorated simply by charity; the Church must become an advocate for justice. A sharp critic of Manchesterian economic theories and practices that were one expression of social Darwinism, Ketteler also battled Marxists and other socialists who wanted to eradicate religion in their liberation of the proletariat, as well as Enlightenment liberals and rationalists who imagined religious conviction a species of self-bondage through self-deception. Ketteler thus anticipated twentieth-century Catholic social doctrine's position ahead of the usual liberal/conservative categories of political and economic analysis and prescription.

The greatest of nineteenth-century Catholic thinkers was John Henry Newman. Like Möhler and Scheeben, Newman was a great advocate of the theology of Church Fathers in the renewal of the Church's mind. He had a unique ability to make Catholicism make sense to people of anti-Catholic Great Britain, and his *Grammar of Ascent*, an imaginative exploration of the relationship between faith and reason, was deliberately aimed at ideological modernity's skepticism about humanity's capacity to get at the truth of anything. At the same time, Newman flatly rejected what he called the "great mischief" of "liberalism in religion," by which he meant "the doctrine that there is no positive truth in religion . . . [that] revealed religion is not a truth but a sentiment and a taste . . . and [that it is] the right of each individual to make it say just what strikes his fancy."[9]

Newman's most significant contribution to the renewal of Catholic intellectual life was his demonstration that Church doctrine develops organically over time. While the Church's mind does not change in any fundamental way, it does grow, such that the Church deepens its insight into the truths bequeathed to it by Christ. In his pathbreaking *Essay on the Development of Christian Doctrine*, Newman identified seven "notes," or criteria, for judging whether any given theological proposal was an authentic deepening of the Church's understanding of God's revelation. These criteria enabled the Church to distinguish true ecclesial developments from breaks with or diversions from the Christian tradition, and helped ensure that developing doctrines were firmly anchored in the truths of the Creed and "the faith which was once delivered to the saints" (Jude 1.3).[10]

Newman, like Möhler, Rosmini, Scheeben, and Ketteler, helped prepare the ground on which the Catholic Church could engage the modern world. That project was advanced by Pope Pius IX's successor, Pope Leo XIII, born Vincenzo Gioacchino Pecci in 1810. During some two decades as bishop of Perugia, where he was sent after his career in Vatican diplomacy stalled, Pecci thought through the challenges posed to Catholicism by both ideological and political modernity. He thus came to the papacy convinced that the defensive approach to modernity characteristic of the pontificates of Gregory XVI and Pius IX between 1830 and 1878 was no longer viable. Elected as an elderly placeholder, Leo XIII reigned for twenty-five years, and his pontificate decisively changed the course of modern Catholic history.

Leo XIII showed his hand early, in a gesture and an encyclical. The gesture was to create John Henry Newman a cardinal on May 12, 1879. By the standards of his age, Newman was an adventurous theologian and therefore a suspect figure to many conservative ultramontanists. For Leo XIII to raise him to the cardinalate was a signal to the entire Church: exploratory theology, anchored in the enduring truths of the tradition and respecting the norms of authentic development, was welcome in the Catholic Church. The implicit message was that if Catholicism were to have any impact in a world that imagined it had outgrown religious faith, it could not go on repeating the formulas that had failed to make any dent on the ideologies of modernity.

The encyclical, issued in August 1879, was *Aeterni Patris*, which promoted the renewal of Christian philosophy. By mandating the close study of the original texts of St. Thomas Aquinas, Pope Leo, himself a longtime student of Aquinas, hoped to develop a Catholic mind capable of grappling with the intellectual, cultural, and social challenges of modernity—just as Thomas had helped medieval Catholicism grapple with the new learning of his day, the recovery of Aristotle.[11] The brilliant Thomistic synthesis of faith and reason might, in Leo's judgment, help Catholicism to address the new learning of his time: to meet the intellectual challenges posed by Enlightenment and post-Enlightenment culture and do so without surrendering to the intellectual confusions of the modern world, as liberal Protestant thinkers such as Friedrich Schleiermacher had done.[12]

Leo XIII's program—the Leonine Revolution—included other intellectual elements that would play large roles in the renewal of the Catholic mind over time.

The Church could not ignore the impact of modern archaeological discoveries, modern studies of ancient languages, and new methods of historical research on biblical interpretation. So Leo, carefully but decisively, supported modern Catholic biblical studies with the 1892 encyclical *Providentissimus Deus*; a year earlier he had given his blessing to the École Biblique in Jerusalem, the Church's first institution of higher study to deploy the new historical-critical and linguistic methods of scriptural analysis.[13] He opened the Vatican Library and the Vatican Secret Archives to scholars of all faiths and none. Such openness to primary-source historical research, which he must have known would demonstrate that Catholic theology, and the Church's relationship to the world, evolved over time, was an implicit critique of the claims by some (including his two immediate papal predecessors) that no such change was possible—a claim which had led to the false notion that attempts to demonstrate development in Catholic self-understanding were inherently disloyal. Building on the work of Ketteler, whom he called his "great predecessor," Leo XIII inaugurated the papal tradition of modern Catholic social doctrine with the 1891 encyclical on capital and labor, *Rerum Novarum*, which championed the rights of workers while sharply criticizing Marxist concepts of the rightly ordered modern economy.[14] And in a series of encyclicals on political modernity, Leo slowly and cautiously opened the door to the possibility of a Catholic rapprochement with democracy and with states that did not privilege Catholicism—an opening influenced by the fact that, in the United States, Catholicism was prospering in a republic whose constitution separated the institutions of Church and state.[15]

Leo XIII's social doctrine was of particular importance for the renewal of the Catholic mind. Having discerned a hollowness at the center of political modernity caused by its skepticism about metaphysics and its focus on institutions and procedures, he worked to fill that emptiness with the deep truths about the person and society that, like Thomas Aquinas, he thought were embedded in the human condition and could be grasped by reason. As a Christian and a churchman, Leo certainly believed that reason ought to be amplified by biblical faith and informed by Catholic doctrine. Yet his social doctrine opened new opportunities for serious conversation between the Church and political modernity by making arguments in a vocabulary of public reason that could be engaged by anyone of goodwill. Thus, in his 1885 encyclical on the Christian constitution of states, *Immortale Dei*, he proposed that "the best parent and guardian of liberty amongst men is truth," understanding as he did that the question "What is truth?" can be asked in a genuinely searching rather than cynical way, and that such sincere questioning can open up the ethical question at the root of all political community, "How should we live together?"

Leo XIII challenged political modernity to think in a deeper way about the nature of law and freedom, about civil society and its relationship to the state, and about the limits and boundaries of state power, all the way down to first principles. In doing so, he devised the intellectual framework for his twentieth-century successors, who would have to develop Catholic social doctrine amid, and in the wake of, the New Thirty Years War.[16]

Pope Leo XIII was no revolutionary in the common sense of that word. He had no interest in kicking over the traces of Catholic doctrine. Rather, he wanted to develop the Church's thinking in order to engage the modern world. He also shared many of Pius IX's criticisms of modernity-as-ideology. His tomb in the Basilica of St. John Lateran, however, embodies the character of the Leonine Revolution, the sea change he effected in the Catholic approach to the modern world. In that funerary monument, a statue of Leo, wearing the papal tiara, stands atop the marble coffin that contains his mortal remains. His right foot is thrust forward, and his right hand is raised in a gesture of invitation, as if to say to modernity, "We have something to talk about. We have a proposal to make." With Leo XIII, a new Catholic era opened: an era in which the Church would engage modernity in an effort to convert it—and perhaps, thereby, help the modern world realize some of its aspirations to freedom, justice, solidarity, and prosperity.[17]

That, at least, was the hope of those who applauded the Leonine Revolution and wanted to develop it after the Pope's death in 1903. That development stalled during the papacy of Pius X, as the Church wrestled, not always wisely, with theological efforts to meet the challenge of cultural modernity that were condemned under the rubric of "Modernism." Because the term "Modernist" has been resurrected as an epithet in various twenty-first-century intra-Catholic conflicts over the intention and teaching of the Second Vatican Council, some clarification of the concerns and proposals of the "Modernists" of the early twentieth century is necessary.

In the 1907 decree condemning Modernist errors, *Lamentabili*, and the 1907 encyclical on Modernist teachings, *Pascendi Dominici*

Gregis, Pius X, who did not share Leo XIII's intellectual interests, and looked askance at aspects of his predecessor's program, condemned "Modernism" as "the synthesis of all heresies."[18] But what, in fact, was this "Modernism"? It is not easy to say, because Modernism was less a doctrine (like Arianism) or a coherent theological movement (like Lutheranism or Calvinism) than a set of intellectual tendencies.

Two of its emblematic figures—the French biblical scholar Alfred Loisy and the English Jesuit theologian George Tyrrell—shared, as historian John W. O'Malley observed, a "desire to help the Church reconcile itself with what they felt was best in intellectual culture" as it had developed in the nineteenth century.[19] Loisy, Tyrrell, and the other Modernists differed on many points, had no coordinated program, and did not conduct partisan campaigns in journals as both liberal and conservative ultramontanists had done in the mid-nineteenth century (especially before and during Vatican I). They did share certain convictions similar to those of liberal Protestant theologians and biblical scholars of the period. They thought that modern linguistic, archaeological, and historical studies had made it impossible to rely on the Bible as a source of historical fact. They could not see beyond what they regarded as Immanuel Kant's demolition of traditional metaphysics; and because of that, they tended to think of religious faith as a sentiment rather than an assent to truths. They displayed a naïve confidence in the natural sciences, thought Darwin had settled the question of human origins, and drank deeply from the wells of Hegelianism: history is all, present experience judges biblical revelation, and thus the Church must adapt itself to the spirit of the age, even if doing so required repudiating much of what Catholicism once thought to be true. Yves Congar, OP, one of the most influential theological advisers at the Second Vatican Council, identified the core problem here in the late 1930s: "Revelation, in the opinion of . . . Loisy, is nothing but human religious intuitions springing up as part of man's effort in search for the true and the perfect.

Dogma is only the authorized explanation of primitive assertions of the 'faith,' that is to say, of the religious consciousness. In Tyrrell's opinion, revelation is a 'prophetic' phenomenon, an internal ethic. The Church's guardianship of this deposit [of faith] is merely a custody of the heritage of an inspiration."[20]

Some of that heritage did require reexamination. It was hardly credible to insist that the entire edifice of Catholic truth stood or fell with maintaining that Moses had written the whole Pentateuch. Nor would it do to repeat the arguments that had sustained Catholic doctrine in the past, if those arguments could no longer be heard. Still, genuine Catholic reformers, such as John Henry Newman and the French philosopher Maurice Blondel (who emerged from much the same cultural milieu as Loisy and Tyrrell), did not share the Modernists' diminished sense of the reality of divine revelation, which reflected a more general skepticism about the supernatural and humanity's connection to the supernatural world. In his *Grammar of Assent*, Newman articulated a sophisticated modern philosophy of religious belief in which faith and reason worked together, challenging the Modernists' imitation of Ludwig Feuerbach in reducing faith to feeling. Blondel worked to construct a new Catholic metaphysics—a new Catholic understanding that there were deep truths built into the human condition and the human person—through his "philosophy of action." The Modernists seemed quite content to see metaphysics of any sort consigned to the rubbish heap of intellectual history.[21]

The Catholic Modernists condemned by *Lamentabili* and *Pascendi* tended to think of the Church as a society of well-intentioned good works rather than as a sacramental communion, brought into being by the incarnate Son of God to continue his redemptive and sanctifying mission in the world. That low ecclesiology or theology of the Church led to a disdain for ecclesiastical authority that amplified the Modernists' conflict with Rome, where Pius X had brought a country pastor's suspicion of intellectual elites to the papacy.

The result was tragedy all around. Loisy and Tyrrell were both excommunicated, and both died unreconciled to the Church. These individual tragedies were compounded by the ferocity with which Pius X and his associates sought to stamp out the "synthesis of all heresies." *Pascendi* set up mini-Inquisitions in Catholic universities and theological faculties to identify and dismiss suspected Modernists and to enforce the "Anti-Modernist Oath" that Pius X demanded of all clerics and consecrated religious in 1910. The innocent as well as the doctrinally dodgy were caught in the dragnet, and internal ecclesiastical and academic politics played unhelpful roles.[22] Matters became even worse when an ambitious Italian curialist who later found a home in the Italian fascist movement, Msgr. Umberto Benigni, formed a network of intellectual vigilantes, the *Sodalitium Pianum*, or Fellowship of Pius, who reported dubious colleagues around the world to the Roman authorities. Scholars of solid orthodoxy fell victim to this purge, and bullying and conspiracy theories too often displaced serious intellectual debate in many Catholic quarters.[23]

The truth of Catholic faith and the integrity of the Church were indeed threatened by the intellectual tendencies of the Catholic Modernists. Many of the ideas that Loisy and Tyrrell promoted as developments of doctrine were incompatible with John Henry Newman's seven "notes" of authentic development, and in fact involved a heretical rupture with settled doctrine. The Modernist crisis also hardened the sense in Rome that the only trustworthy theology was the form of Neo-Scholasticism taught in the various Roman pontifical universities—a way of doing theology that tended to reduce both dogma and theology to exercises in syllogistic logic that could be captured for all time in manuals.[24] This not only stifled the revival of the thought of Thomas Aquinas that Leo XIII sought; it also distorted the Roman cast of mind in the years after the Modernist crisis abated, as the Church's administrative center became habitually suspicious of developments in biblical studies and theology during and after the New Thirty Years War.

That defensiveness, and the resentments it fostered, would lead to an epic confrontation at the Second Vatican Council.

Pope Benedict XV quickly put a stop to the anti-Modernist pogrom when he assumed the papacy following Pius X's death in 1914. Benedict's inaugural encyclical called for an end to the theological civil war within the Church and deprived the *Sodalitium Pianum* of its papal sponsorship. An atmosphere suspicious of innovation, and a tendency to reject any attempt at theological development as a species of "Modernism," remained, however, for some time. So did the Anti-Modernist Oath, which was required of everyone seeking priestly ordination until 1967.

A similar atmosphere of vilification has been revived in the twenty-first century. In some Catholic quarters, the tendency to dismiss or condemn as "Modernism" any theological or liturgical idea deemed distasteful has become a nasty habit, redolent of the conspiracy theories of Umberto Benigni and the *Sodalitium Pianum*.[25] And while there are certainly currents of thought in the twenty-first-century Church that bear an uncomfortable resemblance to Loisy's and Tyrrell's anti-supernatural skepticism about the binding authority of divine revelation, there are ample intellectual resources with which to challenge and correct those tendencies, thanks to the renewal of the Catholic mind that the early twentieth-century Modernist controversy jeopardized. The twenty-first-century *reductio ad Modernismum* in certain circles is typically a substitute for thought, not serious Catholic thinking.

The Modernist crisis and the traumas of the New Thirty Years War notwithstanding, the renewal of the Catholic mind made impressive strides in the middle decades of the twentieth century.

One of the most influential theological movements in mid-twentieth-century Catholicism described itself as *ressourcement*: a Christ-centered return to the primary "sources" of Catholic thought in the Bible, the first-millennium Fathers of the Church, and the medieval theological masters, including Bonaventure, Duns Scotus, and Thomas Aquinas. In fact, though, the term *ressourcement* can be applied to the entire development of Catholic theological reflection in this period. For, according to the most creative Catholic minds of the mid-twentieth century, the "sources" to be conversation partners for theology included literature, modern philosophy, Christian mysticism, and history as well as older forms of theology. Thus, one of the premier *ressourcement* theologians, the Swiss polymath Hans Urs von Balthasar, would engage the thought of Dante, St. John of the Cross, Blaise Pascal, Johann Georg Hamann, Vladimir Soloviev, Gerard Manley Hopkins, and Charles Péguy, as well as the Church Fathers Irenaeus of Lyons and Augustine and the medievals Anselm and Bonaventure, in his massive work on "theological aesthetics," *The Glory of the Lord*.[26]

Although the renewal of Catholic theology took many forms, the different methods and interests of the *ressourcement* thinkers reflected a common, Christocentric conviction: dogma—the truths of Catholic faith—must once again disclose Christ and the Gospel, for the Church began with Christ and Christ's proclamation of the Kingdom of God among us.[27]

The Gospel had, over time, converted a considerable part of the Mediterranean world, leading to the full legalization of Christianity in the fourth century. That new public situation and the Church's expansion under it led to an intense encounter between Christianity and classical culture. Throughout this process, the Christian proclamation or kerygma—"Jesus is Lord"—was "translated" into creed and dogma, not least through the work of the first ecumenical councils. Over time, though, as Catholicism became a dominant cultural, social, and political force, the Church, rather than the Church's Lord, sometimes became the primary focus of belief. Nonetheless, the Gospel kerygma, the proclamation of Jesus Christ, remained the basic reference point for Christian faith, even after a millennium and a half of dogmatic development and definition.

The challenge of modernity-as-ideology did not change that; in fact, meeting that challenge underscored the centrality of Christ. For faith in a modern world, the *ressourcement* thinkers grasped, could not be just an assent to propositions, an agreement to syllogisms, or a surrender to ecclesiastical authority. Christian faith was, and always must be, an encounter with the person of Jesus Christ through the Bible, the sacraments, the preaching, and the witness of the Church. That was the kind of encounter that led to deep conversion—which was what Joseph Ratzinger, in his 1958 *Hochland* article, had found lacking in the seemingly secure Catholicism of Western Europe. The encounter with Christ could lead the Church out of its defensive crouch and reanimate Catholicism for its mission of converting and sanctifying the world, as Hans Urs von Balthasar argued in his 1952 book, *Razing the Bastions*.[28]

This emphasis on the ancient kerygma—the Church's basic proclamation of the lordship of Jesus Christ, crucified and risen—began to influence Catholic theology through the work of the German theologian Karl Adam. In his two most influential works, *The Spirit of Catholicism* (1927) and *Christ Our Brother* (1930), Adam stressed that the Church was first and foremost a community of believers—of people who had heard and accepted the kerygma, who were sacramentally conformed to Christ, and who were united in a communal bond that answered the fragmentation of life often characteristic of modernity: a dissolution in which "we became imprisoned within the walls of our own selves."[29]

Adam's slightly younger contemporary Romano Guardini also stressed the centrality of Christ to the Church's proclamation and proposal. Like Balthasar, Guardini believed that novelists and poets were fit conversation partners for theology, and so his theological work often took place in dialogue with literary figures such as Dante, Fyodor Dostoevsky, Friedrich Hölderlin, Blaise Pascal, and Rainer Maria Rilke. Those encounters led Guardini to challenge what he termed the "interior disloyalty" of modernity-as-ideology.

Modernity-as-ideology denied the objective truths built into the human condition, for which it substituted a Promethean subjectivism. That turn inward, Guardini was convinced, had displayed its lethal historical effects in communism and German National Socialism.

Catechism propositions could not meet the challenge of modernity's radical self-absorption. What the Church must offer, Guardini argued, was a personal encounter with Jesus Christ, the incarnate Son of God, who reveals to us the full truth of our humanity—and thus shows us a path beyond the prison of the self into true community. That community, Guardini believed, was available to all in the Church's worship, its liturgy.[30]

Building on the work of the innovative theologians of the late nineteenth and early twentieth centuries, and contemporaries such as Adam and Guardini, the renewal of the Catholic theological mind followed several paths in the mid-twentieth century. Key to most of these streams of thought was the previously mentioned recovery of the Fathers of the Church as sources of twentieth-century theological reflection and renewal. That retrieval was facilitated by an immense mid-nineteenth-century work of historical scholarship, the *Patrologia Latina* and *Patrologia Graeca* projects of the French publisher Jacques-Paul Migne, which gave scholars ready access to 383 volumes of patristic texts in the original Latin and Greek. As John O'Malley noted, "Nothing was more important than Migne's *Patrologia* in promoting the study of the Fathers from this time forward."[31]

Few made better use of those patristic sources than the French Jesuit Henri de Lubac, who brought the Fathers, as well as the Bible and the great medieval thinkers, into conversation with Blondel's revitalized Catholic metaphysics. In doing so he offered an answer to the false views of the human person that he found in atheistic humanism. Human nature always sought the vision of God, de Lubac taught. The God of the Bible did not intend to enfeeble or dehumanize his human creation, as the atheistic humanists alleged. Rather than entering history to fetch us out of our humanity, the Son of God became incarnate to empower humanity to live toward a nobler destiny: the communion with the Creator that God had intended from the beginning. And the human creature seeks that communion, he wrote in a letter to Maurice Blondel, with an "absolute desire"—a theme he developed in one of his most important (and controversial) works, *The Mystery of the Supernatural*.[32]

Other theologians took up the renewal of Thomistic thought that Leo XIII had promoted, but which had stalled during the Modernist crisis. Marie-Dominique Chenu, OP, believing that Thomas Aquinas had too often been turned into a fossil by a propositional approach to theology, sought to re-center Thomas's theology on Christ, as he believed the Angelic Doctor himself had done in the thirteenth century. Thomas's theology, Chenu argued, ought not be reduced to a closed system in theological manuals. If the Church reappropriated the Christ-centered, sacramental, and contemplative or mystical elements of Thomas's thought and spirituality, settled truths could be presented in a fresh light that was more suitable for proclaiming Christ and Christian truth to modern skeptics.[33]

The Neo-Scholastic Thomistic thought that dominated Roman theology from the Modernist crisis to the Second Vatican Council was exemplified by Réginald Garrigou-Lagrange, OP: the "Sacred Monster of Thomism," as he was dubbed. Garrigou was a stalwart defender of the deductive or syllogistic style of theology and the precise vocabulary it employed, seemingly convinced that neither could be changed without grave damage being done to the truths of Catholic faith. (To take one example: Garrigou criticized the doctoral dissertation of a young Polish priest named Karol Wojtyła because the Pole had not used the term "divine object" of God, preferring to speak of the more personal nature of the human encounter with God.[34]) Garrigou also played a considerable role in the Roman critique of *ressourcement* theology and was thought to have been a driving force behind Pius XII's cautionary 1950 encyclical on what the Pope deemed "false opinions threatening to undermine the foundations of Catholic doctrine," *Humani Generis*, which took particular aim at the work of Henri de Lubac. Long interested in mysticism and the Christian call to holiness, Garrigou was not merely a theological logic-chopper. His identification of the *ressourcement* movement with Modernism was misplaced, however, and Garrigou played no significant role in the preparation of the Second Vatican Council or at the Council itself. Nonetheless, a post-conciliar Church would eventually find use for the finely honed distinctions of the Neo-Scholasticism he embodied, although it was some thirty years after his death in 1964.[35]

The most adventurous of the Thomistic schools of thought in the mid-twentieth century was styled "Transcendental Thomism," a way of placing Thomistic thinking in dialogue with the critical philosophy of Immanuel Kant initiated by the Belgian philosopher Joseph Maréchal, SJ, and developed by the prolific German theologian Karl Rahner, SJ. Like other theologians who would influence the teaching of Vatican II, Rahner stressed that divine revelation was God's self-revelation to humanity: God revealed himself, not merely propositions about himself, to the People of Israel and in the Gospel proclaimed by Jesus of Nazareth. Humanity could "hear" such a word from God because, Rahner taught, there was a "supernatural existential," an instinct for receiving a divine word, built into the human condition.[36] Thus what Catholicism meant by the Incarnation of the Son of God could be expressed, for the modern world, in terms of an ultimate encounter between divinity and humanity: Jesus Christ was he in whom God's self-revelation and the human receptivity to that definitive word of divine revelation met "absolutely" and unsurpassably.[37]

Rahner's philosophical theology was heavily influenced by the Kantian critique of classical metaphysics, even as it sought to mount a philosophically sophisticated theological presentation of Catholic doctrine. Unlike other reformist theologians who would play influential roles at Vatican II, however, Rahner's presentation of Catholic faith was not heavily influenced by Scripture and the Fathers of the Church, to the point where it eventually became clear to the more *ressourcement*-oriented Joseph Ratzinger (who worked closely with Rahner at Vatican II) that the two men "lived on different planets," theologically speaking.[38]

Two French "Neo-Thomist" laymen, the philosophers Jacques Maritain and Étienne Gilson, were not so concerned as Rahner and the Transcendental Thomists with Kant, whom the two Frenchmen did not regard as an insuperable obstacle that had to be acknowledged by twentieth-century Catholic thinkers eager to engage modernity in order to convert it.

Maritain contrasted his Thomistic "existential realism" with the nihilistic existentialism of Jean-Paul Sartre and articulated a philosophical personalism to counter the anorexic accounts of the human person found in the twentieth-century heirs of the nineteenth-century atheistic humanists. There were both material and spiritual dimensions to the human person, and the latter expressed itself in the human yearning for transcendence and encounter: for communion with a reality greater than ourselves and for deep relationships. During and after World War II, Maritain also developed a Catholic theory of human rights and democracy that would influence papal teaching on those subjects and Vatican II.[39]

Étienne Gilson deepened Catholic understandings of the history of philosophy and strove to bring philosophy and a biblically rooted theology into a closer and more dynamic relationship. Gilson insisted that the God who announced himself to Moses in Exodus as "I Am Who I Am," and "I Am" (Exodus 3.14), is identical with the God whom Thomas Aquinas described as *ipsum esse subsistens*: Being itself. This was a key insight in the ongoing Catholic contest with nineteenth-century atheistic humanism and its twentieth- and twenty-first-century epigones, which conceived of God as a kind of super-being who was in constant competition with the world, and thereby demeaned the world and humanity. No, Gilson countered: Thomas's *ipsum esse subsistens*, Being itself, is the very "to be" that makes the world and humanity possible.[40]

French Dominican Yves Congar advanced the theological conversation begun by John Henry Newman in his *Essay on the Development of Christian Doctrine*, emphasizing that true Catholic reform was always re-*form*: a retrieval of some facet of the Church's Christ-given "form" that had been lost or forgotten.[41] Congar also made a significant contribution to the renewal of the Catholic mind by expanding the Church's understanding of what is meant by "tradition." In the Counter-Reformation polemic against Protestantism and its principle of *sola Scriptura*, "Scripture alone," Catholicism had emphasized tradition as a source of God's revelation, parallel to the revelation of God in Scripture; or, as the American theologian Avery Dulles, SJ, put it, tradition transmitted "truths explicitly revealed to the apostles but not consigned to writing in the canonical Scriptures."[42] In the contest with intellectual modernity and in reaction to the Modernist crisis, the official Catholic concept of "tradition" had become somewhat frozen, however, identified with the propositions found in approved (and Neo-Scholastic) theological manuals. Congar, a stringent critic of the Modernists, proposed a different, more dynamic view of tradition, drawing on his comprehensive knowledge of the history of theology to stress the continuing presence of the Holy Spirit in the Church, the social character of tradition as an ecclesial reality, and the importance of the Church's sacramental worship to its developing self-understanding.[43]

"Tradition," Congar wrote, "is not slavish servility but fidelity"—fidelity to the truths learned from the past. "Tradition is memory, and memory enriches experience. If we remembered nothing, it would be impossible to advance; the same would be true if we were bound to a slavish imitation of the past."[44] Thus, for Congar, as for other *ressourcement* theologians, the retrieval of the patristic heritage of the Church was not pious nostalgia but intellectual and spiritual adventure in service to the Church's proclamation of Jesus Christ to the world.[45]

Leo XIII's cautious opening to modernity and his desire to engage modern intellectual life rather than polemicize against it led to other developments in the renewal of the Catholic mind that would have a considerable impact on the Second Vatican Council.

Hubert Jedin, a German diocesan priest whose mother was Jewish, was sacked from his academic post in 1933 as a "non-Aryan" and subsequently arrested by the Gestapo in 1938. Released, he left Germany in November 1939 and took refuge in the Vatican's Collegio Teutonico del Campo Santo. From that base, he took full advantage of Leo's opening of the Vatican archives by spending a decade working on what would become the definitive history of the Council of Trent. He was therefore well positioned, after John XXIII's surprise announcement of a new ecumenical council, to explain historically just what such an assembly was: a task he quickly took up in the book *Ecumenical Councils of the Catholic Church: An Historical Outline*. John XXIII named him an adviser to the Council, and he served in that capacity throughout the Council's preparatory phases and its four periods. Thanks to Jedin, bishops participating in Vatican II could do so within a critical historical understanding of how the previous twenty such assemblies had functioned.[46]

Despite the chill caused by the Modernist crisis, Catholic biblical scholarship made important advances in the mid-twentieth century. Ironically or providentially, the gimlet eye that Roman authorities kept focused on Catholic exegetes prevented Catholic biblical studies from becoming as deconstructive as liberal Protestant scholarship became under the influence of Rudolf Bultmann and others committed to the "demythologization" of the Bible. By focusing on archaeological, linguistic, literary, and historical studies, Catholic exegetes developed an approach to the richness and pluralism of the Bible that would be put to good use by Vatican II, not least in its presentation of the nature of the Church itself.[47]

The green light for the Catholic use of modern exegetical methods was given by Pope Pius XII in the 1943 encyclical on Scripture, *Divino Afflante Spiritu*. Unlike those who insisted that Catholic exegesis must use the Latin Vulgate edition of the Bible, Pius XII stressed the importance of understanding the divinely inspired biblical texts in their original languages and according to the different literary forms used by the biblical authors. This, he wrote, would enable the exegete to understand and present the biblical book's literal sense as the biblical author intended it to be understood. The German rector of the Pontifical Biblical Institute, Augustin Bea, SJ, who helped draft this document, would go on to play a major role in the Second Vatican Council. His collaboration with Pius in the preparation of *Divino Afflante Spiritu* and his work at the institute helped open the door to the flourishing of Catholic biblical scholarship in the post–World War II period.

The Liturgical Movement, which began in the nineteenth century and continued throughout the first six decades of the twentieth, also had a decisive impact on Vatican II. Curiously, a movement that came to be identified in the post-conciliar period with some of the most radical interpretations (and misinterpretations) of the Council was launched by a conservative ultramontanist: the French monk Prosper Guéranger, OSB. Guéranger and his followers believed that the atomistic individualism of modernity was humanly diminishing and socially damaging, and in response taught that authentic human community could be rebuilt through the Church's liturgy: its regular worship, both at Mass and in the Divine Office, the daily hours of prayer to which clerics and religious were bound—and into which lay Catholics should be invited.[48]

That conviction, and the notion that the sacred liturgy should be reformed organically through a retrieval of its medieval and patristic forms, continued into the twentieth century. The Liturgical Movement was a key reference point for the renewal of the Catholic theological mind and was especially important in the reformist theology of Romano Guardini and Joseph Ratzinger. In the liturgy, they argued, the Church was most itself, and the experience of liturgy ought to be brought more directly into the Church's theological self-understanding. A renewed, liturgically centered, and vibrant Church would, the Liturgical Movement's leaders believed, both deepen the conversion of the Church's people to Christ and help bring the leaven of the Gospel to the world. As John O'Malley put it, "What especially drove . . . [the] leaders of the [liturgical] movement . . . was the conviction that the liturgy, when properly and fully appropriated by the faithful, was not simply in principle the center of the devotional life of Catholics but the Church's most powerful instrument for the spiritual rebirth of society at large."[49] Thus in one of its major American centers, St. John's Abbey in Collegeville, Minnesota, the Liturgical Movement was closely connected to efforts to promote Catholic social doctrine.[50]

The renewal of the Catholic mind in the mid-twentieth century also found expression in a transatlantic Catholic literary renaissance. Its key figures in France were the novelists Georges Bernanos and François Mauriac (a Nobel laureate) and the poet Paul Claudel, while across the English Channel Robert Hugh Benson, G. K. Chesterton, Ronald Knox, Graham Greene, Evelyn Waugh, and J. R. R. Tolkien brought a Catholic optic to fiction, journalism, and the art of the essay. Paul Horgan, Flannery O'Connor, and Walker Percy were three distinctive American embodiments of a refined Catholic literary sensibility; O'Connor, like Chesterton and Knox, was also a gifted Catholic apologist.

This flourishing of Catholic literature did not have a direct effect on the Second Vatican Council. It did, however, illustrate how the truths of Catholic faith could engage the concerns of those looking for secure personal and cultural moorings amid and after the New Thirty Years War. The higher Catholic literature of the mid-twentieth century also displayed an acute sensitivity to the dilemmas posed to faith by modernity-as-ideology, which perhaps reflected the fact that many of the period's great Catholic writers were either converts to Catholicism or "reverts," men and women who returned to the Church after excursions into various forms of secularism in which they found no satisfactory answers to the displacements of modern life.

This impressive twentieth-century flourishing of Catholic creativity in philosophy, theology, history, biblical studies, and literature led to a certain confidence about the possibility of Catholic intellectual life charting the path toward a robust Catholic renewal in a Church capable of meeting the challenges posed culturally, by modernity-as-ideology, and socially and politically, by the end of Christendom. That confidence coexisted with the sense among many of the Catholic thinkers noted here that institutional Catholicism was too often stagnant, blind to the realities of encroaching unbelief and spiritual boredom, and given to "smugness . . . the Great Catholic Sin" (according to Flannery O'Connor).[51] Yet despite all that, something fresh and hopeful seemed in the air.

Even when they were studying amid the bombed-out ruins of Munich in the hard years immediately after World War II, Joseph Ratzinger remembered the profound sense of possibility that he and his seminary colleagues experienced. It was, he told his biographer, Peter Seewald, a "great time of breakthrough. . . . We believed we were leading the Church into a new future. . . . [We] really had the feeling that Christianity can be lived anew."[52] During his theological studies, Ratzinger recalled, Romano Guardini's book *The Spirit of the Liturgy* and the thrill of learning theology from great teachers had enkindled in him a new appreciation for the Church's worship and its tradition, understood as a source of what was fresh and faith-affirming: "The Church came alive for us above all in the liturgy and in the great wealth of its theological tradition. . . . [There was] a feeling of breakthrough: a theology asking questions with new boldness, and a spirituality that was doing away with what was fusty and obsolete, to lead to new joy in salvation."[53]

That, after all, was the point—joy in salvation. True, a Catholicism that often emphasized the avoidance of eternal damnation was making the important point that choices in life count. But the more thoughtful existentialists, such as Albert Camus, knew that, at least in terms of life in this world.[54] What was needed to heal the wounds of a modernity still crippled by the knowledge of what it had done to itself in the New Thirty Years War was a positive, ennobling message: a Christ-centered message of the human capacity, under grace, to build a more humane future reflecting humanity's God-given and noble destiny. The renewal of the Catholic mind had refined (and in some cases created) the intellectual tools needed to offer the world a new Christian and indeed Christocentric humanism in response to the defective ideas of the human person that had wrought such lethal damage.

In that sense, the great anthropological question posed to Catholicism by intellectual modernity had been met by the re-centering of Catholic theology and apologetics on Christ as the icon of a true humanism. The Catholic proposal remained to be embodied communally, however. And that would require a resolution of the other great question: the question of the Church.

6

What Kind of Church?

IN ADDITION TO THE CHALLENGE OF PROCLAIMING A NOBLER idea of the human person than that promoted by ideological modernity, twentieth-century Catholicism faced the challenge of developing its own self-understanding, its ecclesiology or theology of the Church, in response to the quest for authentic community that was one reaction to modernity's atomization of society. For as history had demonstrated, that quest could take wrong turns with horrific consequences. Aspects of the ecclesiological development underway in creative Catholic theology have been noted, particularly the emphasis on the Church as a liturgical and sacramental community, not merely a "perfect society" conceived on a political model. The Church's own internal situation and world events also posed a series of problems which the theology of the Church could not ignore.

From Pope Pius IX on, Catholicism became more and more centralized and ever more focused on the person and teaching authority of the pope, who came to embody "the Church" in a historically unprecedented way. Most early nineteenth-century Catholics had little idea who the pope was or what popes did. Thanks to modern communications, the rapid development of inexpensive newspapers, and the persecution he suffered at the hands of Italian secularists, Pius IX became a popular figure—the first pope in history whose picture Catholics displayed in their homes. And the sharp focus of all-things-Catholic on the papacy—what became known as ultramontanism—took root. In due course, ultramontanism took over.

As noted earlier, ultramontanism (which got its name by emphasizing the pontifical figure who lived *ultra montes*, beyond the mountains, i.e., the Alps) began in the nineteenth century on what would now be called the Catholic Left, with the French publicist Hugues-Felicité-Robert de Lamennais. Concerned with what they regarded as Enlightenment rationalism's erosion of society's moral foundations, Lamennais and his followers sought to promote religious renewal in the world and the Church. To effect that reform, to build barriers against the attempts by public authorities to turn the Church into a department of the state, and to prevent Catholicism from decomposing into a loose federation of national churches, the liberal ultramontanists promoted a strong papacy with supreme spiritual authority in the universal Church.[1]

Yet through the vicissitudes of history (and Lamennais's own increasing radicalism), ultramontanism soon migrated to Catholicism's conservative and reactionary sectors and became the theory undergirding the Roman and papal centralization of the Church. By the time of the Modernist crisis, what amounted to papal autocracy, often exercised through a peremptory Roman Curia that identified its role with that of the pope himself, became virtually synonymous with Catholicism, even though different popes exercised their supreme authority with different degrees of vigor.

An autocratic style of governance had its advantages in meeting certain modern challenges. Some of those advantages were embodied by the strong leadership of Pope Pius XI, Bishop of Rome from 1922 until 1939. Papal autocracy permitted Pius XI to ignore the fretting of some Vatican diplomats (and local churchmen) and mount vigorous critiques of fascism, Nazism, communism, and Mexican anticlericalism in the 1931 encyclical *Non Abbiamo Bisogno* and the 1937 encyclicals *Mit Brennender Sorge*, *Divini Redemptoris*, and *Firmissimam Constantiam*.[2] It also enabled him to create hierarchies from native clergy in what had long been mission territories; in this, he followed the lead of his immediate predecessor, Benedict XV, and resisted the efforts of various Great Powers to populate the Catholic hierarchy in their colonies with clergy who, being drawn from the colonizing country, would presumably be submissive to the colonizer's wishes and program.

This forceful action helped prepare the Church to meet the challenges posed by post–World War II decolonization. New nations meant new local Churches. A Eurocentric Church was becoming more and more a world Church, and Catholicism had to adjust its self-understanding and leadership to that historical reality. Otherwise, missionaries risked being identified, as historian John O'Malley noted, as "agents of a foreign culture [rather] than as representatives of a religion that professed universality."[3]

The challenge posed by decolonization was but one facet of the larger and always pressing question of the Church's relationship to the state, especially those modern states loath to recognize any authority other than their own. When the Italian Risorgimento completed the unification of Italy by conquering Rome in 1870, and Pius IX lost the last fragment of the Papal States (once a large swath of the Italian Peninsula), many secular observers believed the curtain to have come down on the Church and the papacy as consequential forces in world affairs. That did not happen, and the new situation that Pope Leo XIII faced upon his election in 1878—the fact of being a pope who did not have considerable territories to govern—liberated the papacy to play a different role on the global stage.[4] The papacy did need some guarantee of its independence from worldly powers, and Pius XI solved that problem with the 1929 Lateran Treaties, which created the micro-state of Vatican City. But from 1870 on, the papacy's role in international public life would shift from that of a class-C European power to the more appropriate role of teacher and moral witness.

In post–World War II Europe, the rise of Christian Democratic political parties claiming inspiration from the social doctrine of

Leo XIII, Pius XI, and Pius XII (whose 1944 Christmas Message opened the door to a Catholic endorsement of the democratic project) was another *novum* in contemporary Catholic history that demanded a development of Catholic church-state theory. The new postwar politics made it necessary to go beyond the spadework that Leo XIII had done in his encyclicals on political modernity, and that Pius XI had continued in his 1931 encyclical on reconstructing the social order, *Quadragesimo Anno*, issued to mark the fortieth anniversary of *Rerum Novarum*.[5] Facing the question of the Church's right relationship to political authority (including its obligation to resist the communist challenge in the postwar world) also required the Church to think more deeply about its own nature—as did the increasing affirmation of religious freedom throughout the democratic world, manifest in the 1948 Universal Declaration of Human Rights (in the drafting of which the Catholic philosopher Jacques Maritain played a role). Catholic political theory could not be detached from Catholic ecclesiology.

Considerable pastoral challenges and other new historical realities intensified the need to develop the Church's self-understanding beyond the juridical-legal model of the *societas perfecta*, the "perfect society." What kind of Church might attract the working classes, who had been abandoning European Catholicism in droves since the Industrial Revolution? What kind of Church could more deeply catechize—and thus hold the allegiance of—the bourgeois societies emerging throughout the West in the aftermath of the New Thirty Years War? Marriage and the family were under new pressures: What kind of Church, offering what instruction and counsel, could revitalize family life and sacramental marriage in the new sexual-cultural environment that had been developing in the West since at least the 1920s?

Questions of the Catholic Church's relationship to other Christian communities had to be addressed as well.

Official Catholicism had been dubious about the modern ecumenical movement's quest to recompose Christian unity, an almost exclusively Protestant enterprise that began with the 1910 World Missionary Conference in Edinburgh. Yet modernity's skepticism about Christianity in general, and Catholicism in particular, was reinforced by the ongoing scandal of Christian division. Moreover, Christians of various communions had supported each other in Stalin's Gulag, in anti-Nazi resistance movements, and in Japanese prison camps during World War II. That experience of Christian solidarity amid denominational difference remained to be inserted in the Catholic Church's self-understanding.

Within the Catholic Church itself, a kind of internal Catholic ecumenism was needed to address the legitimate concerns of the Eastern Catholic Churches, Byzantine in liturgy and governance yet in full communion with Rome: ancient communities that often found themselves treated as second-class Catholics. Did "Catholic" mean "Roman," exclusively? If not, then what was the relationship of "Rome" and the local Catholic Churches of the Latin West to their Greek-influenced Eastern brethren? Despite some theological probes toward a more comprehensive Catholic ecclesiology and spirituality recognizing the importance of the Eastern Fathers of the Church, a developed theory of the universality of the Church remained to be articulated in an authoritative manner.

Then there was the unprecedented and unspeakable horror of the Shoah, the Holocaust of European Jewry. How was the Church to think about itself and its relationship to its religious parent, Judaism, in a world after Auschwitz, Treblinka, and Belsen: a world in which every Christian community was compelled to examine its conscience about the ways in which ancient prejudices had contributed to the cultural conditions making it possible for Hitler to carry out his satanic "Final Solution" to the "Jewish Question"?

A series of questions that could not be ignored had thus emerged from inside the Church and from the flow of history.

Was a thoroughly centralized Catholic Church—in which the pope functioned as a global chief executive officer, and local bishops served as branch managers of Catholic Church, Inc., taking orders from above, but incapable of serious initiatives on their own—the only possible model of authentic Catholicism? It certainly hadn't been the model for most of Christian history: What might be learned from that premodern experience for the third millennium of the Church? Was extreme ultramontanism—of the sort that had led Pope Pius IX to exclaim, "*La tradizione son' io!*" (*I* am the tradition!)—the last word in Catholic ecclesiology?[6] How could Vatican I's teaching on the papacy be completed by a developed understanding of the role of the local bishop in his local Church, and on the relationship between the body of bishops as an order within the Church and the Church's head, the Bishop of Rome?

Catholic theology was evolving, not least because of a deeper understanding of the Bible and the history of doctrine. Could the Church develop its understanding of the truth of Scripture—its inerrancy, to use the technical term—that did not depend on insupportable claims about the timeline of Creation, or the Mosaic authorship of the entire Pentateuch? Could the Church develop a deeper, more nuanced view of theological and even doctrinal development, such that every fresh thought was not automatically labeled "Modernism," and any possible change in doctrinal formulation was not considered the tug on a thread that could unravel the entire tapestry of Catholic faith? Did changing *anything* necessarily mean changing *everything*? If a stolid rejection of any development in Catholic thought and self-presentation was the dominant Catholic cast of mind, how could the Church possibly engage powerful modern intellectual movements such as utilitarianism, existentialism, and Marxism? Out-of-hand condemnations could not be Catholicism's only approach to the various forms of intellectual modernity—so how were the adherents to these alternative faiths to be converted to Christ?

Finally, there were the problems posed by an increasingly irascible and narrow-minded Roman Curia, which was playing an enlarged role in the Church in the latter years of Pope Pius XII as the Pope suffered in the mid-1950s from one illness after another, some exacerbated by incompetent medical care.

The Holy Office—the *Suprema* among the congregations (or cabinet departments) of the Curia—was especially prominent in the hunt for new forms of Modernism in theology and unwelcome departures in biblical exegesis. European *ressourcement* theologians, such as the French Dominicans Marie-Dominique Chenu and Yves Congar, and the French Jesuits Jean Danielou and Henri de Lubac, as well as the American John Courtney Murray, SJ (a leading proponent of a renewed Catholic church-state theory), came under critical Holy Office scrutiny in the 1950s, which led to censorship of, or proscriptions on, their publishing. Criticism of this stifling atmosphere sometimes came from unexpected quarters.

Msgr. Giuseppe De Luca was a stalwart, conservative churchman who had drafted the Holy Office decree that placed works by the French author André Gide (winner of the 1947 Nobel Prize for Literature) on the Index of Forbidden Books. Yet he found the atmosphere in the *Suprema* intolerable, and in 1953 he described the situation and his frustration with it to one of Pius XII's deputies, Msgr. Giovanni Battista Montini, in unambiguous terms: "In this suffocating atmosphere of unctuous and arrogant imbecility, perhaps a scream—chaotic but Christian—would do some good."[7] Internal housecleaning, it seemed to many, was needed.

If the last years of Pius XII brought conservative ultramontanism to both its apogee of power and a point of genuine crisis, however, it was also Pius XII who pointed a path beyond that model of the Church.

That path was charted in the 1943 encyclical on the Mystical Body of Christ, *Mystici Corporis*, a pivotal point in modern Catholic history.

As its name suggests, the teaching of *Mystici Corporis* was built upon a theme in the renewal of Catholic theology that could be traced back to Johann Adam Möhler in the mid-nineteenth century: a theme that was then developed by *ressourcement* theology's retrieval of the teaching of the Church Fathers, both Western and Eastern, on the nature of the Church. *Mystici Corporis* was, however, the first time that an authoritative document of the modern papal magisterium had so focused Catholic self-understanding on this more Christocentric, sacramental, and mission-oriented image of the Church as the continuation in history of Christ's redemptive and sanctifying action in the world. As O'Malley noted, *Mystici Corporis* "described the relationship between head and members [in the Church] in hierarchical and juridical terms." But it located those realities of Catholic life within a wider context that, as O'Malley put it, "insisted on the role of the Holy Spirit in the Church and thus on the balance that needed to hold between the hierarchical structures and the charismatic gifts of the Spirit."[8]

Mystici Corporis took an important (and, as things would turn out, decisive) step beyond the ecclesiology of the Church as the "perfect society." As Christ's living body in history, the Church lives by sacramental grace, and that grace does not work within the Church for the Church's sanctification only. Through the distribution of various spiritual gifts, the Holy Spirit draws the Church closer to Christ, and thereby empowers the Church to proclaim the Gospel, convert the world to Christ, and sanctify the human condition. And while *Mystici Corporis* sharply distinguished the Church's ordained hierarchy and its lay members, the encyclical also taught that all the members of the Mystical Body had important roles that strengthened the Body and facilitated its mission.

In retrospect, *Mystici Corporis* was more than a welcome papal recognition of the evolution of the Church's self-understanding that had taken place in the modern period. By challenging the Church to think about itself less juridically and more sacramentally and spiritually, the encyclical helped Catholicism imagine its relationship to modernity in more evangelical and less defensive terms. By writing it, Pius XII opened a door to the Second Vatican Council.

What Kind of Council?
To What Ends?

Pıus XII died on October 9, 1958. At his death, both casual observers and a good many devout Catholics thought the Church so solid and stable as to be impervious to internal confusion or external pressure. The German magazine *Der Spiegel* voiced this conviction in a February 1962 article, writing, "Currently the Roman Catholic Church—after a 2,000-year-long history—has achieved a unity and consistency in teaching and structure never seen before. Today it presents an unprecedented example of a spiritual community: It possesses 'a single truth' and a single custodian of the truth." Because of that unity of truth and authority, Catholicism was superior to "its only opponent today with similar mass impact: world communism."[1]

Others were not so sure. Six years earlier, Hans Urs von Balthasar had called the Church to be more open to the working of the Holy Spirit, so that Catholicism might be roused "from the bed of historical sleep for the deed of today." The world needed the Gospel, perhaps as never before. Christendom was finished. As impressive as the accomplishments of Counter-Reformation Catholicism had been, "the splendor of [that] salvage operation" was "over."[2] Joseph Ratzinger had parallel concerns, and in 2012 recalled how things looked to him at the end of the Pius XII era: "Christianity, which had built and shaped the West, seemed increasingly to be losing its defining power. It seemed to have grown tired, and the future seemed to be determined by other spiritual forces."[3] It is not hard to imagine that similar intuitions and judgments were behind John XXIII's decision to summon a new ecumenical council, which came as such a shock to those accustomed to thinking of Catholicism as the unchanging, unassailable institution described by *Der Spiegel*.

The development of Catholicism's understanding of the roots of the modern crisis in inadequate or false ideas of the human person and human community, and the Christocentric renovation of Catholic ecclesiology implied in *Mystici Corporis*, suggested that a bold initiative was necessary: for the Church's sake but also for the world's. If the Church was no longer the sacramental sector of Christendom because there was no more "Christendom," then what was it? If the Church was the living presence of Christ in the world for the sanctification of the world, how was it to be that, both *ad intra* (internally, in terms of worship, self-concept, and governance) and *ad extra* (beyond itself, in terms of mission, evangelization, and service)? How might the Church make the Gospel compelling again, in a world that imagined itself to have outgrown religious faith?

That was why a council was necessary: to find answers to those questions and thereby empower a revitalized Church to offer the modern world a path beyond incoherence—or, worse, self-destruction—through an encounter with Jesus Christ, the incarnate Son of God.

But what kind of council, working to what ends?

Only three of the twenty previous ecumenical councils had met in the second half of the second millennium: Lateran V (1512–1517), usually regarded as a failure; Trent (1545–1547, 1551–1552, 1562–1563), which created the Counter-Reformation Catholicism to which every Catholic, at the time of John XXIII's election, was accustomed; and Vatican I (1869–1870), which had been interrupted by the Franco-Prussian War before its work was done. As previously noted, some imagined that the need for such deliberative assemblies had ended with Vatican I's definition of the pope's universal jurisdiction and infallible teaching authority: if a problem were so urgent as to need definitive and binding settlement, the pope could handle it. That view notwithstanding, both Pope Pius XI and Pope Pius XII considered the possibility of convening an ecumenical council.

Pius XI, thinking that Vatican I might be reopened and brought to a proper conclusion, asked various curial cardinals in 1923 what they thought of the idea. Cardinal Louis Billot, a French Jesuit, was decidedly unenthusiastic and put his dubieties in frankly ultramontanist terms. Reconvening Vatican I would be ill advised, he wrote, because "it would be impossible to conceal the existence of profound differences, within the episcopacy itself, on social, political, and economic questions, and their relations with morality and the rule of faith. Because of their complexity, these questions will be presented under different aspects depending on the country, and they will give rise to discussion that will run the risk of being extended and prolonged indefinitely." The bishops, in other words, could not be trusted to maintain the façade of the solidity of the Church; they might expose the fact that there were in fact different Catholic approaches to the relationship between Catholic truth and modernity in its many forms.

But Billot's real fear was that a council would be the opening wedge to his (and others') bête noire, Modernism:

> The most important reason that would seem to me to militate absolutely against the idea [of a council] . . . is that the resumption [of Vatican I] is desired by the worst enemies of the Church, that is, by the Modernists, who are already prepared—as the most certain information testifies—to take advantage of the general situations in the Church in order to start a revolution, the

new French Revolution of their hopes and dreams. . . . [T]hey will not succeed, but we will relive the sorrowful days of the end of the reign of Leo XIII and the beginning of the pontificate of Pius X; we will see even worse, and it will be the total destruction of the happy fruits of the encyclical *Pascendi* which had reduced [the Modernists] to silence.[4]

The chilly reception Pius XI received to the idea of reopening Vatican I put an end to that possibility in his pontificate. Then came the crisis of totalitarianism and the Second World War, which obviously precluded any gathering of the world episcopate. The archives of the Vatican's Holy Office reveal, however, that Pius XII also considered holding an ecumenical council.

The suggestion had come to the Pope from a very conservative cardinal, Ernesto Ruffini of Palermo. Pius XII seemed taken with the idea and appointed a commission to explore the possibility of resuming Vatican I. The commission was led by Cardinal Alfredo Ottaviani, the de facto head of the Holy Office (the pope being the *Suprema*'s de iure leader). Ottaviani was not averse to a council; he believed there was a "need to clarify and define several doctrinal points, given the heap of errors that are becoming widespread in philosophical, theological, moral, and social matters." Pope Pius's commission met secretly between February 1949 and January 1951, but it could not agree on the kind of council needed: a brief, one-month session to ratify by acclamation previously developed materials, or a lengthy council structured around open-ended discussion of materials developed over a long preparatory process. "Faced with these differing opinions," historian Robert de Mattei noted, "Pius XII preferred to set aside the project."[5]

Cardinal Ottaviani would later report that he and Cardinal Ruffini had raised the issue again with Cardinal Angelo Giuseppe Roncalli on the night before his election as John XXIII. In a private meeting in Roncalli's small room, they suggested that "it is necessary to think about a council," and Roncalli had responded positively to the proposal.[6] No one knows whether this idea had occurred to Roncalli before; by his own later testimony, the idea of a council came to him early in his pontificate as an unexpected inspiration that he believed to have come from the Holy Spirit. But if in human terms the idea had first been planted in Roncalli's mind by Cardinals Ottaviani and Ruffini, then there was irony indeed. These two conservative ultramontanists were almost certainly proponents of the notion of a short, brisk council that would condemn the theological errors of the age (and perhaps philosophical, political, and economic errors for good measure), after which everyone would return home with the Catholic status quo reaffirmed by the authority of an ecumenical council.

John XXIII had something else in mind.

Some months after the January 1959 announcement of his intention to summon an ecumenical council, John XXIII made clear that this would not be a resumption of Vatican I but a new council, the Second Ecumenical Council of the Vatican.[7] Five days earlier, he had reflected in his diary that he imagined the Council as "an invitation to spiritual renewal for the Church and the world."[8] Such an invitation would be issued in positive terms, as Pope John emphasized in his announcement of the Council on January 25, 1959: his Council would encourage "the enlightenment, edification, and joy of the entire Christian people," and it would "extend a renewed cordial invitation to the faithful of the separated communities to participate with us in [the] quest for unity and grace, for which so many souls long in all parts of the world."[9] In other words: no condemnations, and no anti-Protestant or anti–Eastern Orthodox polemics. The open hand, not the clenched fist, would characterize Vatican II.

The preparatory process John XXIII established reflected the approach to a council proposed by the more open-minded members of Pius XII's secret exploratory commission in 1949–1951.

Thus, in the Council's antepreparatory phase, the entire world episcopate was consulted about the topics for discussion at the Council, as were the superiors of religious orders of men (but not women) and pontifically chartered university faculties throughout the world. Historian John O'Malley noted that the letter of invitation to submit discussion topics was sent "to 2,598 ecclesiastics and elicited 1,988 responses (77 percent). The responses varied in length from six lines from the bishop of Wollongong, Australia, to twenty-seven pages from the cardinal-archbishop of Guadalajara, Mexico. When printed after the Council, the responses filled eight large-format volumes, totaling well over 5,000 pages." Within that mass of material, opinions as to what Vatican II should discuss, and how the various topics should be coherently focused, varied considerably. Many responses reflected a satisfaction with the Catholic status quo, which might be strengthened by conciliar condemnations of modern errors (including communism) and new Marian doctrines. According to O'Malley, "A few responses were more venturesome, particularly in asking for greater responsibilities for the laity in the Church and for an extension of the use of the vernacular [i.e., local languages] in the Mass. . . . A very few bishops from non-western countries or regions asked for modification or abrogation of celibacy for priests."[10]

These patterns of response reflected a lack of the sense of urgency that had motivated John XXIII to summon the Council—which was perhaps understandable, given the prevailing sense of Catholic solidity, stability, and ecclesial impregnability. The Pope's interest in a council that would grapple with serious problems in world civilization had not yet been internalized by many in the world episcopate, at least as judged by the general character of the bishops' submissions of discussion topics. Moreover, John XXIII had only defined the Council's purposes in general terms.

One response gave sharper focus to John XXIII's hopes for Vatican II, however. It came from an obscure Polish bishop, about whom no one in Rome had likely had a thought since July 4, 1958, when he became one of Pius XII's last nominees to the episcopate: Karol Wojtyła, the auxiliary bishop of Kraków. Unlike some of his episcopal colleagues around the world, he did not send in a laundry list of ecclesiastical housekeeping matters for the impending council to resolve. Instead, he submitted a kind of philosophical essay that reflected the concerns that had focused his teaching at the Catholic University of Lublin, which was influenced by his extensive pastoral experience—and then filled out that analytic framework with specific suggestions for issues the Council should address.

"Above all," Bishop Wojtyła wrote, "people today seek an answer to the problem of the human person and [our] place in the world." Failed or "exaggerated" humanisms had not answered modern humanity's deepest questions; they had, "very often," resulted in "despair" about "human existence." This was the core civilizational issue that the Council must address. It would best do so by a fresh presentation of "Christian personalism," which it seemed "fitting and timely to delineate in doctrinal terms."

Human beings were inherently theotropic: "The human personality is made manifest first and foremost in the relation of each and every person to the personal God." To scoff at that deep truth of the human condition (as the atheistic humanists had done), or to criminalize the actions of those who recognized it (as communism was doing), was to demean the human person, "distinct from other beings of the physical world" precisely by reason of this capacity for "participation by grace in the divine nature and in the life of the Most Holy Trinity." That theotropic instinct for the divine could not be eradicated; humanity was created for union with God, and such communion with divinity fulfilled the true meaning of being human. The Church's moral teaching should therefore be framed in a personalistic fashion, rather than as a matter of rules laid down by an authority external to the human experience. The moral law was a set of guideposts leading to human flourishing and, ultimately, to communion with God:

"Catholic moral doctrine sets forth rules for using things without abusing them and for loving persons."

The modern world, in Wojtyła's judgment, was suffocating from "materialism in its several varieties—scientific, positivistic, dialectical." Confronted by that crisis, the Church must propose a Christ-centered humanism that lifted humanity up by restoring a sense of the "transcendental spiritual order" within the human person, "who is created in the image and likeness of God," and is thereby constituted as a person—a creature who reflects the personhood of that trinity of divine persons who compose the Godhead. Atheistic humanism claimed to liberate humanity from the shackles of an immaturity imposed by biblical religion. Christian personalism accepted that challenge (not least by admitting the Church's own failures to be transparent to the Gospel) and refuted it by displaying a vision of human possibility that was more compelling, because it was nobler, than anything being offered by utilitarianism, existentialism, or Marxism.

To do that, the Church itself needed renewal and reform. The "doctrine of the Mystical Body of Christ" called the Church to a new ecumenical engagement, for those separated from Catholicism did not "cease to be members, in some sense, of Christ's Body." Therefore, Catholic ecumenism should put "less emphasis on those things that separate us" while "searching . . . for all that brings us together."

The Council should remind lay Catholics that they were not mere objects of the clergy's pastoral attention but baptized members of the Mystical Body with a "specific responsibility . . . in the various occupations of secular life, in which they are responsible for the Church and its witness." For this "mutual effort of the laity with the clergy for the building-up of the Body of Christ" to take place, priests and bishops must understand their vocation—which was "not merely a job or a form of social work"—as an exercise of spiritual "fatherhood." Priests must "steer clear of 'defensive' or 'patriarchal' postures . . . and also steer clear of a kind of apartheid over against the laity, all of which runs counter to the building-up of the Mystical Body."

This focus, in turn, would require a reform of the "formation and training" of priests, both diocesan clergy and those in religious orders. The priest of the future must understand his task as the sanctifying of all of life, including those activities—"intellectual pursuits, the arts, and . . . even . . . sports"—that may "not have an outwardly religious or sacral character," but can nonetheless be sanctified "indirectly," and thereby reinforce the Christian human-ism that proposes to humanity a world open to signals of transcen-dence. The intellectual formation of priests must therefore be given greater emphasis in seminaries, and "the minds and consciences of seminarians" should be directed to a sense of "apostolic mis-sion" from "the very beginning" of seminary formation. Seminaries ought not be "simply professional schools" or trade schools, but "true academies . . . comparable to universities" in their intellectual seriousness.

As to formation in religious orders, that, too, should be oriented to mission: to an understanding that "the life of monks, nuns, and religious constitutes the front rank of the Church Militant, pointed at the kingdom of God and of Christ in this world." Even contem-plative communities withdrawn from "the world" should under-stand their life of cloistered prayer and penance as empowering the mission of the laity, the clergy, and the active religious orders.[11]

In light of John XXIII's vision of its purpose as grasped by Karol Wojtyła, how should the Second Vatican Council speak? How should the Council address the crisis of civilization, which Ro-mano Guardini had presciently described as the "interior disloy-alty of the modern world," in ways that modernity could hear and engage—and thus consider the possibility of its conversion and redemption? Future conciliar adviser Joseph Ratzinger knew that, as the German theologian put it, there could be "no return to the *Syllabus*," however necessary many of its strictures might have been in the mid-nineteenth century.[12] As Ratzinger argued in a lecture he delivered a few months before the Council opened, something far more evangelical and kerygmatic was needed: "The world does not await further refinements of the [ecclesiastical] system from us; it awaits the answer of faith at a time of unbelief," particularly in response to the dilemmas that modernity had created. It awaited a presentation of what Hans Urs von Balthasar had called "the glory of God, which pervades . . . revelation as a whole," and "the glory of creation . . . which shone through the whole theology of the Fathers of the Early and High Middle Ages."[13]

As both Ratzinger and John XXIII would put it, Church and world awaited "a new Pentecost."[14] That yearning underscored the necessity of Vatican II.

PART II

WHAT VATICAN II TAUGHT

8

The Council's Distinctive Features

ALTHOUGH THE SECOND VATICAN COUNCIL IS OFTEN RE-garded as the first "modern" council, that distinction belongs to the First Ecumenical Council of the Vatican, which challenged various aspects of modernity in a rather modern way in 1869–1870.[1]

In an era of expanding parliamentary power and great international conferences, Vatican I was the largest deliberative assembly of the time, with more than 700 bishops participating. They came from the Western Hemisphere, Africa, and Asia as well as from Christianity's European heartland, making Pius IX's council a far larger and more international gathering than Klemens von Metternich's Congress of Vienna or Otto von Bismarck's Congress of Berlin. The ancient tradition of lay sovereigns attending Church councils and having a voice in their deliberations was abandoned— an important break with one feature of the old altar-and-throne arrangements. Vatican I was also the first ecumenical council to be a media event: the debate over papal infallibility was carried out in newspapers, magazines, and journals, including the semi-official Jesuit-edited publication *La Civiltà Cattolica*, established in Rome in 1850 to give a platform to extravagantly ultramontanist views.[2] Embodying the papacy's new prominence in the Church, Pius IX took a far more assertive role in the Council's deliberations than his predecessors had done at the Council of Trent. And, as philosopher Russell Hittinger noted, "the greatest indication of the Council's modernity was its fundamental mission. What could be more modern than an assembly convening to claim natural and divine rights against state despotism?"[3]

Even if Vatican II cannot claim the distinction of being the first "modern" Council, this twenty-first ecumenical council, meeting to consider the Catholic Church's role in a post-Christendom world—a world in which defective ideas of the human person and human community had created an ongoing civilizational crisis—displayed many distinctive features of its own.

The first was its sheer size.

From December 8, 1869, until October 20, 1870, Vatican I had met in the north transept of St. Peter's Basilica, into which the Council's membership fit comfortably. By contrast, the bishops attending Vatican II occupied the basilica's entire nave—a span some 700 feet long in which two parallel tiers of seats, resembling upholstered bleachers, had been built. The tiered seating in the conciliar *Aula* (hall) extended from the basilica's entrance, and the red porphyry disk on which Pope Leo III had crowned Charlemagne as Holy Roman Emperor, to just short of the high altar and the table where the Council's presiding officers sat.

The diversity of bishops at the Second Vatican Council was also unprecedented.

Forty percent of the bishops at Vatican I had been Italians, and some 75 percent of the bishops present in 1869–1870 were Europeans. By contrast, 64 percent of the bishops attending Vatican II came from *outside* Europe.[4] Some 2,800 bishops in total attended the Council, with an average of 2,400 present at any given moment—making the Council the largest deliberative assembly with real decision-making authority in history. Those bishops, according to conciliar historian John O'Malley, "came from 116 different countries, with more or less the following geographic distributions: 36 percent from Europe, 34 percent from the Americas, 20 percent from Asia and Oceania, and 10 percent from Africa."[5] There were no bishops present from China, North Korea, or North Vietnam, as those countries' communist governments blocked their participation. Warsaw Pact communist regimes made participation difficult for their bishops but not impossible (the exceptions being the Hungarian cardinal, József Mindszenty, a refugee in the U.S. embassy in Budapest, and several clandestine bishops of the Greek Catholic Church conducting underground ministries in Ukraine, who could not attend).

Vatican II also broke precedent in that invited observers from other Christian communities attended all four periods of the Council. The presence of religious and intellectual leaders from outside the Catholic Church had real effects, for these honored guests did not just "observe" but were participants in various ways in the event of Vatican II. As O'Malley noted, "The decision to admit non-Catholic observers . . . allowed the deliberations of the Council to be reviewed by scholars and churchmen who did not share many of the basic assumptions upon which Catholic doctrine and practice were based . . . [and did not allow] the attention of the Council to focus on issues of concern only to Roman Catholics—or only to Roman Catholic prelates."[6]

There had been theological advisers present at previous councils, and while O'Malley has argued that the *periti* (theological advisers) "played a lesser role at Vatican II . . . than they had at the Council of Trent," there is no question that they made significant contributions to the Council's work. They served on various commissions, acted as advisers to and speechwriters for bishops, and were key participants in the "Off Broadway" council of official press briefings and unofficial seminars held in such venues as the Dutch Documentation Center and the Foyer Unitas, both located in the Palazzo Pamphilj on the Piazza Navona. Among the theologians who left an imprint on the Council's texts were men whose professorial careers were just beginning, such as Joseph Ratzinger, and others who had been under Holy Office scrutiny in the previous decade, including Henri de Lubac, Karl Rahner, Yves Congar, Marie-Dominique Chenu, John Courtney Murray, and the Flemish Dominican Edward Schillebeeckx. The most mediagenic of the *periti*, the Swiss theologian Hans Küng, had the least impact on the Council's actual work, while a Belgian, Gérard Philips, was arguably the most influential theologian at Vatican II, even as his efforts went largely unremarked at the time and are typically forgotten today.[7]

Vatican II was also distinctive in that it cost a lot of money. Reconfiguring St. Peter's by installing tiers of seats, coffee bars, a new sound system, and multiple lavatories was very expensive. Moreover, the Vatican had to cover the travel and housing expenses of half the participating bishops. The Vatican's own outlay came to over $7 million (a lot of money in the early 1960s), and the costs incurred by the bishops able to pay their own way likely doubled or tripled that figure.[8]

And then there was the media presence at Vatican II.

Newspapers and magazines had been part of the external debate surrounding Vatican I, but the media presence at Vatican II was far greater and had more impact.[9] At Vatican I, the press's primary interest was the controversial question of papal infallibility: Was this a settled matter of Catholic faith? If so, was it opportune to define it at this moment in history? What would such a definition mean for the Vatican's relationship with civil authorities, and for Catholics' lives as citizens? Moreover, the debate on those questions interested a rather narrow band of churchmen and partisans of one position or another; ordinary Catholics were not breathlessly awaiting newspaper reports on the debates taking place in the north transept of St. Peter's, or in tales of behind-the-scenes maneuvers.

At Vatican II, by contrast, virtually every issue on the Council's agenda was of interest to the media, and, thanks to radio and television, the conciliar debates and the tensions they revealed were instantaneously transmitted throughout the world. This new reality inevitably created a feedback loop into the Council itself, where media perceptions of the issues and descriptions of the Council's internal dynamics were more important than they had been at Vatican I.

As a glance through old issues of *Life* magazine and a review of grainy films from the years of Pius XII demonstrate, the Western media was enamored of the postwar Catholic Church as great theater: a display of lavish pageantry, with brightly hued costumes and stately rituals suggesting a Renaissance court returned vividly to life. That imagery dominated the earliest reporting on Vatican II, not least its extraordinary opening, when some 2,500 bishops, vested in white copes and miters, processed out of the Apostolic Palace, through St. Peter's Square, and into the great basilica in a ceremony that lasted almost five hours. The bishops were followed by Pope John XXIII, who was carried on a portable throne, the *sedia gestatoria*, and surrounded by uniformed guards carrying halberds and *flabella*, large ceremonial fans made of white ostrich feathers. In an era of big-screen CinemaScope movies, often based on biblical themes, here was a contemporary analogue, live and in brilliant color. The focus on the pageantry likely had something to do with the fact that much of the immediate reporting missed the key themes of Pope John's opening address to the Council.

But after the pageantry, then what?

Like its twenty predecessors, Vatican II conducted its debates in an ecclesiastical and theological vocabulary that most twentieth-century reporters were ill equipped to understand. Something more familiar quickly emerged, however, when the Council's first working sessions demonstrated that the dominant media image of the Catholic Church—as an unchanging (and indeed unchange-able) monolith—was woefully inadequate in grasping the reality of the historic moment at hand. As those first sessions revealed tensions and conflicts within the Church, a story line on Vatican II began to take shape for much of the international press: what was afoot in St. Peter's was a form of politics, a contest for power. And politics was something the media thought it understood and knew how to make interesting for a general audience.

Since the 1789 division of the French National Assembly into those who took an anti-monarchist and anticlerical position on the "left" of the chair, and royalists and supporters of the Church on the chair's "right," politics had often been assumed to be a matter of liberals versus conservatives: the proponents of change versus the defenders of the status quo. However much this dyad obscured the nuances along the spectrum of political opinion, it was useful as the era of cheap newspapers dawned later in the nineteenth century: it simplified matters for a mass readership and offered the attractive possibility of painting one's political opponents in an unfavorable moral light. The tendency to divide virtually everything into these simple categories was deeply ingrained in Western culture and in the Western press. It would come to frame much of the media coverage of Vatican II.

There was something peculiar about this. By the time Vatican II met, the fourteenth Dalai Lama, the spiritual leader of Tibetan Buddhism and the embodiment of Tibetan national identity, had become an international figure, especially because of the brutal repression of Tibetan religion and national aspiration under Chinese communism. At the time of the Dalai Lama's escape to India in 1959, no one thought to describe him as a "liberal Buddhist" or a "conservative Buddhist," presumably because of a sense that the complex religious tradition he represented could not be parsed in such terms. Yet that essentially political taxonomy came to dominate media coverage of Vatican II. It distorted the event of the Council and has continued to do so ever since.

In the Anglosphere, and especially in the United States, the left/right division of all things Catholic was quickly set in reportorial and editorial concrete by the work of the pseudonymous author who styled himself "Xavier Rynne": in reality, Francis X. Murphy, an American Redemptorist priest based in Rome, whose reports on the Council in the *New Yorker* helped create the analytic framework for many others working in Rome during the conciliar years. Father Murphy was a competent theologian and able writer with a gift for making sense of doctrinal and theological fine points to those outside the Church. At the beginning, he tried to present a balanced explanation of Catholicism to a general audience; in his first set of *New Yorker* essays, for example, he explained the grave errors of the Modernism condemned by Pius X and defended Pius XII's 1950 encyclical *Humani Generis*, noting its "paternal spirit" and its encouragement of the theological "investigation of modern problems, merely cautioning against bizarre attempts to accommodate Catholic teaching to contemporary philosophical fads and materialistic errors."[10] Yet as the Council continued (and fruitless Holy Office attempts to identify and muzzle the mysterious and popular "Xavier Rynne" multiplied), Father Murphy's *New Yorker* reports became "blatantly biased," as O'Malley put it.[11] Adding a moral overlay to the political taxonomy in order to portray a Church divided between good liberals and evil conservatives made the dyad even more attractive to reporters and commentators eager to identify protagonists and antagonists in a stirring drama.

The media presentation of Vatican II as a power struggle between open-minded liberals committed to reform and close-minded conservatives defending a sclerotic status quo certainly had some effect within the Council itself: How many bishops wanted to find themselves portrayed in the press as mindless reactionaries? Nonetheless, the impact of the liberal/conservative taxonomy on the Council's actual products—its sixteen documents—was likely less significant than is sometimes suggested, whether by defenders or critics of Vatican II. For both John XXIII and Paul VI were determined that Vatican II not operate on a simple majoritarian principle but instead aim to reach the greatest possible consensus in its teaching—a goal they largely achieved, as the final votes on the Council's sixteen texts attest.

What that distorting liberal/conservative lens did do, however, was invert the notion of "reform" as previously understood at ecumenical councils. In the past, council-mandated "reform" was an ecclesiastical term for a tightening of discipline, especially among the clergy. That was the case at the Council of Trent, for example.[12] "Xavier Rynne" and the other proponents of the liberal/conservative schema as a one-size-fits-all explanation for everything Catholic helped turn "reform" into code for something quite different.

To note these media distortions and oversimplifications is not to deny that there were contending factions and parties at Vatican II. There certainly were (as there had been at every previous council), and the clashes among them could be fierce (as was also the case at every previous council).[13] The diversity of the world episcopate and pent-up frustrations with Roman heavy-handedness in the latter years of Pius XII led at least one experienced churchman to expect a donnybrook at Vatican II. For on the night that John XXIII announced his intention to summon an ecumenical council, the archbishop of Milan, Cardinal Giovanni Battista Montini, called an old friend, Father Giulio Bevilacqua, and said, "This holy old boy doesn't realize what a hornet's nest he's stirring up."[14]

On October 13, 1962, Montini's prediction was borne out. At the beginning of Vatican II's first working session, Archbishop Pericle Felici, the Council's general secretary, announced that the bishops would proceed immediately to elect members of the commissions that would refine texts for the Council to discuss, by filling out ballots with the names of 160 potential commission members. The announcement was not well received, as the bishops, most of whom had just arrived in Rome, were largely unaware of each other's views and capacities. A chaotic scene followed, which included elderly men calling out to each other for suggestions across the capacious nave of St. Peter's. Cardinals Achille Liénart of Lille and Josef Frings of Cologne, two of the Council's board of presidents, rose to protest the rushed election (which some thought to be an effort by the Roman Curia to dominate the commissions). Liénart and Frings were vigorously applauded. A quick meeting among the ten Council presidents (including Liénart and Frings) led to an agreement to postpone the voting for several days, so that the bishops could consult one another and reach a more considered decision. It was the first signal that the Council would, as John O'Malley put it, "run its own business in its own way, and not meekly assent to what was handed to it"—which was, of course, what some had hoped would happen in the plan for a quick council they had proposed to Pius XII.[15]

The hornet's nest was stirred up again nine days later. Pope John XXIII had established a Secretariat for Christian Unity to help prepare for Vatican II, but without specifying the scope of the new organization's competence. What he had done, however, was name a formidable cardinal as its head: Augustin Bea, former rector of the Pontifical Biblical Institute and confessor to Pius XII. In the months before the Council opened, the new Secretariat had clashed with the pre-conciliar Theological Commission, led by the conservative ultramontanist Cardinal Alfredo Ottaviani, over the question of whether the Secretariat could propose for conciliar debate a document on religious freedom. Ottaviani rejected this out of hand, saying that the subject was doctrinal and came under the authority of the Theological Commission, which he deemed superior to, and indeed independent of, all other preparatory bodies. Bea pushed back, and the issue of his Secretariat's status was unresolved when the Council began its work. Then, on October 22, 1962, John XXIII settled the dispute, giving the Secretariat for Christian Unity the prerogatives of a full conciliar commission—a seemingly mundane procedural decision, but another blow to the commanding position the curial party had assumed for itself and an important step toward Vatican II's teaching on church-state issues.[16]

Another important papal intervention a month later stirred the hornet's nest again. During the immediate pre-conciliar decades, the question of the relationship between Scripture and Tradition in the Church's understanding of divine revelation had become a litmus test separating the Roman theology of the day and *ressourcement* theologians.[17] The Theological Commission's draft of a conciliar document on revelation, reflecting only the Roman theological view, was not enthusiastically received: 62 percent of the bishops voted to send the document back for redrafting rather than having the Council give it formal consideration. The voting process was confused (deliberately, some charged), but as a two-thirds majority was required for rejection of the proposed draft, it seemed as if the 37 percent minority in favor of proceeding to a formal discussion of the draft had carried the day.

John XXIII intervened again, and a surprise announcement was read to the Council by General Secretary Felici on the following day, November 21, 1962. The Pope, he said, had gotten the impression that further discussion of the Theological Commission's draft text on revelation would not be productive, so he had withdrawn the document from the Council's consideration and assigned its redrafting to a special commission to be led by Cardinals Ottaviani and Bea.[18] In the judgment of Joseph Ratzinger, Yves Congar, and many others, this was *the* decisive turning point at Vatican II, not only procedurally but substantively. For the question at issue was how God made his purposes known to humanity in a binding way that was authoritative for the Church over time. The resolution of that question over the next two and a half years would produce one of the Council's two chief documents.[19]

The hornet's nest continued to be stirred up throughout the Council's second period in the fall of 1963, with numerous clashes

among the bishops on the nature of their own office and its relationship to the papacy. The fractious buzzing reached a dramatic
crescendo on November 19, 1964, toward the end of the Council's
third period: "Black Thursday," in the jargon of some conciliar
historians. On that day, Paul VI agreed with the decision of the
Council's cardinal-presidents to defer a vote on a draft declaration
on religious freedom to the Council's fourth period, the following
year. Following a scene of some pandemonium in the *Aula*, during
which hard words were said, a petition signed by 441 bishops,
asking the Pope *"instanter, instantius, instantissime"* (urgently,
very urgently, most urgently) to reconsider, was hand-delivered to
the papal apartment by three irate cardinals from North America:
Joseph Ritter of St. Louis, Albert Meyer of Chicago, and Paul-
Émile Léger of Montreal.[20] The Pope heard the cardinals out but
said the postponement of the vote was in accord with the Council's rules; he further promised that religious freedom would be
the first topic to be discussed in the fall of 1965. When tempers
cooled, it became clear that Paul VI had shown a deft hand here,
for the draft document proposed to the Council in 1965 was a
major improvement over the document on the table in 1964. The
revised draft passed by an overwhelming majority despite continued dissent from bishops who preferred the old altar-and-throne
arrangements.[21]

The hornet's nest of controversy and contention that Cardinal
Montini feared in 1959 was thus stirred up at the very beginning of the Council's first period and continued to be stirred up
over the next three periods—presided over by Montini himself as
Pope Paul VI. Indeed, the hornet's nest continues to be stirred up
today, and serious consideration of the Council's teaching and its
implications for pastoral practice has not been made easier by the
ongoing habit of parsing Catholic controversy in the political categories of liberal and conservative, typically translated into moral

categories of good and evil. That unfortunate habit began at the Council itself. But political categories cannot adequately express the reality of an ecclesiastical event. There were "politics" and factions at the apostolic proto-council in Jerusalem in the mid-first century AD. But when that assembly made its decisions known, it expressed its consensus decision in explicitly religious terms: "It has seemed good to the Holy Spirit and to us" (Acts 15.28).

Any deliberative assembly composed of human beings who hold diverse, competing, and sometimes conflicting views cannot help but be political: proponents of different views will form groups that seek to persuade others of the truth as they understand it. There were "politics" of this sort at every episcopal assembly subsequent to the apostolic meeting in Jerusalem recounted in Acts, including not only the twenty ecumenical councils, but also numerous regional and national councils (including the seven provincial and three plenary councils of Baltimore, held by the American episcopate in the nineteenth century). To imagine any episcopal assembly without "politics" in this sense is to imagine that Church councils are not populated by fallible human beings subject to all the temptations of ignorance, ego, and power to which humanity is susceptible.

Nonetheless, to parse the Second Vatican Council in the overtly politicized and moralistic categories created in the Anglosphere by "Xavier Rynne" is to fail to deal with Vatican II on its own terms. Remedying that deficient analysis requires another kind of exercise in *ressourcement*: a "return to the sources" of Vatican II, to Pope John XXIII's statements of purpose for the Council, and to the Council's principal documents. By doing so, we can better understand what the Council's founding father intended for this distinctive assembly, as well as what the Council actually taught—which will help clarify the vital legacy of Vatican II.

9

John XXIII's Original Intention

JOHN XXIII'S PURPOSES IN SUMMONING THE SECOND VATI-can Council and his hopes for what it might achieve come into focus through four important texts: the apostolic constitution *Humanae Salutis*, dated December 25, 1961, by which he solemnly convoked the Council; his address to the final session of the Council's Central Preparatory Commission on June 20, 1962; the papal radio message of September 11, 1962, a month before the Council's opening; and, above all, *Gaudet Mater Ecclesia*, John XXIII's opening address to Vatican II on October 11, 1962.

As the Latin title of the apostolic constitution *Humanae Salutis* clearly signals, John XXIII understood the purposes of the Second Vatican Council as Christocentric, evangelical, and soteriological, or salvific: the primary purpose of Vatican II would be to enrich and intensify the Church's proclamation of the salvation won for humanity by Jesus Christ. That was the reason for the Church's existence:

The divine Renovator of human salvation, Jesus Christ, who . . . conferred on the Apostles the mandate to preach the Gospel to all peoples, to support and guarantee their mission made the comforting promise: "Behold, I am with you all days even unto the consummation of the world" [Matthew 28.20]. This divine presence . . . is noticeable above all in the gravest periods of humanity. Then it is that the bride of Christ shows herself . . . as the teacher of truth and minister of salvation [by deploying] all her power of charity, prayer, sacrifice, and suffering, the same invincible spiritual means used by her divine Founder, who in his life's solemn hour declared, "Have faith, for I have overcome the world" [John 16.33].[1]

The world was in great need of the good news of the Gospel, Pope John continued, for there was a "crisis . . . [within a modernity] that boasts of its technical and scientific conquests but also bears the effects of a temporal order that some have wanted to reorganize by excluding God." In *The Drama of Atheistic Humanism*, Henri de Lubac had described where that led, and John XXIII agreed with the French *ressourcement* theologian: it led to a world of "great material progress, but without a corresponding advance in the moral sphere"; it led, as de Lubac had warned, to human beings organizing the world against each other. Yet it would not do to repeat condemnations of this sad state of affairs, and the reason was Christological: "While distrustful souls see nothing but darkness falling upon the face of the Earth, we prefer to restate our confidence in our Savior, who has not left the world he redeemed."

Faced with the challenges of modernity, the Church could not be, and indeed had not been, inert: "She has decisively opposed . . . materialistic ideologies," not least through the witness of her modern martyrs, who "are displaying a heroism that equals that of the most glorious periods of the Church." Moreover, the Church had witnessed "the rise and growth within herself of immense energies of the apostolate, of prayer, of action in all fields," not only within the clergy but also among "a laity which has become ever more conscious of its responsibilities within the Church." The Christian community, the Pope believed, had been "strengthened in its social unity, reinvigorated intellectually, [and] interiorly purified" as the Leonine Revolution had worked its way into the texture of Catholic life.

Therefore? Therefore, a council. On assuming the papacy, John XXIII had felt "at once" the "urgent duty to call our children together in order to give the Church the possibility to contribute more effectively to the solutions of the problems of the modern age." So he had thought "the time was now ripe to offer the Church and the world the gift of a new ecumenical council." The Council would "promote the sanctification" of the Church's members and accelerate "the spread of revealed truth." It would promote Christian unity through "doctrinal clarity and . . . mutual charity." And it would meet the world's need for a witness to peace, "a peace which can and must come above all from . . . human intelligence and conscience guided by God, Creator and Redeemer of humanity." The dangers threatening the human future came from false conceptions about the human person; the Council would respond to those dangers by "giving life to the temporal order by the light of Christ." That was the Church's mission: by preaching Jesus Christ and offering friendship with the incarnate Son of God, the Church would "[reveal] men to themselves, leading them to discover [anew the truth of] their own nature, their own dignity, their own purpose."

The initial preparatory work had been arduous and would continue, but now "the moment has come to convoke the Second Vatican Ecumenical Council . . . for the coming year, 1962 . . . which will be held in the Vatican basilica." Let the Church, and other Christians, pray, then, for a new, Pentecostal experience of the mystery and glory of salvation—an experience like that of the first Christians: "May the divine Spirit deign to answer in a most comforting way the prayer that every day rises to him from every corner of the world: 'Renew your wonders in our time, as though in a new Pentecost, and grant that [the] Holy Church . . . may spread the Kingdom of the divine Savior, a Kingdom of truth, of justice, of love, and of peace. Amen.'"

In his address to the final meeting of the Council's Central Preparatory Commission, held on June 20, 1962, John XXIII thanked the commission's members for their work on the many possible agenda items for Vatican II, which included "the relations between Church and state, the need for the Church, the ecumenical question, ecclesiastical discipline in connection with the relations between bishops and religious, the training of clerics, Catholic schools, Catholic associations . . . and . . . the apostolate." There would be much to discuss and determine at the Council, to be sure. At the same time, and precisely because of the conciliar bustle he foresaw, Pope John called the members of the commission and the world's bishops to a kind of extended spiritual retreat in preparation for the Pentecostal event of Catholic renewal for which he hoped:

> We have reached, then, the final . . . stage in our work of preparation, and now you have three months in which to collect your thoughts . . . [as] the Fathers [bishops] in every part of the world will have time to give intensive, energetic consideration to the great work in hand. . . .
>
> Get everyone to pray more and more fervently; to unite their prayers with ours. . . . The Mass, the Divine Office, the Rosary; these are the things that give us strongest support; these are the things which feed the fervor of Christendom, strengthen souls, and make them responsive to the spur of holy joy.[2]

Much had already been written about Vatican II and the expectations for it in various sectors of the Church and throughout the world. These proposals had been an "intellectual treat indeed," the Pope said, and they "command respect." He had, he continued, "read as many of them as possible," and was "greatly consoled" by what he had read. But a different kind of preparatory reading was now required. So John XXIII wished to "conclude this address with one final suggestion offered to you in fatherly love. . . . We wish you, during this time of preparation for the Council . . . to read each day a few pages of St. John's gospel, and to meditate on them for a while," for there, "the heavens are opened for us and we are allowed to contemplate the mystery of God's Word."

In those daily readings from the fourth gospel, the Council fathers would be brought face to face with the two great biblical personalities from whom John XXIII had taken his regnal name: John the Baptist and John the Apostle and Evangelist. As the Council drew ever closer and the challenge of proposing a new Christian humanism came into closer focus, Pope John hoped that the Council fathers would find inspiration, as he had, in John the Baptist, the "forerunner" of "the true Light" who was "still heralding and proclaiming his unassailable witness of justice and freedom," and "John, the holy apostle whom Jesus loved," who "hands on to every age the deepest mysteries revealed by Jesus in intimate conversations with his apostles." Under their influence, the impending council would leaven the world with holiness, the fruit of truth and charity. Vatican II might make needed adjustments in the Church's internal life. Its overarching purpose, however, was to fit the Church to be an even more effective instrument of the world's sanctification, to lift up a true humanism, and to embody authentic human community.

On September 11, 1962, precisely a month before the Council convened, Pope John XXIII gave an important radio address that further underscored his Christocentric, evangelical intention for Vatican II. He had undoubtedly read the draft schemas and other documents for the Council and may have been struck by their tendency to speak in a formal and abstract vocabulary. The

Council itself would decide whether that was the Church's appropriate voice. Before the Council got down to business, however, Pope John wanted to stress that he had something beyond didacticism in mind for Vatican II. To that end, he put considerable time into the preparation of this radio address, which he evidently wanted the bishops about to gather in Rome to regard as an interpretive key for pondering—and accepting or rejecting—the draft documents prepared for their consideration.

John XXIII's radio address was the most overtly kerygmatic statement of his intentions for Vatican II—and in that sense it was the fruit of the renewal of the Catholic mind that had begun with Karl Adam and Romano Guardini before reaching its first maturity in the kerygmatic emphasis of *ressourcement* theology. The Church's basic proposal to the world was the proclamation made by Christ himself: "The Kingdom of God is in the midst of you" (Luke 17.21). And that, John XXIII said, must be the message of the Council: "This phrase, 'Kingdom of God,' expresses fully and precisely the work of the Council. 'Kingdom of God' means and is in reality the Church of Christ, one, holy, catholic, and apostolic, the one which Jesus, the Word of God made man, founded and which for twenty centuries he has preserved, just as still today he gives her life by his presence and grace." That encounter with the incarnate Word of God had been the purpose of every previous council: "What in fact has an ecumenical council ever been but the renewing of this encounter with the face of the risen Jesus, glorious and immortal king, shining upon the whole Church for the salvation, joy, and splendor of the human race?"

Then came John XXIII's precise definition of Vatican II's raison d'être: "Of fundamental importance is what is said about the very reason for the Council's being held: at issue is the response of the whole world to the testament of the Lord which he left us when he said, 'Go, teach all nations . . .' *The purpose of the Council is, therefore, evangelization.*"[3]

As if to make sure that no one missed the Christocentric core of that conciliar purpose, John XXIII reminded a group of young people five days later that the gist of his September 11 radio broadcast was "*Ecclesia Christi lumen gentium* [The Church of Christ, the light of the nations]."[4] Two years later, *Lumen Gentium* (Light of the Nations) would become the Latin title of one of Vatican II's two most authoritative texts.

When he solemnly opened the Second Ecumenical Council of the Vatican on October 11, 1962, John XXIII knew that his personal pilgrimage was drawing to a close. Shortly after the private retreat he made in the Vatican's Torre San Giovanni from September 10 to 15 to prepare himself for the Council, the Pope underwent a battery of medical tests to determine the cause of the gastric pain he was experiencing. On September 23, the Pope received the physicians' verdict: he had cancer, and it would likely kill him within a year. That evening, he went into the grottoes beneath St. Peter's to pray at the tombs of Popes Pius XI and Pius XII. Perhaps while there, he reflected on the new and more dramatic meaning of an observation he had made a few weeks earlier to Cardinal Léon-Joseph Suenens of Belgium, when they met at Castel Gandolfo: "I know what my part in the Council will be. . . . [I]t will be to suffer."[5] The facts of the octogenarian pontiff's declining health were closely held, though, as Pope John did not want the Council's initial period to be disrupted by pre-conclave speculations and maneuverings.

Given that John XXIII understood that his opening address to Vatican II would also be, in all probability, his last extended word to the Council, that address, *Gaudet Mater Ecclesia* (Mother Church Rejoices), should be read as the culmination of his series of pre-conciliar reflections and the definitive statement of his intention for the great assembly he was inaugurating. The address took thirty-seven minutes to deliver, and the Pope spoke in Latin, which meant that the full import of his message was not immediately grasped by some, perhaps many. Sixty years later, *Gaudet Mater Ecclesia* is chiefly remembered for a brief passage in which John XXIII lamented those "prophets of doom" who, despite their "religious fervor," nonetheless saw "only ruin and calamity in the present conditions of human society." No doubt Pope John intended that these words carry a sting. But to reduce *Gaudet Mater Ecclesia* to a moment of papal reprimand is to ignore the theological and spiritual richness of the rest of the text—and to miss its significance, given the Pope's perilous health. *Gaudet Mater Ecclesia* therefore repays a close reading, for, more than any other source, its key themes define John XXIII's vision for the Council.[6]

Vatican II, the Pope began, stood in a line of Christocentric continuity with the ecumenical, provincial, and regional councils of the past twenty centuries, whose "lively and encouraging voices" had testified time and again to the fact that the "Church of Christ . . . takes her name, her grace, and her total meaning from the divine Redeemer." Many things had changed over the past two thousand years, but the most important thing had not changed and never would: "Christ Jesus still stands at the center of history and life." And in him, as ever, would be found the answers to "the very serious matters and questions which need to be solved by the human race."

Therefore, the Council, like the Church itself, must be radically Christ-centered. The intense focus on the Church and its institutional structures that had been so prominent in Catholicism's self-understanding over the past century had served its purpose: the bastion Church had defended itself institutionally against the various assaults of modernity, especially political modernity. Now, however, that ecclesiocentrism had to give way to the Christocentrism from which the Church began. For the Church was not an end in itself; it was an instrument proclaiming the truth about humanity and its history, which is fully revealed in Christ.

"History," the historian-pope continued, "is the great teacher of life." And if the Council were reminded by that history that the Catholic Church must constantly preach and witness to "the glory of Christ the Lord, unconquered and immortal King of ages and peoples," then Catholicism could "look to the future without fear," as the Church would "bring individuals, families, and nations to turn their minds to the things that are above," preparing them to meet history's Lord. The Christocentric Church must always be an evangelical Church, a Church permanently in mission.

The Church had a proposal to make, a proposal that "embrace[d] the whole human person, body and soul." To make that proposal under the conditions of modernity did not require inventing anything, but it did require careful thought about the ways in which the Church's proposal was best made. So the Council's "greatest concern" must be "that the sacred deposit of Christian doctrine . . . be more effectively defended *and presented*"; the Council must "transmit whole and entire and without distortion the Catholic doctrine which . . . has become the common heritage of humanity." To be sure, some had not recognized this doctrine as a "very rich treasure." Yet, even faced with resistance, the Church must continue to offer the Gospel to the world, not merely defend its doctrine: the Church's task was "not only to guard this precious treasure, as if we were concerned only with an antiquity." Nor would a repetition of past formulas of faith suffice to meet the world's present need; the Council could not simply "discuss some of the chief articles of the Church's doctrine or repeat at length what the Fathers and ancient and more recent theologians [had] handed on." The Council must do more: "What instead is necessary today is that the whole of Christian doctrine . . . be more fully and more profoundly known. . . . What is needed is that this certain and unchangeable doctrine . . . be investigated and presented in the way demanded by our times. For the deposit of faith, the truths contained in our venerable doctrine, are one thing; the fashion in which they are expressed, but with the same meaning and the same judgment, is another thing."[7]

So the Church would propose, not impose, and the Catholic proposal ought to be made in a vocabulary that the people of the late twentieth century could hear and engage. The Council was not summoned, however, to change the truths the Church had proposed for two millennia. For, as the Pope said, "it is clearer than ever before that the truth of the Lord remains forever [Psalm 116.2]." And that "truth of the Lord" is, in fact, the Lord himself: "To the human race, laboring under so many difficulties, [the Church] says, as Peter once did to the unfortunate man who begged him for alms, 'Silver and gold have I none, but what I have I give you: in the name of Jesus Christ the Nazarene, rise and walk' [Acts 3.6]."

The world was sorely in need of such a witness to Christ, who reveals the truth about humanity and its noble destiny. There was nothing new about that neediness, John XXIII insisted: "Indeed, as age succeeds age, we see the uncertain opinions of men take one another's place and new-born errors often vanish as quickly as a mist dispelled by the sun." The Church had "in every age . . . opposed these errors and often . . . even condemned them, and indeed with the greatest severity." Sometimes that had been necessary. But something different was required now in addressing modernity's inadequate and often quite false ideas about the human person and human community: "At the present time, the spouse of Christ [i.e., the Church] prefers to use the medicine of mercy rather than the weapons of severity." There were false doctrines afoot in the world, to be sure, but they had caused such suffering that they condemned themselves. As Catholicism proposed a more noble understanding of "the dignity of the human person," the Church should do so as "the most loving mother of all, kind, patient, and moved by mercy and goodness."

To be a Christocentric, missionary Church in the distinctive circumstances of the modern world, Catholicism had to deepen its perception that history, including the present moment, is *History*: God's story. Discerning the "signs of the times" in the New Testament meant learning to see the Kingdom of God breaking into history through the presence of the incarnate Son of God. Christ always remained with the Church, however, so discerning the contemporary "signs of the times" required the Church to look into the present for openings through which the Gospel could be proclaimed and friendship with Christ offered. There was reason for hope here, the Pope noted, because "in the present course of human events, by which human society seems to be entering a new order of things, we [can] see . . . the mysterious plans of divine Providence." In recent history, "countless obstacles have been taken away with which the children of the world used once to impede the free activity of the Church." And while it should always be remembered that previous ecumenical councils "were often celebrated amid serious difficulties and sufferings caused by the undue interference of civil authorities," and that painful instances of that interference remained in the case of those bishops "who for the sake of faith in Christ are in prison," or who were otherwise impeded from participating in Vatican II, it was, nevertheless, "a hopeful thing to see that the Church, finally free from so many profane hindrances of the past, can from this Vatican basilica, as if from a second apostolic cenacle, through you raise her majestic and solemn voice." No king, prince, emperor, president, or dictator would participate in, much less determine, the course of the Council. And that was a blessing.

However challenging the times, then, they had also opened "new avenues for the Catholic apostolate." And in her work of proclaiming Christ and the Gospel, the Church should strive to see that "the wonderful discoveries of human genius" never lead to a self-absorbed Prometheanism, an auto-deification in which humanity imagines itself its own redeemer. There was one Redeemer of humanity, Jesus Christ. And in proposing him and his Gospel under contemporary circumstances, the Church must look toward an expansion of "the spaces of Christian charity," as "nothing [was] more fit to uproot the seeds of error and nothing more effective [in promoting] concord, a just peace, and fraternal unity among all."

Among Christians, that unity must always be a "unity in truth," for, as the Pope reminded the Council, God "wills all persons to be saved and to come to the knowledge of the truth [1 Timothy 2.4]." The Catholic Church, through the Council just beginning, would take up anew her "duty to work actively to fulfill this mystery of that unity for which Christ Jesus ardently prayed [to] the heavenly Father on the eve of his sacrifice." By working to foster Christian unity, the Council and the Catholic Church would help spread "the message of salvation . . . preparing and consolidating the path that can bring about that unity of the human race which is the necessary foundation if the earthly city is to be ordered into a likeness of the heavenly city, 'whose king is truth, whose law is love, and whose length is eternity' [St. Augustine, *Epistle 138, 3*]."

The Second Ecumenical Council of the Vatican should therefore be an event that "breathes holiness and stirs up joy." For the Council would meet as an expression of what the Creed called the communion of saints. And "that is why it can be said that heaven and earth are uniting in celebration of the Council. The saints of heaven are here to protect our work; the faithful are here to continue to pour out their prayers to God; all of you are here so that, readily obeying the heavenly inspirations of the Holy Spirit, you may eagerly set to work so that your efforts will appropriately respond to the desires and needs of the various peoples."

Then John XXIII concluded as he had begun: "To Jesus Christ, our most loving Redeemer, immortal king of peoples and ages, be love, power, and glory forever and ever. Amen."

A careful reading of *Gaudet Mater Ecclesia* will note that Pope John spoke of "celebrating" the Council. This new Pentecost for which he hoped was not a business meeting in which the branch managers of a global enterprise came together with their chief executive officer to discuss ways to increase market share. First, foremost, and always, Vatican II was intended by John XXIII as an event in the realm of the spirit: an event at which the Catholic Church, through its ordained leadership, would relive the outpouring of the Holy Spirit that Christ had promised his first followers, a promise kept on the first Christian Pentecost.

In sum, then, John XXIII's original intention for Vatican II was that it be Christocentric and mission-focused. Just as through the councils of antiquity the Church had learned how to make the Gospel come alive in classical culture, and just as the Council of Trent helped the Church make the Gospel come alive in the centuries after the various Reformations, this twenty-first ecumenical council should ponder ways to propose the salvific good news of the Gospel in ways that could be engaged by modern humanity—thereby demonstrating that Jesus Christ is not just "Christ yesterday," but "Christ yesterday, today, and forever," as the Letter to the Hebrews proclaimed him (13.8). In doing so, the Council and the Church would be responding to late twentieth-century humanity's two greatest dilemmas: its defective understandings of the human person, and its failed efforts to create authentic human community. Those defects and failures need not be condemned in the style of the *Syllabus of Errors*, for history itself had made those errors clear. What was needed was a fresh presentation of the truths of Catholic faith, fashioned so that those truths could be grasped as lifelines: as answers to the great questions of contemporary human life; as demonstrations that human beings were not merely congealed stardust and that humanity's destiny was not oblivion. The first of those truths was that, in Jesus Christ, humanity discovered both the truth of God's passionate love for the world and the truth about the dignity and destiny of the human person. The second of those truths was that the Church, the continuation of Christ's presence in the world, embodied the genuine community for which humanity longed.

The path of Christ-centered, evangelical mission thus lay through proposing the truth, embodying it in the works of charity and justice, and striving to heal those wounds of division within Christianity that impeded the proclamation of the Gospel.

It is one of the ironies of modern Catholic history that the pope who was a keen student of one of the most important Counter-Reformation implementations of the Council of Trent should be the pope who decisively accelerated the Church's journey to a post-Counter-Reformation future. John XXIII was too good a historian, and too much a product of that Counter-Reformation way of being Catholic, to gainsay or deprecate the strong, institutional base that Counter-Reformation Catholicism had built.[8] That base was not impregnable, however, and elements of it needed renovation, for, as the Pope said at an audience in November 1962, "The Christian life is not a collection of ancient customs."[9] *Gaudet Mater Ecclesia* suggested that the Church's institutions, rather than being defensive bastions, ought to be turned into staging grounds and launching pads for a mission of conversion in which the Church would propose a renewed humanism rooted in the dignity of the human person revealed in Christ—a renewed humanism that would be embodied in the Church's works of mercy and solidarity.

The new Pentecost for which John XXIII prayed in *Gaudet Mater Ecclesia* was not to be a momentary experience of spiritual euphoria, although he did want the bishops gathered in St. Peter's to experience in a fresh way the joy of the Gospel, which he knew to be the infallible sign of God's presence in the world. Rather, through the new Pentecost experienced by the Church's bishops gathered in ecumenical council, the entire Catholic Church was to be animated with that pentecostally inspired evangelical zeal which had led the first Christian community on a mission of evangelization. Christianity had begun in mission, and Catholicism must become, once again, a community of missionary disciples.

That was the message of *Gaudet Mater Ecclesia*. The recovery of that Christocentric, evangelical imperative was Pope John XXIII's original intention for the Second Vatican Council. And that is why *Gaudet Mater Ecclesia* is the clearest interpretive lens through which to read Vatican II, beginning with its two most important achievements, the Dogmatic Constitution on Divine Revelation and the Dogmatic Constitution on the Church.

10

The Word of God Breaks Through the Silence

The Dogmatic Constitution on Divine Revelation

CONCILIAR HISTORIES AND COMMENTARIES OFTEN PRESENT *Dei Verbum*, Vatican II's Dogmatic Constitution on Divine Revelation, as an academically oriented document, written to resolve controversies that had been roiling Catholic theology and Catholic biblical studies.

The first involved the question of how divine revelation was transmitted, which was sharply posed during the Protestant Reformations of the sixteenth century and remained a contested issue five hundred years later: Was Scripture the sole "source" of divine revelation? Or did God reveal saving truths through both Scripture and the Church's Tradition, those truths of apostolic faith that were not consigned to writing in the Bible? And if the latter was the case, what was the relationship between Scripture and Tradition?

Another brace of pressing issues involved the science of biblical interpretation. Modern linguistic studies, modern archaeology, and modern methods of analyzing ancient texts had dramatically changed humanity's understanding of the written artifacts of antiquity. How were these methods of inquiry to be deployed by Catholic biblical scholars who believed that they were seeking to understand the Word of God written in human words? Enlightenment rationalism dealt with ancient religious texts as literary cadavers to be dissected; the Church obviously could not accept that. But how could the vitality of Scripture be recovered, so that God's words in the Bible might break through the silence of a world that imagined itself to have outgrown religion—in part, because of its skepticism about the veracity and historical reliability of the Bible? Was it possible to use modern tools of biblical interpretation without reducing the Bible to a collection of legends and fables, and if so, how?

These were important questions. Resolving them was essential if the Catholic Church was to proclaim Christian truth confidently in the modern world. The dogmatic constitution found answers to these questions, which will be explored in a moment. At the outset, though, it is important to recognize that there is a more compelling way to read *Dei Verbum*.

If the dogmatic constitution is read through the lens of John XXIII's original evangelical intention for the Council, echoed and amplified in Bishop Karol Wojtyła's memorandum urging Vatican II to rescue the Western humanistic project through the bold proclamation of a Christian humanism centered on the person of Jesus Christ, the very title of the document—*Dei Verbum*, "Word of God"—comes into sharper focus. So does the Council's achievement in this seminal text, which touched upon matters of great consequence, not simply academic questions of primary interest to scholars.

In *Dei Verbum*, the Catholic Church affirmed that humanity does not live in a claustrophobic world: a world of self-creating, self-contained, autonomous human beings, caught in a narcissistic trap of reflection; a world of self-absorption, silence, and darkness. Rather, the bishops of Vatican II taught, we live in a world open to transcendence, to that which is greater than ourselves. Modernity's misconceptions had not changed the fact that the human world is a world with windows, door, and skylights, even if it seemed that ideological modernity had painted over the windows, closed the skylights, and bolted shut the doors. The human world and human history were neither absurdities nor the exhaust fumes of impersonal economic forces. The human world, the Council taught, was intrinsically open to a divine word spoken into it: a word spoken by a God who entered history to show the path toward a truly humane future and who invited men and women to follow humanity's Creator on that journey, which ultimately led to communion with the divine.

Dei Verbum thus challenged the Promethean narcissism that had led to the self-destructive cataclysms of the New Thirty Years War and its Cold War aftermath. History had proven the truth of Henri de Lubac's observation that a humanity without God could only organize itself as a circular firing squad: a Hobbesian world of constant conflict, human beings endlessly pitted against each other. So perhaps, the Council hoped, the world was ready to consider things anew and to listen for a divine word within history that pointed toward the redemption of history. Perhaps modern men and women, frightened and disoriented in a world of silence, were not all that different from those first-century Romans to whom St. Paul had written that "creation awaits with eager longing for the revealing of the sons of God" (Romans 8.19).

For a Church on the cusp of its third millennium, *Dei Verbum* also reaffirmed the ancient truth, first grasped by the patriarch Abraham, that authentic religion is not a matter of men and women searching for God, but of men and women accepting the God who comes into history in search of them. That God first made himself known to the children of Abraham, the People of Israel, to whom, through Moses, essential truths for righteous living were revealed.[1] That God then revealed himself in an unsurpassable way in the person of Jesus of Nazareth, the incarnate Son of God. True religion, *Dei Verbum* taught, was not a matter of looking inward but of looking forward, of hearing the word of

God spoken to Israel and by Jesus Christ, seeing God's deeds in Israel and in the Lord Jesus, and then following the path into the future that God had charted and that God continues to illuminate.

Dei Verbum thereby recovered the deep anthropological truth described by Augustine in his *Confessions*, a truth that, forgotten, had led to a grave crisis in the civilizational project of the West: "*Tu nos fecisti ad te et cor nostrum inquietum est donec requiescat in te*" (Thou hast made us for Thee and our hearts are restless until they rest in Thee).[2]

The Dogmatic Constitution on Divine Revelation had a complex gestation that lasted through all four periods of Vatican II before *Dei Verbum* was finally promulgated on November 18, 1965, three weeks before the Council ended.

As previously noted, the first draft submitted to the Council was severely criticized. Pope John XXIII withdrew it from discussion in November 1962 and assigned its revision to a "mixed commission," composed of members of the Council's Theological Commission and its Secretariat for Christian Unity and chaired by Cardinals Alfredo Ottaviani and Augustin Bea. Although the new commission met amid some controversy, the text it proposed struck Joseph Ratzinger, among others, as a considerable improvement, because it discussed divine revelation through the prism of salvation history, meaning both the deeds and words by which God made himself known to humanity. The Council discussed this new draft during its second period, in the fall of 1963. Enough dissatisfaction remained that it was agreed to put the topic over to the Council's third period, in the fall of 1964, where, as the new pope, Paul VI, promised, it would be a priority. This was a decisive move, Ratzinger later wrote, because it eventually led to a far better document, in which it was made clear that "the Church . . . is not there for its own sake, but only to lead to him to whom all honor is due, God the Lord."[3]

A third draft text, discussed during the fall of 1964, still did not achieve the broad consensus Pope Paul wanted, so the Pope intervened again, continuing the discussion and allowing for the document's refinement in Vatican II's fourth period in the fall of 1965. Further debate and emendation finally produced a text that Ratzinger described as "a synthesis of great importance," to which an overwhelming majority of the bishops at the Council could assent: the decisive vote was 2,344 in favor and 6 against.[4]

As finally adopted and promulgated, *Dei Verbum* made several great affirmations crucial to the Second Vatican Council's project of renewing a Christocentric Catholicism permanently in mission—a Catholicism that could offer the world a path beyond civilizational crisis.

First, *Dei Verbum* taught that divine revelation is real. What St. Paul said to the fractious paleo-Christians of Asia Minor—"I would have you know, brethren, that the Gospel which has been preached by me is not man's Gospel. For I did not receive it from man, nor was I taught it, but it came through a revelation of Jesus Christ" (Galatians 1.11–12)—remained true two millennia later. Catholicism proposes to the world the truths bequeathed to it by God, not inventions of its own cleverness. God's word had truly broken through the world's silence and entered history, both in God's self-revelation to the People of Israel and through God's Son, the incarnate Word of God and Second Person of the Trinity.

So "revelation" is not, in the first instance, a catalog of knowledge, but a personal encounter with the living God, of the kind experienced by Abraham, by Moses, by David, by the prophets of Israel, and, above all, by the apostolic band gathered by Jesus of Nazareth, which then took the Gospel of Christ to all the nations. As biblical scholar Francis Martin has explained, "Because of God's action in Christ, anticipated in the Old Dispensation and perfected in the New, [God] addresses himself to the very depth of the human person. This makes of revelation a speaking and an answering of a profoundly unique kind: It is a friendship and a dialogue."[5]

At the very beginning of *Dei Verbum*, then, the Second Vatican Council confidently declared that the God of the Bible was neither a human projection nor an oppressor of humanity but the Creator who wished to call humanity into communion with himself and did so through what we know as salvation history—a history that continues down to our time:

> It pleased God, in his goodness, to reveal himself and to make known the mystery of his will [cf. Ephesians 1.9]. His will was that men should have access to the Father, through Christ, the Word made flesh, in the Holy Spirit, and thus become sharers in the divine nature [cf. Ephesians 2.18; 2 Peter 1.4]. By this revelation, then, the invisible God [cf. Colossians 1.15; 1 Timothy 1.17], from the fullness of his love, addresses men as his friends [cf. Exodus 33.11; John 15.14–15], and moves among them [cf. Baruch 3.38], in order to invite and receive them into his own company. . . . The most intimate truth which this revelation gives about God and the salvation of man shines forth in Christ, who is himself both the mediator and the sum total of revelation.[6]

God's self-revelation, *Dei Verbum* taught, began in the very process of creation, which God saw was "good" (Genesis 1). It continued when God disclosed himself to primitive humanity, embodied in the figures of Adam and Eve, to whom God promised "redemption[,] . . . for he wishes to give eternal life to all those who seek salvation by patience in well-doing." Then God "called Abraham and made him into a great nation [cf. Genesis 12.2]," and "after the era of the patriarchs, he taught this nation, by Moses and the prophets, to recognize him as the only living and true God, as a provident Father and just judge." Thus "throughout the ages he prepared the way for the Gospel."[7]

That Gospel and the Redeemer who proclaimed it, Jesus Christ, stand at the center of history, for in Christ the deepest truths about the world, its origins, and its destiny were made known to humanity:

> After God had spoken many times and in various ways through the prophets, "in these last days he has spoken to us by a Son" [Hebrews 1.1–2]. For he sent his Son, the eternal Word who enlightens all men, to dwell among men and to tell them about the inner life of God. Hence Jesus Christ, sent as "a man among men," speaks the words of God [John 3.34], and accomplishes the saving work which the Father gave him to do [cf. John 5.36, 17.4]. As a result, he himself—to see whom is to see the Father [cf. John 14.9]—completed and perfected revelation and confirmed it with divine guarantees. . . . He revealed that God was with us, to deliver us from the darkness of sin and death, and to raise us up to eternal life.[8]

In *Dei Verbum*, then, the Second Vatican Council taught that God reveals himself, not just propositions about himself, and does so through both deeds and words in a process that culminates in Jesus Christ. In this teaching, as theologian Aidan Nichols, OP, has argued, Vatican II took a position ahead of, rather than between, the previously contending parties in Catholic theology. In *Dei Verbum*, the Council intended to "move beyond a purely propositional idea of revelation, as often entertained by traditionalists." But the dogmatic constitution did so "not by *rejecting* the way of propositions . . . but rather by *englobing* the propositional element within a wider whole."[9]

In a similar way, Vatican II resolved the debate over whether divine revelation had one source or two: Scripture alone, or Scripture and Tradition. That debate, *Dei Verbum* suggested, was miscast.

There is one "source" of revelation, God himself. And God makes himself (not just ideas about himself) known to humanity through both Scripture and those truths that come to us through the apostolic Tradition of the Church, describing their relationship and dogmatic unity in these terms:

> Sacred Tradition and sacred Scripture, then, are bound closely together, and communicate with each other. For both of them, flowing out from the same divine well-spring, come together . . . and move towards the same goal. Sacred Scripture is the speech of God as it is put down in writing under the breath of the Holy Spirit. And Tradition transmits in its entirety the Word of God which has been entrusted to the apostles by Christ the Lord and the Holy Spirit. . . . Sacred Tradition and sacred Scripture make up a single sacred deposit of the Word of God.[10]

Vatican II's second great affirmation in *Dei Verbum* was that God's self-revelation is valid for all times and peoples and continues to be made available to humanity through the Church: "God graciously arranged that the things he had once revealed for the salvation of all peoples should remain in their entirety throughout the ages and be transmitted to all generations." That was why Christ, "in whom the entire revelation of the most high God is summed up," created a missionary Church: he "commanded the apostles to preach the Gospel," through which they were "to communicate the gifts of God to all men." By their preaching, their witness, and the communities they founded, the apostles gave to others the gifts they had received, "whether from the lips of Christ, from his way of life and his works, or [what] they had learned . . . at the prompting of the Holy Spirit."

Some of what had been learned in this intensely Christocentric revelation of "saving truth" was, "under the inspiration of the . . . Holy Spirit, committed to . . . writing," and the Christian

Scriptures were born. Other facets of what had been learned were passed along through apostolic succession: "In order that the full and living Gospel might always be preserved in the Church the apostles left bishops as their successors." Those men and their successors had created what the Church knows as its Tradition. Scripture (in both the Old and New Testaments) and Tradition, therefore, "are like a mirror, in which the Church, during its pilgrim journey here on earth, contemplates God, from whom she received everything, until such time as she is brought to see him face to face as he really is [cf. John 3.2]." Through Scripture and Tradition, the Church remains in living and vital contact with its origins, such that "the Church, in her doctrine, life, and worship, perpetuates and transmits in every generation all that she herself is, all that she believes."[11]

The Scriptures are a permanent reality in the Church, in that new books are not added to the Bible over time; yet the Church's understanding of the Word of God in the Bible develops. Likewise, the revealed truths that the Church hands on from generation to generation in her Tradition are not a static patrimony. For as the First Vatican Council had affirmed in its Dogmatic Constitution on the Catholic Faith, the Church's understanding of the truths given to it "makes progress in the Church, with the help of the Holy Spirit." So there is "a growth in insight into the realities and words that are being passed on." Catholicism is a dynamic reality, and "as the centuries go by, the Church is always advancing toward the plenitude of divine truth, until the words of God are fulfilled in her."[12]

Doctrinal development was just that, however: development, not rupture with the past in the form of paradigm shifts. And the guardian of the authentic development of doctrine was not the theologians' guild; it was the "living teaching office" of the Church, located in the pope and the bishops by the will of Christ. That teaching office, or "magisterium," had "the task of giving an authentic interpretation of the Word of God, whether in its written form or in the form of Tradition." Yet the magisterium "is not superior to the Word of God but its servant. It teaches only what has been handed on to it . . . and all that it proposes for belief as being divinely revealed is drawn from this single deposit of faith." Scripture, Tradition, and the Church's teaching authority were "so connected and associated that one of them cannot stand without the others."[13]

Divine revelation is real; the Church's understanding of divine revelation is dynamic and developing. In the final analysis, however, revelation judges the Church and history. Absent that tether to revealed truth, the faith dissolves, and the Church with it.

The third critical teaching of *Dei Verbum*—a cluster of related affirmations, actually—restored the Bible to the people of the Church, put the Bible at the heart of Catholicism's evangelization and catechesis, and declared Scripture to be "the very soul of . . . theology."[14]

The Bible had not been especially prominent in Catholic piety since the sixteenth-century Reformations, and Catholics were rarely encouraged to become biblically literate; in the Counter-Reformation Church, Catholics learned catechism answers more than biblical quotations. In its apologetics, the Church tended to use the Bible as a quarry to be mined for proof-texts; but when modernity questioned the reliability of the Bible as a historical record and then proceeded to "demythologize" Scripture and reduce Jesus of Nazareth to a moral paragon and wisdom teacher, the proof-text approach to the Bible became less than persuasive. Dogmatic theology played a greater role than biblical studies in seminary training, and Catholic preaching suffered as a result.

The *ressourcement* theologies of the twentieth century recognized the deficiencies in all this, and the principal *ressourcement* theologians worked hard to give Catholic thinking a firmer biblical foundation. Their work was vindicated by Vatican II, as the Christocentricity that John XXIII urged the Council to adopt reverberated in *Dei Verbum*. There, the Council made its own the blunt dictum of Latin Christianity's first great biblical scholar, St. Jerome: "Ignorance of the Scriptures is ignorance of Christ."[15]

For the Second Vatican Council, then, the Bible was not a venerable text to be honored for its age, for the poetic beauty of some of its books, and for its occasional insights into the human condition. Yale's George Lindbeck, a Lutheran observer at Vatican II, often described the Bible as the "master code of reality," and that was the approach the Council adopted.[16] And if the Bible offered the key to understanding things as they are, then the Bible also offered a template for constructing a true humanism. How was that template or master code to be understood?

To begin with, it was to be understood as of divine origin: the Church, "relying on the faith of the apostolic age, accepts as sacred and canonical the books of the Old and New Testaments, whole and entire, with all their parts, on the grounds that, written under the inspiration of the Holy Spirit, . . . they have God himself as their author, and have been handed on to the Church as such." The divine author worked through human instruments, who wrote as men, not as machines taking dictation: "To compose the sacred books, God chose certain men who, all the while he employed them in this task, made full use of their powers and faculties so that, though he acted in them and by them, it was as true authors that they consigned to writing whatever he wanted written, and no more." From this inspired cooperation between God and men of faith, the Scriptures drew their distinctive authority, which was an authority in the realm of religious and moral truth: "The books of Scripture firmly, faithfully, and without error teach that truth which God, for the sake of our salvation, wished to see confided to the sacred Scriptures."[17]

The Bible was not, then, in competition with astronomy, astrophysics, history, geology, or any other human science. The "inerrancy" of the Scriptures involved the salvific truths contained in the biblical texts.[18] As for the four canonical gospels, the Council taught this about their historical reliability, the creativity of their authors, and their character as a written form of kerygmatic proclamation:

> Holy Mother Church has firmly and with absolute constancy maintained and continues to maintain that the four gospels . . . faithfully hand on what Jesus, the Son of God, while he lived among men, really did and taught for their eternal salvation. . . . [Then] the apostles handed on to their hearers what he had said and done, but with that fuller understanding which they, . . . enlightened by the Spirit of truth, now enjoyed. The sacred authors, in writing the four gospels, selected certain of the many elements which had been handed on, either orally or already in written form; others they synthesized or explained with an eye to the situation of the churches, the while sustaining the form of preaching, but always in such a fashion that they have told us the honest truth about Jesus.[19]

While constantly keeping in mind the critical question—"What is God saying to us in the inspired Scriptures?"—Catholic biblical interpretation ought to make use of various analytic tools, many of modern design, in order to grasp the truths the Bible intended to convey. The Council urged Catholic exegetes to distinguish among the various literary forms found in Scripture: historical writing, epistolary instruction, poetic expressions, prophetic proclamations, and so forth. Through that kind of careful analysis, *Dei Verbum* taught, the biblical scholar could "search out the meaning . . . which God had thought well to manifest through the medium of the [biblical author's] words." Moreover, biblical interpreters should pay close attention to the "unity of the whole of Scripture," rather than analyzing the various books of the Bible as if they had no relationship with each other. Biblical exegetes should also remember that they were engaged in a task within the Church and for the Church: biblical scholarship was an ecclesial discipline, and the Church's Tradition had much to teach modern biblical exegetes and theologians in drawing "true meaning from the sacred texts."[20] *Dei Verbum* thereby affirmed the insights of those *ressourcement* thinkers who had recovered the riches of patristic and medieval biblical interpretation for contemporary theology.

The Bible was not for scholars alone, however. The Scriptures should animate "all the preaching of the Church," and indeed "the entire Christian religion." Those afforded the privilege of preaching in the Church should make it their task to "distribute fruitfully the nourishment of the Scriptures" to all the Church's people, a nourishment that "enlightens the mind, strengthens the will, and fires the hearts of men with the love of God." Biblical preaching, in its turn, should inspire the Christian people to make full use of the "access to sacred Scripture," which, the Council taught, "ought to be open wide to the Christian faithful." Scholars, preachers, and lay Catholics alike should also recognize that "prayer should accompany the reading of sacred Scripture, so that a dialogue takes place between God and man."[21]

Through these affirmations—that the gospels are reliable accounts of the truths taught by Jesus Christ; that the Bible is a unity; that the New Testament is most fruitfully read "through" the prism of the Old Testament; that the Bible belongs to the whole Church, not just to clergy and scholars; that biblical preaching offers the Church's people an encounter with the living Word of God and empowers them for mission; and that Tradition helps us read Scripture thoughtfully, such that, as Tradition develops, so does the Church's understanding of Scripture—the Second Vatican Council both affirmed the reality of divine revelation and positioned Scripture as an integral part of the Church's evangelical mission. That affirmation was expressed at both the end and the beginning of the Dogmatic Constitution on Divine Revelation. In *Dei Verbum*'s prologue, Vatican II taught that the one "deposit" of the Word of God, composed by Scripture and Tradition, calls the Church into mission and proclamation: "Hearing the Word of God with reverence, and proclaiming it with faith, [this Council] assents to the words of St. John: 'We proclaim to you the eternal life which was with the Father and was made manifest to us—that which we have seen and heard we proclaim to you, so that you may have fellowship with us; and our fellowship is with the Father and with his Son, Jesus Christ' [1 John 1.2–3]."[22] The same note was struck in the dogmatic constitution's concluding section, where *Dei Verbum* expressed the conviction that, "by the reading and study of the sacred books, 'the Word of God may speed on and triumph' [2 Thessalonians 3.1] and the treasure of revelation entrusted to the Church may more and more fill the hearts of men."[23] The Catholic Church does not "own" divine revelation as a privilege peculiar to itself, for that would be like the fearful servant in Luke 19.12–27, who hid the treasure his master had entrusted to him, rather than putting it to work and increasing its value. Rather, the truths bequeathed to the Church in divine revelation call the Church into mission, for these truths about human nature and human community are meant to be shared with others for the sanctification and salvation of the world.

Enlightenment rationalism, especially in its nineteenth-century form, denied the reality of divine revelation: the reality of God's speech into the world's silence. Modern historical-critical study of the Bible either bracketed the question of Scripture's relationship to a divine word spoken into history or so diminished the truth-content of biblical revelation as to reduce the Bible to an occasionally insightful literary artifact from a distant past. Despite their claim to have liberated humanity from the chains of superstition, these tendencies in modernity-as-ideology diminished, rather than ennobled, the human condition. The denial of divine revelation, or its reduction to a few (increasingly contested) moral injunctions, was one facet of the crisis of Western humanism. As Solzhenitsyn, de Lubac, and others had argued, the rejection of any notion of a divine word of truth spoken into history was no small part of the self-destructive crisis of Western civilization. Confronted with these challenges, *Dei Verbum* and the Second Vatican Council proposed an ampler view of the human condition. The Council robustly and unabashedly affirmed the reality of divine revelation while refreshing the Catholic Church's understanding of how God deals with humanity, and asked modernity to consider whether it had not prematurely and preemptively narrowed the bandwidth of human knowledge.

The God of the Bible does not address humanity from outside history, *Dei Verbum* taught. In his self-revelation, he invites men and women into a personal encounter in which truths are disclosed: truths about God, to be sure, but also truths about humanity, its origins, its destiny, and its capacity to form genuine community. Those truths are *true*, the Council insisted, even if they do not satisfy atheistic humanism's concept of "truth." There is more to the truth than what is empirically verifiable, *Dei Verbum* insisted, and human beings diminish their humanity by positivistic reductions of what can be confidently known in this world.

In recognizing the importance of modern methods of analysis for a proper understanding of the Bible, and in its teaching on the distinctive character of religious knowledge, the Second Vatican Council was not reluctantly surrendering ground to intellectual modernity: it was calling modernity to a more capacious understanding of truth and knowledge. It did so by extending and deepening Catholicism's traditional understanding of faith. For as Pope John Paul II wrote in the 1998 encyclical on faith and reason, *Fides et Ratio*, the Second Vatican Council reaffirmed what the First Vatican Council had taught in its Dogmatic Constitution on the Catholic Faith in continuity with the teaching of the Council of Trent: "The truth attained by philosophy and the truth of revelation are neither identical nor mutually exclusive."[24]

Faith and reason both lead us to the truth about God and the truth about ourselves. There is no zero-sum competition here, for faith and reason, working together, expand humanity's horizons. Thus, as John Paul put it, echoing the teaching of *Dei Verbum*, faith and reason "are like two wings on which the human spirit rises to the contemplation of truth; and God has placed in the human heart a desire to know the truth—in a word, to know himself—so that, by knowing and loving God, men and women may also come to the fullness of truth about themselves."[25]

D*ei Verbum* also clarified just what Church doctrine is for. Divine revelation, the Council taught, is a matter of encountering a personal mystery of love before it is a matter of embracing a system of thought. Human beings being what we are, however, that mystery demands to be understood, and deepening human understanding of the mystery of love who is the God of the Bible is an evangelical imperative: How could Catholics proclaim and offer to others the gift they have received without ideas? That is why the Church formulated creeds and defined doctrines. Those creeds and doctrines exist so that, throughout history, men and women in any age can encounter God, even amid the silence of a world turned in upon itself. And in that encounter, human beings can enter into communion with God and "become sharers of the divine nature," as *Dei Verbum* put it.[26]

In this striking affirmation, based on its Christocentric conviction that "the most intimate truth" which divine revelation gives about God and us "shines forth in Christ[,] . . . the sum total of revelation," *Dei Verbum* cut to the heart of the challenge to both the Church and humanity posed by atheistic humanism and other forms of ideological modernity.[27] In doing so, the Second Vatican Council made its own one of those teachings from the Fathers of the Church retrieved by twentieth-century *ressourcement* theology: as St. Athanasius put it, the Son of God, the divine Word, became man "so that we might be made God."[28] Here was a humanism far bolder than anything proposed by Voltaire, Comte, Feuerbach, Marx, or Nietzsche. And the icon of this radical Christian humanism was Jesus Christ, crucified and risen.

Such boldness was not accidental. For, as Joseph Ratzinger, the conciliar *peritus* who had perhaps more influence on the development of *Dei Verbum* than any other theologian, remembered, bold teaching was exactly what John XXIII wanted from the Council. In Pope John's vision of Vatican II, the Council was to "radicalize" the faith, not weaken it by making concessions to modern intellectual sensibilities and shibboleths. That radicalization, in turn, would reinvigorate the Church for mission. Thus *Dei Verbum* and the Council it anchored Christologically should be read according to Pope John's original intention, as "the beginning of a new evangelization of the world."[29] That new evangelization had to be anchored in revealed truth—a concept under assault by the high culture of the West for two hundred years. By affirming boldly the reality of divine revelation and its enduring authority over time, Vatican II solidified the foundation of the Church's mission to convert and ennoble the world while calling Catholic theologians to challenge the cramped positivism that was enervating intellectual life and souring the human spirit.

The Second Ecumenical Council of the Vatican produced two dogmatic constitutions, the highest form of conciliar teaching—*Dei Verbum* and the Dogmatic Constitution on the Church, *Lumen Gentium*. These constitutions have equal authority in the Catholic Church's understanding of the relative weightiness of different types of conciliar texts. Read through the prism of John XXIII's original intention—that the Council lead to the sanctification of the world in response to the crisis of Western humanism and its lethal effects—*Dei Verbum* emerges as *the* fundamental achievement of Vatican II: the clarifying lens through which the rest of the Council's texts should be read.[30]

11

Sacrament of Authentic Human Community

The Dogmatic Constitution on the Church

A T THE END OF HIS BRIEF SURVEY OF THE CHURCH'S twenty previous ecumenical councils, historian Hubert Jedin noted in 1959 that "no truth of the faith is in greater need of a clear definition than the concept of the Church."[1] The Second Vatican Council offered no "definition" of the Church similar to the definition of Mary as *Theotokos* (God-Bearer) at the Council of Ephesus, or the carefully crafted definition of papal infallibility at Vatican I. Vatican II did something just as significant, however. In its Dogmatic Constitution on the Church, *Lumen Gentium*, the Council offered the Church and the world a biblically enriched, theologically deepened, and mission-driven portrait of Catholicism in all its dimensions. This was of paramount importance for Catholic self-understanding. It was also an essential pastoral response to one of modernity's greatest needs and an evangelical corrective to some of modernity's greatest failures.

Ideological modernity's often disparaging critique of traditional forms of community—familial, religious, political—and the dramatic weakening of many of those communities had led to a widespread sense of social fragmentation, especially in Europe after World War I. Ignoble and often lethal forms of ersatz community were one by-product of that disorientation. Totalitarianism—whether

Mussolini's fascism, the *Volkische* community of German National Socialist racial theory, or the dictatorship of the proletariat celebrated (if never achieved) by Marxism-Leninism—was one political expression of this ultramundane quest for authentic human community. In *Lumen Gentium*, the Second Vatican Council boldly proclaimed Catholicism's conviction that the human yearning for authentic community could be satisfied in the Church, the Mystical Body of Christ: a communion of disciples, empowered by the Holy Spirit and animated by right worship, that continued and extended Christ's presence and mission in the world.

That communion, the Council affirmed, transcended every boundary of race, class, or condition—and always had. As St. Paul insisted to the first-century Galatians, among those baptized into Christ there is "neither Jew nor Greek, there is neither slave nor free, there is neither male nor female," for all are "one in Christ Jesus" (Galatians 3.27–28). Thus the communion of the Church, *Lumen Gentium* taught, embodies the unity of the human race as no other. Because of its unity in Christ, "the Church . . . is in the nature of a sacrament—a sign and instrument . . . of communion with God and of unity among all men."[2]

That striking claim was one result of the renewal of the Catholic mind that had taken place from the mid-nineteenth through the mid-twentieth centuries.

The two-edged assault on Catholicism by Enlightenment rationalism and political modernity put the Church's official (or "Roman") ecclesiology into a defensive crouch, heavily focused on the Church as an institution with specific institutional prerogatives.[3] Reflecting Catholicism's long post-Constantinian entanglement with state power, this Roman theology typically presented the Church in essentially juridical and legal terms: the Catholic Church was the *societas perfecta*, the "perfect society," self-contained and self-governing, and adherence to it was defined by obedience to the perfect society's laws. In this perspective, the theology of the Church was the stepchild of canon law. And in this way of thinking, the Church's self-understanding was dominated by its hierarchical structure and its legal system, such that incorporation into the Church was largely conceived in terms of submission to ecclesiastical authority.

Yet while the dominant Roman ecclesiology hardened, and sometimes atrophied, in response to modernity's attacks, the nineteenth and twentieth centuries were a rich season of ecclesiological reflection in the Catholic Church.

The mid-nineteenth century was the era of Johann Adam Möhler and the retrieval of the first-millennium Fathers of the Church as sources for a renewed theology of the Church that went beyond the fine-tuning of a structure and a legal system. It was the time of Antonio Rosmini-Serbati and his call for Catholicism to disentangle itself from state power and become again a Church of evangelical persuasion. Matthias Scheeben, for whom Catholicism's raison d'être was the sanctification of a humanity primordially created to share in God's life, introduced the idea of the Church as Christ's "Mystical Body" in the world: an ecclesiology linked to an enriched Christian anthropology and ordered to mission and evangelization. Wilhelm Emmanuel von Ketteler promoted the idea of a public Church that, as an advocate for justice, challenged the social, political, and economic status quo even as it did the works of charity. In the twentieth century, Karl Adam and kerygmatic theology tied Catholicism's self-understanding closely to the Church's responsibility to proclaim Jesus Christ and the Gospel. In that proclamation, and in a Church empowered for mission by its liturgy, Romano Guardini saw the Catholic answer to the lethal Prometheanism of the age.

These Catholic thinkers set the stage for a more thorough *ressourcement* of ecclesiology. Yves Congar deepened the Church's understanding of the character of its Tradition. Henri de Lubac recovered the idea of the Church as mother (*mater ecclesia*) from the patristic theology of Origen and Cyprian. And Hans Urs von Balthasar developed Marian theology in an ecclesiological direction, stressing Mary's *fiat* ("Let it be to me according to your word" [Luke 1.38]) as the paradigm of all discipleship and the essential form of the Church. Many of these developments helped prepare the theological ground for Pius XII's 1943 encyclical *Mystici Corporis*, which pointed the Church toward a more Christocentric and sacramental self-concept and self-presentation.

These developments in turn set the theological stage for the conciliar debates that shaped *Lumen Gentium* in the definitive form in which it was promulgated on November 21, 1964, at the end of Vatican II's third period.

The draft text on the Church, *De Ecclesia*, written by one of the Council's preparatory commissions, was heavily influenced by the dominant Roman theology of the Church as a *societas perfecta* over against the world. It was not well-received, and no less stalwart a churchman than the formidable Cardinal Stefan Wyszyński criticized it for its shallowness. The Church, the primate of Poland insisted, had more to say to the modern world than that it was a "Church Militant" (the title of *De Ecclesia*'s opening chapter) in combat with the principalities and powers. Bishop Émile De Smedt of Belgium was even harsher, charging that the draft text was riddled with "triumphalism," "clericalism," and "legalism."[4]

Those critiques notwithstanding, certain themes in *De Ecclesia* carried over into the subsequent drafts of what eventually became *Lumen Gentium*. Some of them might surprise those who parse everything about Vatican II in terms of reactionary curial traditionalists versus broad-minded, transalpine liberals. For these themes suggest how the renewal of the Catholic mind in the nineteenth and twentieth centuries had begun to reconfigure the ecclesiological thinking of traditionally minded churchmen.

The draft text, for example, included a chapter on the imperative of Catholic social action by the laity, which would have been inconceivable ninety years earlier at Vatican I. It included a chapter on ecumenism, which would have been just as inconceivable at Pius IX's council. Moreover, the Curia-influenced draft of *De Ecclesia* recognized that Vatican I, short-circuited by world events, had ended before its doctrine on the papal teaching office could be complemented by a parallel teaching on the role of the bishops in the Church. As theologian Aidan Nichols noted, "the draft schema already had it in mind to declare the . . . order [of bishops] the sacramental continuation of the ministry of the apostles—such that the 'college' of bishops . . . can be said to succeed to the place enjoyed by the college of the apostles in the Church of the beginnings."[5]

Roman ecclesiologists had been among the principal critics of the interpretation of Pope Leo XIII's church-state theory by the American Jesuit John Courtney Murray and others working to develop a Catholic theory of religious freedom. Yet the curial draft of *De Ecclesia* (in addition to a predictable defense of Catholic rights in a non-Catholic state) included a reflection on religious tolerance in a Catholic state. Perhaps even more surprisingly, given the increasing prominence of Marian piety in Catholicism after the apparitions at La Salette (1846), Lourdes (1858), and Fátima (1917), the preparatory commission did not recommend a separate document on Mary (as many Mariological theologians and episcopal devotees of the Virgin wanted); rather, it included a Mariological "appendix" to *De Ecclesia*. The door was thereby opened for Vatican II to treat the Church's understanding of Mary as a crucial element within Catholicism's understanding of itself, not as a topic separate from the Church. The argument on this front—a separate conciliar document on Mary or a Marian component within a comprehensive conciliar reflection on the Church—continued for three years but was finally resolved when *Lumen Gentium* did more than the original draft of *De Ecclesia*

had proposed, affording Mary the dogmatic constitution's concluding chapter rather than an "appendix."[6]

The original draft of *De Ecclesia* was nonetheless framed in
predominantly institutional terms, and that framing is what
changed during the evolving conciliar debate on the nature of the
Church. Primate Wyszyński was vindicated: the Church did have
more to say to the world than the first draft text suggested. And
the first thing the Church said to the world was that Catholicism
is because of Jesus Christ. So the Church is, in theological terms, a
mystery: not in the sense of a puzzle to be solved, but in the sense
of a spiritual reality to be encountered in the experience of God's
love entering and reshaping history. The Church is a unique form
of human community, rooted in God and in God's salvific plan for
humanity. Before the Church is a structure or an organization, it is
an essential part of salvation history.[7]

Lumen Gentium begins, therefore, not with a definition of
what the Church is but with a declaration of faith in who Jesus Christ is: "Christ is the light of the nations" (*lumen gentium*,
the dogmatic constitution's *incipit*). And the "heart-felt desire" of
the Council was that, "by proclaiming his Gospel to every creature . . . it may bring to all men the light of Christ which shines
out visibly from the Church."[8] The Church is a communion of the
disciples who have made Christ's cause their own; whose task it
is to invite humanity into union with God; and who, in doing so,
invite the human world to be made holy—and thereby satisfied in
its desire for true community.

This intimacy between God and humanity is reflected in the
authentic community found among men and women who have
learned their full dignity through their relationship to God. The
communion of disciples that is the Church therefore embodies a
true humanism that finds the truth about our humanity in Christ,
which creates a different kind of society, a "sacramental society . . .
with a program for the sanctifying permeation of [the] human
environment."[9] That program is the Catholic response to the di-

lemma of an ultramundane world capable only of creating societies in which human beings are set against each other in perpetual conflict.

Theologian Avery Dulles stressed that this ecclesiology of sacramentality—*Lumen Gentium*'s teaching that "the Church . . . is in the nature of a sacrament"[10]—was of "foundational importance" for Vatican II and marked the decisive move by which Vatican II developed Catholicism's self-understanding beyond the juridical/legal model of the *societas perfecta*.[11] To describe the Church as a "sacrament"—the outward sign or embodiment of the mystery of Christ's continuing, salvific presence in the world—is to say that, before the Church is a hierarchically structured society governed by law, it is a community or communion formed by grace: by a participation in the very life of God. Or, as *Lumen Gentium* teaches, the Church is "the Kingdom of God now present in mystery," such that by proclaiming the Gospel and offering it without reservation to all humanity, the Church "becomes on earth the initial budding forth of that Kingdom."[12]

The Church has a structure or constituting form given it by Christ, and *Lumen Gentium* discussed the components of that constituting form and their interaction in considerable detail, setting the theological baseline for Vatican II's teaching on various Catholic vocations and states of life in five of its decrees. Within that hierarchical structure, the dogmatic constitution proposed the restoration of the diaconate—an order with New Testament roots that had become, in second-millennium Latin-rite Catholicism, a sacramental way-station for men en route to the priesthood—as a "proper and permanent rank of the hierarchy."[13] That important step notwithstanding, *Lumen Gentium* is quite clear in its teaching that the Church's hierarchical structure is not the starting point for the Church's self-understanding; Christ and the Gospel are. Moreover, the structures given by Christ to the Church—including the episcopate, the priesthood, and the diaconate—are for the sake of the Church's preservation in the truth and the Church's mission.

Over the past six decades, the title of *Lumen Gentium*'s second chapter, "The People of God," has often been taken as a populist counter to Pius XII's emphasis, in *Mystici Corporis*, on the distinction between the ordained hierarchy and the laity. Unpacking the teaching of *Lumen Gentium* this way tends to obscure more than it illuminates. Aidan Nichols's discussion of the dogmatic constitution's evolution helps clarify the meaning and significance of that second chapter, which was intended to "fill out" *Lumen Gentium*'s teaching, in its first chapter, on the "mystery" of the Church as a sacramental communion that reflects Christ, the light of the nations. After noting that the final form of *Lumen Gentium* "reverses the order of the 1963 draft text[,] which treated the Church's hierarchical structure before dealing with 'The People of God and the laity in particular,'" Nichols continued with the necessary correction:

> This reversal was later seen as a victory for lay people. Yet in fact *Lumen Gentium*'s chapter on the People of God pays no special attention to the laity when compared with any other component of the Church. What became a typical post-conciliar journalist's habit of calling the laity "the People of God" is without foundation in the conciliar texts. In chapter two of *Lumen Gentium*, the phrase "People of God" denotes the Church totality of which the laity constitute one part—albeit, of course, numerically speaking the predominant part.[14]

In *Lumen Gentium*, then, the "People of God" is the whole Church, to which "all men are called to belong," which is "present in all the nations of the earth . . . [and which] purifies, strengthens, and elevates" the "abilities, the resources and customs of peoples." The Church's universality is not of its own devising, nor is it an accident of history. It is "a gift from the Lord himself," so that authentic human community might be formed "under Christ the Head in the unity of his Spirit."[15]

Christ also gave a structure or order to this universal fellowship or communion of disciples, and *Lumen Gentium* developed the Church's understanding of that "ordering" in several ways.

With the First Vatican Council, the Second Vatican Council in *Lumen Gentium* affirmed the unique authority of the Bishop of Rome, the pope: "The Roman Pontiff, by reason of his office as Vicar of Christ . . . and as pastor of the entire Church, has full, supreme, and universal power over the whole Church, a power which he can always exercise unhindered."[16] Yet *Lumen Gentium* did not define that authority in autocratic terms. During the final phase of its development, Pope Paul VI proposed that chapter three of the dogmatic constitution include a sentence teaching that the pope "is accountable to the Lord alone." The Council's Theological Commission, on which traditional churchmen of ultramontanist views were represented, rejected that formulation of papal accountability, calling it "oversimplified," for "the Roman Pontiff is also bound to revelation itself, to the fundamental structure of the Church, to the sacraments, to the definitions of earlier councils, and other obligations too numerous to mention."[17]

Lumen Gentium then completed the interrupted work of Vatican I by teaching that the Church's bishops are true heirs of the apostles; that the "college" of bishops today is the successor of the apostolic "college" described in Acts 15; and that this college, with and under its head, the Bishop of Rome, has "supreme and full power over the universal Church."[18] Local bishops are true vicars of Christ in their particular Churches and are ordained to teach, govern, and sanctify; they do not simply execute instructions from Catholicism's Roman headquarters. Like the office of bishop itself, the episcopal college is ordered to mission: like the apostles, the bishops, by "sharing in [Christ's] power," are ordained to make "all peoples [Christ's] disciples . . . and thus spread the Church . . . until the end of the world." In doing so, the Catholic episcopate witnesses to the fact that "the Gospel, which [the apostles] were charged to hand on, is, for the Church, the principle of all its life for all time."[19] Therefore, among the many responsibilities conferred on bishops by episcopal ordination, "preaching the Gospel has pride of place."[20] Catholic bishops have administrative responsibilities for the oversight of their local Churches. Bishops are primarily teachers, though, not managers. And through their teaching and their sacramental sanctification of the Church, they should empower all the people of the Church to be effective witnesses to Christ in the world and effective proponents of authentic human community.

Lumen Gentium insisted that the evangelical responsibility to offer the Gospel to others belongs to all the People of God. For "God willed to make men holy and save them, not as individuals without any bond or link between them, but rather to make them into a people who might acknowledge him and serve him in holiness." Laypeople are the Church's principal instruments for the sanctification of the world, for "every individual layman must be a witness before the world to the resurrection and life of the Lord Jesus, and a sign of the living God."[21] Moreover, lay Catholics receive this apostolic commission to "nourish the world with spiritual fruits"[22] from their baptismal incorporation into the Mystical Body of Christ, not by delegation from the Church's ordained leadership:

> The apostolate of the laity is a sharing in the salvific mission of the Church. Through Baptism and Confirmation all are appointed to this apostolate by the Lord himself. . . . The laity, however, are given this special vocation: to make the Church present and fruitful in places and circumstances where it is only through them that she can become the salt of the earth. Thus every lay person . . . is at once the witness and the living instrument of the mission of the Church itself "according to the measure of Christ's bestowal" [Ephesians 4.7].[23]

The laity—incorporated into Christ at Baptism, consecrated by the Holy Spirit in Confirmation, and nourished by the body and blood of the Lord in the Eucharist—therefore participates in the Church's messianic character. Which means that every baptized Catholic shares in the three offices (*munera*, in the technical Latin term) of Christ: priest, prophet, and king. Being conformed to Christ in Baptism, every Catholic (and indeed every Christian) can worship in the truth (the priestly office), proclaim the truth (the prophetic office), and serve their brothers and sisters, in the Church and the world, in truth (the kingly office).[24]

Conformity to Christ in Baptism and the other sacraments of initiation (Confirmation and the Holy Eucharist) calls all the faithful into mission: to offer others friendship with Christ and membership in his Mystical Body as the fulfillment of the world's longing for a noble humanism capable of creating authentic human community:

> Christ is the great prophet who proclaimed the kingdom of the Father both by the testimony of his life and by the power of his word. Until the full manifestation of his glory, he fulfills this prophetic office, not only by the hierarchy who teach in his name and by his power, but also by the laity. He accordingly both establishes them as witnesses and provides them with the appreciation of the faith . . . and the grace of the word . . . so that the power of the Gospel may shine out. . . .
>
> Therefore, even when occupied by temporal affairs, the laity can, and must, do valuable work for the evangelization of the world.[25]

For their part, the Church's pastors "should recognize and promote the dignity and responsibility of the laity in the Church" in a mutual exchange of the Holy Spirit's gifts. In a proper relationship between pastors and people, the pastors should look to their people for advice and "give them the courage to undertake works on their own initiative." In this way, the lay sense of responsibility for the Church's mission is strengthened as their apostolic zeal is encouraged, while the pastors, "helped by the experience of the laity, are in a position to judge more clearly and more appropriately in spiritual as well as temporal matters." Thus "strengthened by all her members, the Church can . . . more effectively fulfill her mission for the life of the world."[26]

The sacramental communion that is the Church measures its fidelity to the mission Christ gave it by spiritual criteria. In a modern world often deaf to religious argument, the Church's proposal, Vatican II recognized, is best embodied by the quality of the lives of the Church's people. The noble, more humane manner of living displayed by Christians was what impressed and converted much of the Mediterranean world during the first great evangelization, in the centuries immediately following Christ.[27] Such a witness, the Council taught, must be revitalized in the Church on the edge of its third millennium.

Underscoring this point at length, the fifth chapter of *Lumen Gentium* insisted that all the baptized are called to a radical, Christlike holiness: as the dogmatic constitution put it, "all Christians in any state or walk of life are called to the fullness of Christian life and to the perfection of love, and by this holiness a more human manner of life is fostered also in earthly society."[28] Sanctity is not for the church sanctuary alone: the sanctification of the world is *the* Christian mission, in which all members of the Church share. And that mission can only be carried out by a holy people. So holiness, rather than being the preserve of a few exceptional people, is the ordinary measure of Christian life: "All the faithful," *Lumen Gentium* taught, "are invited and obliged to holiness."[29]

Holiness takes many forms in the Church: in marriage and family life; in the consecrated life vowed to poverty, chastity, and obedience; in celibate love and its exercise of that charity that displays "the same mind that Christ Jesus showed." The witness of martyrs is the "greatest testimony to love," for through it the disciple is made "like his master, who willingly accepted death for the salvation of the world." And while that dramatic form of holiness is "given to few," nevertheless all the baptized "must be prepared to confess Christ" before the world "and to follow him along the way of the cross amidst the persecutions which the Church never lacks."[30]

The universal call to holiness finds a brilliant exemplar in the Blessed Virgin Mary, to whom *Lumen Gentium* devoted its eighth and concluding chapter. By locating the Mother of God within the Church, Vatican II intended to reset one part of the ecumenical dialogue with those Christian communities who feared that Catholicism somehow put Mary above or outside the Church. At the same time, *Lumen Gentium* deepened the Church's Marian theology by considering "the Mother of the Lord . . . as the supreme icon of the pilgrim Church," in whom is previewed the destiny of the entire Church "in reaching the heavenly homeland rather than simply aspiring to it."[31]

Mary, the dogmatic constitution taught, is "the pre-eminent and . . . wholly unique member of the Church," who "occupies a place in the Church which is the highest after Christ and also closest to us," and her primordial discipleship stands as the Church's "type" and "its outstanding model in faith and charity."[32] In Mary's Assumption into heaven, defined as dogma by Pope Pius XII in 1950, the Church sees its own future. For as Mary was the first disciple of her Son by reason of her acceptance of the divine call in the Annunciation, so Mary, assumed body and soul into heaven, is the first of Christ's disciples to enjoy what awaits all in the fullness of the Kingdom of God. *Lumen Gentium* thus taught that "the Mother of Jesus in the glory which she possesses in body and soul in heaven is the image and beginning of the Church as it is to be perfected in the world to come . . . as a sign of certain hope and comfort to the pilgrim People of God."[33]

In its reflections on the Church, the Second Vatican Council had to confront the reality of a divided Christianity, and therefore had to define more precisely Catholicism's relationship to other Christian communities. The pursuit of Christian unity was high among Pope John XXIII's priorities for the Council. If the Council was to advance that cause, it had to find a way to "fit" those Christians who were not in full communion with the Catholic Church into Catholicism's understanding of the Church as the Mystical Body of Christ, which in *Lumen Gentium* "remains the principal form of Catholic ecclesiology, serving as a summation of the meanings of the many biblical images" of the Church that the dogmatic constitution surveyed in its opening chapter.[34]

For Pius XII in *Mystici Corporis*, this was a simple matter: the Catholic Church *is* the Mystical Body of Christ, full stop. As Aidan Nichols observed, however, that sharp delineation "appeared to deny any 'ecclesiality' or 'Church value' to non-Catholic Christian communities—even to the Eastern Orthodox, whose continuance of the apostolic succession had never been denied" by Catholicism. After no little discussion and controversy, Vatican II developed a more nuanced formula by teaching that the one Church of Christ "subsists in," but is not completely identical in every respect with, the Catholic Church (the Church that is "governed by the successor of Peter and by the bishops in communion with him"[35]). Nevertheless, *Lumen Gentium* immediately continued, "many elements of sanctification and truth are found outside" the "visible confines" of Catholicism, and these are spiritual gifts belonging to the one Church of Christ.

In the six decades since the Council, more ink was likely spilled over those two words, "subsists in" (*subsistit in*, in the conciliar Latin), than any other phrase in the sixteen documents of Vatican II. As noted by Aidan Nichols, some bishops found that phrasing too weak (even though it had been proposed in the Council's Theological Commission by Father Sebastian Tromp, SJ, a stout defender of *Mystici Corporis*[36]), and wanted to add qualifiers such as "in a complete way" or "by divine right." Nichols then defended the formulation in these terms:

> But the Theological Commission of the Council refused to accept these modifications. It argued that the phrase in the text was strong enough as it was . . . [and] the commission was right. It *was* a strong formulation. It replaced a weaker formula earlier suggested in the debate. This was *adest in*, meaning "is present in." On this view, the Mystical Body, the Church of the Creed, is present in the Catholic Church but without any suggestion that this could not be said in comparable terms of other Christian bodies. *Subsistit in* means that the being (the "subsistence") of the Mystical Body is found in the being of the Catholic Church but that [ecclesial reality] could be found in other [Christian bodies] as well.[37]

These seemingly abstract distinctions were and are crucial. The Catholic Church could not and would not say that it was anything other than the fullest expression in history of the one Church of Christ, such that Catholicism lived the life of the Mystical Body in a singular way. Yet a council determined to insert Catholicism into the ecumenical movement could not deny ecclesial weight to those Christian communities with which it wanted to be in dialogue. Nor could a council that described the Church in sacramental terms deny the efficacy of Baptism, properly conferred, in other Christian confessions. *Subsistit in* was not intended to deny or diminish the Catholic Church's sense of itself. Rather, the Council's intention was to incorporate within that Catholic self-understanding the reality of Christian communities that, as *Lumen Gentium* would acknowledge, baptize in the name of the Trinity, revere the Scriptures, pray, and worship liturgically—and who are therefore "in some real way joined to us [the Catholic Church] in the Holy Spirit for, by his gifts and graces, his sanctifying power in also active in them."[38]

A Church understanding itself as a "sacrament" or "sign" of "unity among all men" also had to clarify its relationship to "those who have not yet received the Gospel"—those who did not believe in Christ, those who conceived of God differently, and those who did not believe in God at all. What was the relationship between these men and women and the People of God?[39] *Lumen Gentium* described those relationships within the context of salvation history while setting the baseline for Vatican II's further teaching on this subject.

First, the dogmatic constitution recognized the unique role of the Jewish people in the history of revelation and salvation: "that people to whom the covenants and promises were made, and from which Christ was born according to the flesh." God does not repent of his gifts, the Council taught, and therefore the Jewish people are "most dear" to the People of God.[40]

The divine "plan of salvation" also included "those who acknowledge the Creator, in the first place amongst whom are the Muslims," who "together with us . . . adore the one, merciful God, mankind's judge on the last day." Then, taking a cue from St. Paul in Acts 17, *Lumen Gentium* taught that God remains close to "those who in shadows and images seek the unknown God," the God who enlivens all creation, for "the Savior wills all men to be saved [cf. 1 Timothy 2.4]." God's salvific will also extends to "those who, through no fault of their own, do not know the Gospel of Christ or his Church, but who nevertheless seek God with a sincere heart, and, moved by grace, try in their actions to do his will as they know it through the dictates of conscience." God even offers "the assistance necessary for salvation" to those who, "without any fault of theirs, have not yet arrived at an explicit knowledge of God and who . . . strive to live a good life." In the perspective of salvation history, the truths that nonbelievers come to know, and the good they do, are a "preparation for the Gospel"; those truths, and that goodness, reflect the divine love "given by [Christ] who enlightens all men that they may at length have life."[41]

To recognize God's salvific care for all humanity ought not, however, weaken the Church's commitment to evangelization and mission. The "Evil One" darkened human minds with error, and the Church had to challenge those errors with the truth of the Gospel, which was the truth about humanity and its destiny. The Gospel also had to be proposed to those tempted to "ultimate despair" in a world of silence. Therefore, the Church must take "zealous care" to be about the work of evangelization, so that it might be faithful to the Lord who had solemnly commanded his friends to "preach the Gospel to every creature [Mark 16.16]." When it does so, "whatever good is found . . . in the minds and hearts of men or in the rites and customs of peoples" is "purified, raised up, and perfected for the glory of God, the confusion of the devil, and the happiness of men." Therefore, to take seriously the divine will that all be saved must mean to take just as seriously the fact that "each disciple of Christ has the obligation of spreading the faith to the best of his ability."[42]

In *Lumen Gentium*, the Catholic Church recognized both the universality of the divine will to save and the unique role of the Church as the embodiment in history of that salvific design. Thus, in concluding its reflection on the Church as the People of God, the Council taught that the Church must pray and work so that "the fullness of the whole world" is incorporated into that People. For then, in Christ, the messianic head of the People of God, "all honor and glory [will] be rendered to the Creator, the Father of the universe."[43]

A Church dedicated to the conversion of modernity inevitably opens itself to the cultural pressures of modernity, including modernity's inbred skepticism about institutional authority. In the post-conciliar years, submission to those pressures (either conscious or unwitting) gave rise to what might be thought of as Liquid Catholicism: a Catholicism that rushes ahead of God in search of secular relevance, thereby embracing the spirit of the age rather than challenging that spirit and its manifestations in culture and society with the truths of the Gospel. Liquid Catholicism claims to be, and its proponents doubtless want it to be, pastorally sensitive and responsive. But a Church without form, a community constantly reinventing itself because of an incapacity or unwillingness to define and adhere to settled doctrinal and moral boundaries, cannot offer what is being sought by a world disoriented by its own formlessness and searching for authentic community.

By contrast, *Lumen Gentium*, which reflects a genuine development of Catholic self-understanding and offers a far richer ecclesiology than the fossilized concept of the Church as a *societas perfecta*, reaffirmed the classic Catholic conviction that the Church has a permanent form or constitution given it by Christ, and that all authentic Catholic reform is a renewal of that constituting, Christocentric form. In doing so, *Lumen Gentium* strengthened the foundations from which an effective mission to sanctify the world, creating authentic human community in place of social fragmentation, could be launched.

12

To Worship the One Worthy of Worship

The Constitution on the Sacred Liturgy

THE "LITURGY WARS" THAT HAVE RIVEN THE CATHOLIC Church since the Second Vatican Council have obscured the intent and the teaching of the Council's Constitution on the Sacred Liturgy, known by its Latin *incipit* as *Sacrosanctum Concilium*. And it is essential for understanding Vatican II to grasp *Sacrosanctum Concilium* for what it really is.

The Constitution on the Sacred Liturgy is not a stand-alone text. *Sacrosanctum Concilium* is intrinsically connected to *Dei Verbum*, *Lumen Gentium*, and John XXIII's original intention for the Council: that Vatican II revivify Catholicism as a Christocentric, sacramentally ordered, and evangelically vibrant movement for the world's conversion and sanctification. Such a movement needs nourishment. That nourishment comes from right worship.

Humanity is constantly tempted to idolatry, which is the worship of that which is not worthy of worship. Modernity confers no immunity to that temptation; indeed, modernity's solipsism and narcissism amplify the form of idolatry dramatically expressed when Israel worshipped a golden calf in Exodus 32.7–20. Joseph Ratzinger's exegesis of that famous scene demonstrates how eerily "modern" it can seem:

The worship of the golden calf is a self-generated cult. When Moses stays away for too long, and God himself becomes inaccessible, the people just fetch him back [through the image of the bull calf]. Worship becomes a feast that the community gives itself, a festival of self-affirmation. Instead of being worship of God, it becomes a circle closed in on itself. . . . The dance around the golden calf is an image of this self-seeking worship. It is a kind of banal self-gratification.[1]

Over the centuries, modernity cast up many false deities: the nation, the state, the revolution, science, the *Führer*, Lenin's mummy, wealth, and the pleasure principle. In each instance, the worship of that which was not worthy of worship led to personal decadence and social decay; in some cases, it led to mass slaughter. In postmodernity, the object of false worship is analogous to Ratzinger's description of what was happening in the incident of the golden calf, for the postmodern world worships the imperial, autonomous, self-constituting Self—the god of Me.

In this perspective, *Sacrosanctum Concilium* and Vatican II's effort to deepen and revitalize the Church's worship was both an effort to remind the Church of its essence as a Christ-centered sacramental communion and a crucial part of the Catholic proposal for a renewed and ennobled humanism. Human beings, theotropic creatures, are going to worship *something*. A liturgically enlivened and evangelically vibrant Catholicism could, the Council hoped, invite an often confused humanity into true worship, the kind of worship that leads to the flourishing of the individual and to authentic human community in social solidarity: the worship of the One who alone is worthy of worship.

For all the sometimes bitter controversy over the implementation of the liturgical reforms mandated by *Sacrosanctum Con-*

cilium, there was little contention over the document during the conciliar debates of 1962 and 1963. According to Aidan Nichols, the original draft, written by members of the Roman Curia before the Council opened, survived "largely intact" once the Council convened, the theological *periti* analyzed it, and the bishops debated it.[2] That should be remembered in any attempt to grasp the teaching of *Sacrosanctum Concilium*. The reasons for it are not hard to identify.

Pope Pius XII's 1947 encyclical on liturgical renewal, *Mediator Dei*, was well received throughout the world Church; it vindicated and further energized a Liturgical Movement active since the nineteenth century, especially in Europe. That movement achieved one of its principal objectives in Pius XII's reforms of the liturgy of Holy Week in 1951 and 1955. These developments in papal teaching and actual liturgical practice predisposed many of the bishops coming to the Council to expect, and welcome, further liturgical development as a result of Vatican II's deliberations—an openness strengthened by the concerns of missionary bishops for a liturgical renewal that addressed their specific needs.[3] That such changes were welcome was clearly indicated by the vote in which *Sacrosanctum Concilium* was approved during the Council's second period: 2,174 to 4.

What did *Sacrosanctum Concilium* teach?

The constitution's brief first paragraph set the context by summarizing John XXIII's *Gaudet Mater Ecclesia*: the purposes of the "Most Sacred Council" were to "impart an ever-increasing vigor to the Christian life of the faithful"; to make the Church a more effective instrument of sanctification by adapting "to the needs of our age" those facets of Catholic life that can and ought to be developed; to promote unity "among all who believe in Christ"; and to do all this in order to "strengthen whatever can call all mankind into the Church's fold," and thus into a true (because Christocentric) community. "Undertaking the reform and promotion of the liturgy," the Church's worship, would serve the sanctification and renewal of Catholic life for the sake of Catholicism's mission of sanctifying the world.[4]

Sacrosanctum Concilium immediately went on to position the liturgy at the very center of Catholic life. In a beautifully crafted expression of Catholicism's nature and purpose in a world longing for contact with the transcendent, the constitution described the Church's worship as an enlivening, humanizing meeting of the finite with the infinite:

> For it is the liturgy through which, especially in the divine sacrifice of the Eucharist, the work of our redemption is accomplished, and it is through the liturgy, especially, that the faithful are enabled to express in their lives and manifest to others the mystery of Christ and the real nature of the true Church. The Church is essentially both human and divine, visible but endowed with invisible realities, zealous in action and dedicated to contemplation, present in the world, but as a pilgrim, so constituted that in her the human is directed toward and subordinated to the divine, the visible to the invisible, action to contemplation, and this present world to that city yet to come, the object of our quest. The liturgy daily builds up those who are in the Church, making of them a holy temple of the Lord, a dwelling place for God in the Spirit, to the mature measure of the fullness of Christ. At the same time [the liturgy] marvelously increases their power to preach Christ and thus show forth the Church, a sign lifted up among the nations, to those who are outside, a sign under which the scattered children of God may be gathered together until there is one fold and one shepherd.[5]

Liturgy, or right worship, is not just what the Church does at certain times and in certain places. The Church's worship is the fullest expression of what the Church *is*. The Church is the continuation of Christ's redemptive work in the world for the sanctification of humanity. The Church is the locus of authentic human community and the agent of genuine human flourishing. The Church is the herald of a true humanism because it is a place of encounter with the transcendent: with a God who ennobles us rather than diminishing us.

Understanding *Sacrosanctum Concilium*'s theology of the liturgy is thus crucial to grasping its intention.

Vatican II's liturgical theology recapitulated and developed Pius XII's teaching in *Mediator Dei*, which, as its *incipit* suggests, stressed Jesus Christ as the priestly mediator between God and humanity. As Aidan Nichols put it, *Sacrosanctum Concilium* reiterated *Mediator Dei*'s teaching in asserting that "the liturgy . . . is an exercise of the priestly office of Christ," the public worship offered to the Father "by the Mystical Body of Jesus Christ, that is, by the Head and his members."[6] As for development, *Sacrosanctum Concilium* laid greater stress than *Mediator Dei* on the eschatological character of the liturgy: the liturgy as an anticipation of life within the Kingdom of God in its fullness. In one of its most notable sections, the Constitution on the Sacred Liturgy, drawing on various Eastern traditions of Catholic worship, such as the Divine Liturgy of St. John Chrysostom, described the eucharistic celebration of the Mass in these vibrantly eschatological terms:

> In the earthly liturgy we take part in a foretaste of the heavenly liturgy which is celebrated in the Holy City of Jerusalem toward which we journey as pilgrims, where Christ is sitting at the right hand of God, minister of the Holy of Holies and of the true tabernacle. With all the warriors of the heavenly army we sing a hymn of glory to the Lord; venerating the memory of the saints, we hope for some part and fellowship with them; we eagerly await the Savior, Jesus Christ, until he our life shall appear and we too will appear with him in glory.[7]

The liturgy does not take the Church "out" of the world. Rather, it offers the Church an experience of the amplitude within which this world exists. And that experience is ordered to mission—to sharing with others the gifts of grace conveyed in the liturgy. Having experienced through their worship the glory and joy of life in the Kingdom, which is life within the light and life of the Triune God, the people of the Church can "announce the good tidings of salvation to those who do not believe, so that all men may know the one true God and Jesus Christ whom he has sent."[8]

Liturgy is right worship, which means giving God what God is due. That right worship is ordered to mission because God has commanded the Church through his crucified and risen Son to "go and make disciples of all nations" (Matthew 28.19). As Nichols commented, "the framers of the constitution saw this eschatological orientation as vital for the Church's outward mission and not just for her inner contemplative side. It is from the forming of the faithful in this essentially heavenly orientation that the Council Fathers hoped to see the introduction of what the constitution calls a 'fortification' of the power to preach Christ and to exhibit the mystery of the Church to those outside."[9] Rightly understood, then, the liturgical renewal mandated by *Sacrosanctum Concilium* is intrinsically linked to John XXIII's intention that Vatican II promote a Christocentric humanism and authentic human community amid the civilizational crisis of late modernity.

Sacrosanctum Concilium's stress on the eschatological or Kingdom character of the Church's public worship also reflected Vatican II's emphasis on salvation history. Throughout the liturgy, but especially in the Mass, the Church is reminded that salvation history is the inner dynamic of world history. In the Eucharist, the Church reads the Scriptures of the Old and New Testament, retelling the stories of God's self-revelation in history through the People of Israel and through the incarnate Word of God, Jesus Christ. That divine self-disclosure reaches its fulfillment in the Paschal Mystery of Christ's passion, sacrificial death, resurrection, and ascension, which the Mass both commemorates and makes present anew.[10] Through the experience of the Eucharist, the people of the Church are reminded that salvation history—the history that unfolds under the chapter headings Creation, Fall, Promise, Prophecy, Incarnation, Redemption, Sanctification, the Kingdom of God—does not run parallel to world history (the history that unfolds under the chapter headings Ancient Civilizations, Greece and Rome, the Middle Ages, Renaissance and Reformation, the Age of Reason, the Age of Revolution, the Space Age, the Digital Age). Salvation history is what is unfolding inside "world history," giving that history its true meaning viewed against its proper horizon.

The loss of that sense of an inner, salvific history of the world was, and is, one reason for the civilizational crisis that Vatican II was summoned to address.[11] In the eucharistic experience of biblical word and sacramental sacrifice, the Church experiences the full panorama of salvation history, which begins with God's acts and words in the Old Testament, reaches its apogee in the Incarnation of the Son of God and his salvific death and resurrection, and continues after his ascension through the vivifying work of the Holy Spirit, who empowers the Church to teach the world the truth about its inner story.[12] That is why the liturgy, according to *Sacrosanctum Concilium*, "is the summit toward which the activity of the Church is directed" as well as "the fount from which all her powers flow."[13]

Several of the constitution's other contributions to the renewal of Catholic worship demonstrate its relationship to Pope John XXIII's original intention for Vatican II.

The Constitution of the Sacred Liturgy emphasized the Christocentricity of Catholic worship and thus the liturgy's capacity to foster a true humanism. *Sacrosanctum Concilium* did this by identifying the many ways in which the Head of the Mystical Body is present to the members of the body in the liturgy, filling them with the grace of the divine life and enabling them to live the truths of their human dignity:

> Christ is always present in his Church, especially in her liturgical celebrations. He is present in the Sacrifice of the Mass, not only in the person of his minister . . . but especially in the eucharistic species [the consecrated bread and wine]. By his power he is present in the sacraments so that when anybody baptizes, it is really Christ himself who baptizes. He is present in his word since it is he himself who speaks when the holy scriptures are read in the Church. Lastly, he is present when the Church prays and sings, for as he has promised, "where two or three are gathered together in my name there I am in the midst of them" [Matthew 18.20].[14]

Sacrosanctum Concilium also taught the imperative of the Catholic people's "full, conscious, and active participation" in the Church's liturgical celebrations, not as a concession to modern or populist sensibilities but because such participation is "demanded by the very nature of the liturgy" as Christian worship. In Baptism, the Christian people are constituted as "a chosen race, a royal priesthood, a holy nation, a redeemed people [1 Peter 2.9, 4–5]," and therefore have a "right and obligation" to participate in the Church's public worship.[15] Post-conciliar misconceptions notwithstanding, this was neither a radical nor a new idea: in his 1929 apostolic constitution on the Church's divine worship, *Divini Cultus*, Pope Pius XI taught that the Catholic faithful ought not be "strangers or silent spectators" at the Eucharist, an admonition picked up word for word by *Sacrosanctum Concilium*.[16] Neither was the constitution's teaching that, at Mass, the Catholic people offer Christ, "the immaculate victim," to the Father, "not only through the hands of the priest" celebrating the Mass, "but with him," such that they should, through this offering of Christ, "learn to offer themselves." Pius XII had made a similar point in *Mediator Dei*.[17]

While those three adjectives—"full, conscious, and active"—have been almost as controverted as *Lumen Gentium*'s teaching that the one Church of Christ "subsists in" the Catholic Church, *Sacrosanctum Concilium*'s purposes in this matter seem clear. Building on the work of the Liturgical Movement as validated by Pius XII in *Mediator Dei*, *Sacrosanctum Concilium* intended to foster and enhance a profound sense of the sacramental liturgy, and especially the Eucharist, as the entire Church's participation, through its worship, in the mystery of God's salvific presence in history. Such a recovery was necessary after a period in which "liturgy" meant the performance of certain rites by priests: something the laity, acting as spectators, attended because of legal obligation. For decades, the Church had worked to inculcate a sense of liturgical empowerment in the laity, by, for example, promoting the use of missals at Mass, so that the worshipping congregation could follow the words and actions of the liturgy in their own language while the priest celebrated the Eucharist in Latin. *Sacrosanctum Concilium* confirmed and extended that effort while also linking active participation in the liturgy to empowerment for mission, another point stressed by the Liturgical Movement.

Questions about certain ways in which the Council's injunction to facilitate "full, conscious, and active participation" was implemented are legitimate subjects of post-conciliar debate. There should be no controversy, however, about the nature of the liturgy as a communal act in which priest-celebrant and congregation play distinctive roles while acting together as the People of God offering right worship to the One worthy of worship. Nor should there be serious controversy over the linkage *Sacrosanctum Concilium* drew between a laity participating in the offering of Christ to the Father in the Eucharist and a laity that, having received Christ back from the Father in Holy Communion, takes Christ back into the world in mission. These were quite traditional Catholic themes.

The constitution's re-centering of the rhythms of the Church's liturgical year on Sunday also deserves attention. "The Lord's Day," *Sacrosanctum Concilium* taught, is "the original feast day, and it should be proposed to the faithful and taught to them so that it becomes in fact a day of joy and of freedom from work." Because Sunday is "the foundation and kernel of the whole liturgical year," its celebration ought not be replaced by other feasts "unless they be truly of the greatest importance" (such as the celebration of a parochial or diocesan patron saint).[18] This provision of the constitution was intended to animate the laity for mission. Immersing themselves in the Paschal Mystery on Sunday, the "Easter" of every week, and receiving Christ's gifts in his eucharistic body and blood, the people of the Church would be further empowered to make their lives into gifts for others through works of charity and evangelization. The weekly renewal of faith through the Church's anticipatory participation in the eternal banquet of heaven, which is beyond history, would help the People of God find intensified purpose within history.

Living a sacramentally energized life in mission requires knowing the story the Church proposes to the world as the world's true story. *Sacrosanctum Concilium* therefore stressed the intimate and unbreakable linkage between the Church's liturgical worship and the Scriptures:

> Sacred scripture is of the greatest importance in the celebration of the liturgy. For it is from it that lessons are read and explained in the homily, and psalms are sung. It is from the scriptures that the prayers, collects, and hymns draw their inspiration and their force, and that actions and signs derive their meaning. Hence in order to achieve the restoration, progress, and adaptation of the sacred liturgy it is essential to promote the warm and lively

appreciation of sacred scripture to which the venerable tradition of Eastern and Western rites gives testimony.[19]

The constitution thus mandated a richer menu of biblical readings in both the Mass and the Divine Office (the Church's official daily prayer, which is required of deacons, priests, bishops, and those in consecrated religious life). By opening "the treasures of the Bible . . . more lavishly," the reformed liturgy was intended to immerse the people of the Church in the story of salvation history, and to help missionary disciples "see" the world they are called to convert and sanctify through a biblical lens.[20] The constitution further urged that the Church's deacons, priests, and bishops, in their homilies and sermons, teach "the mysteries of the faith and the guiding principles of the Christian life" through the biblical readings assigned to each liturgical celebration.[21] The model here seems to have been the expository preaching of the first-millennium Fathers of the Church, to which those in Holy Orders were to be regularly exposed through the revised Divine Office.[22] Preaching ought to foster not just understanding, but greater holiness. For, as *Lumen Gentium* taught, only a holy people can be a people in mission.

Holiness is nourished by prayer, which is why the Council also recommended the Divine Office (usually referred to since Vatican II as the Liturgy of the Hours) to all the people of the Church, so that "the whole course of the day and night [could] be consecrated by the praise of God."[23]

Sacrosanctum Concilium subordinated the liturgical year's sanctoral cycle—the Church's celebrations of the feast days of the saints—to the salvation-history cycle of the great liturgical seasons of Advent, Christmas, Lent, Easter, and the Sunday celebration of the Eucharist. The Council did not, however, minimize the importance of celebrating the saints, whose lives "proclaim the wonderful works of Christ in his servants and offer to the faithful fitting examples for their imitation."[24] The sanctoral cycle of the liturgical year teaches that holiness is available to everyone, even as the variety of saints celebrated remind the Church that there is no one model of Christian sanctity.

On the question of the language in which the Church's liturgical celebrations should be conducted, there was a wide spectrum of opinion during the conciliar debate that led to *Sacrosanctum Concilium*. Some bishops wished to retain Latin throughout the liturgy, arguing that it was an important means of expressing the Catholic Church's unity amid its increasing diversity. Other bishops called for some use of vernacular languages in the liturgy, including the Mass. The conciliar decision on this point was something of a muddle. In section 36, *Sacrosanctum Concilium* laid down that "the use of the Latin language, with due respect to particular law, is to be preserved in the Latin rites." Then, three sentences later, the door was opened to what would eventually become a complete "vernacularization" of Latin-rite Catholicism, when the constitution decreed that it was for the "competent territorial ecclesiastical authority"—which came to mean national bishops' conferences—"to decide whether, and to what extent, the vernacular language is to be used." A similar compromise formula was used to settle the question of the degree to which the Roman Rite could be "adapted" to local cultural conditions. While affirming the need to maintain "the substantial unity of the Roman Rite," the constitution also allowed those "competent territorial ecclesiastical authorities" to undertake some "adaptations" of the Roman Rite, or even "more radical adaptations," in which "elements from the traditions and cultures of individual peoples might appropriately be admitted to divine worship." Another door was thereby opened, in this case to both legitimate adaptations and grave confusions.

Viewed through the prism of John XXIII's original intention for Vatican II, *Sacrosanctum Concilium* comes into focus as the Second Vatican Council's effort to invite the modern world beyond idolatry and to consider the possibility of living within a more truly humanistic concept of time. By teaching that, in the course of the liturgical year, the Church "unfolds the whole mystery of Christ from the incarnation and nativity to the ascension, to Pentecost, and [to] the expectation of the blessed hope of the coming of the Lord," the Council also reminded Catholics that, through the liturgy and its seasons, "the riches of the Lord's powers and merits . . . are in some way made present for all time"—including this time.[25] To live liturgically is to live in a different time zone, one in which salvation history is perceived to be the inner dynamic of world history, such that the imperatives of the moment "in the world" appear in sharper relief. To live liturgically is to live in a temporal environment in which Christ himself is constantly present, continuing his work of redemption.[26]

By describing the liturgy, the Church's public worship, as the "fount" and "summit" of the Church's life, *Sacrosanctum Concilium* and Vatican II called modernity beyond its flattening out of the world, as *Dei Verbum* called modernity to recognize the openness to transcendence built into the human condition. In right worship, the men and women of modernity encountered the truth that salvation history is at work within history, giving "the world" a new depth and texture. The teaching that this encounter took place liturgically was an invitation to modernity to widen the aperture of its perceptions of reality through an immersion in the divine mystery by which everything came to be and is held in being.

In the text of *Sacrosanctum Concilium*, none of this reimagining of the liturgy implied a negation of the past. The liturgical constitution was a vindication of Pius XII and "the crowning of his labors," as one of the drafters of the constitution put it.[27] It was also a "reappropriation of the patristic vision of the theological nature of the liturgy" that cannot be set over against the Council of Trent or the Tridentine liturgy that was a result of that

Council. As liturgical scholar Pamela Jackson put it, "those who drafted *Sacrosanctum Concilium* saw themselves as building on the teaching of Trent and deepening it." Thus the bishop who presented the constitution's draft sections on the Eucharist to Vatican II "explained that there was no need to repeat everything that the Council of Trent had already stated so well."[28] Under the pressures of the various Reformations, Trent had to clarify the Catholic understanding of each element in the sacramental system and the Church's worship. Vatican II sought to bring that, and what had been learned since, into a synthesis of the Church's liturgical self-understanding that ordered right worship to a deepening personal conversion into Christ and to a more effective exercise of the Church's evangelical mission.

The evangelical intention of *Sacrosanctum Concilium* and its genuine theological achievements should be kept in mind when considering the many obstacles encountered in its implementation, which continue six decades after its promulgation.[29]

13

Design for a Christocentric Humanism

The Pastoral Constitution on
the Church in the Modern World

WHILE EVERY DOCUMENT PROMULGATED BY THE SECOND Vatican Council should be read in reference to the dogmatic constitutions *Dei Verbum* and *Lumen Gentium*, in no case is this more important than in considering *Gaudium et Spes*, Vatican II's Pastoral Constitution on the Church in the Modern World, which takes its Latin *incipit* from the "joy and hope" of modern humanity: themes the text addresses (along with modernity's "grief and anguish") in considerable detail.

Because *Gaudium et Spes* delves into historical analysis and public policy far more than any other conciliar document, the temptation to interpret the text through a political or ideological lens has often proven irresistible. That temptation must be resisted if the pastoral constitution is to be properly understood and its various proposals for the human future thoughtfully assessed. The most significant affirmations in *Gaudium et Spes*—largely found in its first part, "The Church and Man's Vocation"*—come into

---

* *Gaudium et Spes* (and the translation of it used here) was written decades before the use of the term "man" for "the human person of either sex as a unique creature" became fraught in various ways. As no other translations of the Latin *homo* is without its own difficulties, "man" is retained here to refer both to all human beings, without regard to their biological sex, and to the individual human person.

clearer focus when it is read as a pastoral development of Vatican II's doctrinal teaching in *Dei Verbum* and *Lumen Gentium*. The time-conditioned and sociologically dependent second part of the pastoral constitution, "Some More Urgent Problems," is of less concern for the Church in the twenty-first century than it was in the twentieth, although it is not without insight.[1]

The Pastoral Constitution on the Church in the Modern World had an exceptionally complicated gestation during the four periods of Vatican II and the intervening conciliar intersessions.[2] That complex history notwithstanding, *Gaudium et Spes* was always intended to meet John XXIII's hopes for advancing a new Christian humanism. That intention is demonstrated in its tenth section, which sets the essential Christocentric framework for the lengthy text that follows:

> The Church believes that Christ, who died and was raised for the sake of all, can show man the way and strengthen him through the Spirit in order to be worthy of his destiny: nor is there any other name among men by which they can be saved. The Church likewise believes that the key, the center, and the purpose of the whole of man's history is to be found in its Lord and Master. . . . And that is why the Council, relying on the inspiration of Christ, the image of the invisible God, the firstborn of all creation, proposes to speak to all men in order to unfold the mystery that is man and cooperate in tackling the main problems facing the world today.

Those sentences outline the twofold analytic approach *Gaudium et Spes* would take to understanding the challenges of the late modern world: Jesus Christ reveals in himself the truth about the human person and the trajectory of human history; that Christocentric understanding of the deep truths of the human condition is essential to a proper analysis of the "joys and hopes, the grief and anguish," of late modern humanity, and to finding remedies for humanity's contemporary dilemmas. Everything of enduring value in the pastoral constitution flows from this radical Christocentricity, which the *ressourcement* theologians who worked on the text for over four years insisted upon. Concerned that a document drawing heavily on the social sciences could lose its proper kerygmatic foundation and evangelical orientation, conciliar theological advisers such as Yves Congar and Jean Danielou (in league with Henri de Lubac, and, later, the archbishop of Kraków, Karol Wojtyła) argued that the constitution should be "built on the bedrock doctrine of Christian anthropology—namely, the doctrine of man as made in the image and likeness of God." Parallel concerns raised by an ecumenical observer, the Calvinist theologian Lukas Vischer, led to additions on "the unmistakably supernatural theme of the Lordship of Christ [as revealed] through the Paschal Mystery" of Christ's passion, death, resurrection, and ascension—thereby illustrating the impact that Protestant observers could have on the Council's teaching.[3]

In addressing the problems created by forms of humanism that hollowed out and diminished humanity, *Gaudium et Spes* proposed a Christian anthropology that laid heavy emphasis on the inherent dignity of the human person. In the technical vocabulary of philosophy, the pastoral constitution's philosophical anthropology was thus "dignitarian." In reading the constitution, though, it is important to bear in mind that the Second Vatican Council was not simply affirming human dignity in a content-free or sentimental way. As Catholic social ethicist J. Brian Benestad has pointed out, *Gaudium et Spes* "has a lot to say about the foundation, meaning, permanence, and *perfecting* of human dignity."[4]

The vision of individual human possibility and integral human community that the Council wished to propose rejected any notion of an infinitely plastic and malleable human nature; the Council did not accept a relativistic concept of ethics, nor did it assume that all social ills were "structural." Rather, the vision of the human person and the human future sketched in *Gaudium et Spes* was based on the conviction that the "grief and anguish" of a fractured modern social order had a lot to do with disordered human souls, lost because of their ignorance of (even disdain for) the deep truths built into the human condition. Those truths can be discerned in the person of Christ and in the life of his Mystical Body, the Church. And while those truths are disclosed most fully in divine revelation, many are also accessible to human reason. In that crucial respect, *Gaudium et Spes* built on, even as it built out from, the key doctrinal and theological affirmations of *Dei Verbum* and *Lumen Gentium*: that revelation is real and speaks authoritatively into the silence of a skeptical late modern world; that a Christocentric and sacramentally enriched Church in mission nourishes the truly liberated human person and offers both a model and an experience of authentic human community.

While it recognizes, without grimacing, that Sigmund Freud and Charles Darwin altered humanity's self-understanding, and that Edwin Hubble and Albert Einstein irreversibly changed humanity's concept of its place in the cosmos, *Gaudium et Spes* is a rather traditional Catholic reflection on the human condition and the social order in several striking ways.

The pastoral constitution taught that disordered societies are in large part a result of divided hearts and souls marred by sin. It insisted that righteous living, not just a properly designed political and economic system, is essential for a just social order. The constitution grounded human dignity in human nature, not human autonomy, and insisted that the fullness of human dignity derives from our being created in the image of God, redeemed by Christ, and destined for eternal life in the Kingdom of heaven. *Gaudium et Spes* taught that the perfection of human dignity (in any state of life) involves growth in wisdom and virtue, and challenged the sexual revolution by teaching that the dignity of the human person involves the chaste use of the gift of human sexuality within the bond of faithful and fruitful marriage. It praised the dignity of the human conscience but insisted that conscience must attend to the truths that God built into the human person and the human condition. For it is the voice of God, not simply the human psyche, that speaks through conscience.[5]

Recognizing that the act of faith faced many challenges under modern cultural conditions, the document also taught that "atheism must . . . be regarded as one of the most serious problems of our time," for the human person "cannot live fully according to truth" absent an acknowledgment of the divine love that created humanity and sustains it in being.[*] And while not blinking at the fact that "it is in regard to death that man's condition is most shrouded in doubt," *Gaudium et Spes* also noted that "a deep instinct" leads men and women "to shrink from and to reject the utter ruin and total loss" of a personal existence. Without embarrassment at the scoffing of some moderns, the pastoral constitution taught that the "seed of eternity" within every human being is not an illusion: "God has created man in view of a blessed destiny that lies beyond the limits" of life on Earth—a life whose reality

---

[*] It is often said in criticism of Vatican II that it never condemned communism, because the Holy See had agreed to avoid any such condemnation in order to gain permission from communist authorities for Warsaw Pact bishops and observers from the Russian Orthodox Church to attend the Council. Yet section 20 of the Pastoral Constitution on the Church in the Modern World had this to say about systematic, programmatic, state-sponsored atheism of the sort espoused by communist regimes: "Among the various kinds of present-day atheism, that one should not go unnoticed which looks for man's autonomy through his economic and social emancipation. It holds that religion, by its very nature, thwarts such emancipation by raising man's hopes for a future life, thus both deceiving him and discouraging him from working for a better form of life on Earth. That is why those who hold such views, wherever they gain control of the state, violently attack religion, and in order to spread atheism, especially in the education of young people, make use of all means by which the civil authority can bring pressure to bear on its subjects." Only the dimmest minds could fail to recognize what was being severely criticized here.

has been made historically manifest in Jesus Christ, crucified and risen; a life that is divine and forever "free from all decay."[6]

The rich and complex Christian anthropology of the pastoral constitution is summed up in two brief passages that would be frequently cited by Pope John Paul II (who may have helped craft them during the preparation of the final draft text). First, the Council taught that Christ reveals both the face of the merciful Father, creator of heaven and earth, and the truth about the human person: "In reality it is only in the mystery of the Word made flesh that the mystery of man truly becomes clear. For Adam, the first man, was a type of him who was to come. *Christ the Lord, Christ the new Adam, in the very revelation of the mystery of the Father and of his love, fully reveals man to himself and brings to light his most high calling.*"[7]

Then the Council described the Christian understanding of genuine liberation: an essential theme in any humanism capable of speaking to the modern world. And in filling out its dignitarian portrait of the liberated human person, *Gaudium et Spes* added a communitarian dimension by drawing on classic Trinitarian theology. If humanity is created in the image and likeness of a God who is a trinity of persons, and if those persons eternally express their divine love in self-giving and receptivity, that must open up "new horizons" for humanity, the Council proposed. Thus when Christ prayed at the Last Supper that his disciples may be one, as he and God the Father are one, he was suggesting that "there is a certain parallel between the union existing among the divine persons and the union of the sons of God in truth and love." It follows from this, *Gaudium et Spes* taught, that *"man can fully discover his true self only in a sincere giving of himself"* to others.[8]

Self-giving, rather than Promethean or Nietzschean self-assertion, is the fullest expression of human dignity and the noblest expression of freedom, according to the Pastoral Constitution on the Church in the Modern World. True freedom is neither willfulness nor personal autonomy, but a life lived according to the commandment to love one's neighbor as oneself. That gift of self, reciprocated, creates authentic human community. A fully embodied dignitarian concept of the human person leads directly to a communitarian understanding and experience of personhood and freedom: an experience of the solidarity in community that God intended for humanity.[9]

Given this understanding of the human condition, what did the Church, bearer of a Christocentric concept of human dignity and a Trinitarian vision of self-giving and receptivity as the essential dynamic of authentic human community, offer the world through the teaching of *Gaudium et Spes*?

The Church offered a new dialogue between religion and science that would benefit both parties, because Catholicism was convinced that, while scientific inquiry has its own proper methods and procedures that religion must respect, scientific investigation takes place against its most ample (and indeed humanistic) horizon when it is recognized that "methodical research in all branches of knowledge . . . can never conflict with the faith, because the things of the world and the things of faith derive from the same God."[10] Christians, for their part, ought to acknowledge that "the achievements of the human race," including scientific insights and the technological achievements that flow from them, "are a sign of God's greatness and the fulfillment of his mysterious design."[11] Concurrently, the Church, drawing on a wealth of experience as well as the truth of revelation, counseled the world to resist the temptation to imagine progress as inevitable because of science and technology. Sin and evil are always real factors in human affairs; to ignore them is to succumb to "a spirit of vanity and malice" that distorts humanity's activity and imperils its solidarity.[12]

The Church in *Gaudium et Spes* offered a divinely warranted ground for equality among all peoples, a concept that modernity proclaimed as one of its political aspirations but often found difficult to explain or justify. And for good reason. The everyday experience of humanity is that there is great inequality among people: some people are more intelligent than others, some more creative than others, some more beautiful than others, some more athletic than others. How, then, to assert the essential moral, legal, and political equality of all these manifestly unequal people? By recognizing, *Gaudium et Spes* taught, that "all men are endowed with a rational soul and are created in God's image; they have the same nature and origins and, being redeemed by Christ, they enjoy the same divine calling and destiny."[13] Failing to recognize this inherent dignity can lead to "forms of social or cultural discrimination in basic personal rights on the grounds of sex, race, color, social conditions, language, or religion."[14] Something more sturdy and resilient than a pragmatic accommodation to the facts of human difference ("Things just work better if we assume everyone is equal . . .") must be the ground of human equality, including equality before the law.

The Church offered a vision of solidarity in community—the pursuit of the common good—that is more comprehensive than the mere acquisition of material wealth. In the first instance, as J. Brian Benestad put it, "the Council points out that the development of the human person depends on the health of the family, [free] associations, and the state," all of which must contribute, in their distinctive ways, to advancing the common good: which *Gaudium et Spes* defined as "the sum total of the social conditions which allow peoples, either as groups or as individuals, to reach their fulfillment more fully and more easily."[15] That definition was, admittedly, somewhat vague. But throughout the pastoral constitution, the Church taught a capacious view of the "common good" that included the pursuit of "truth, justice, love, virtue, and duty in the social order, in addition to a productive economy, environmental protections, proper health care, and the legal protection of basic human rights."[16] Moreover, *Gaudium et Spes* insisted that "respect for the human person" and the duty to "make ourselves the neighbor of every man" had specific applications to both the public moral culture and the laws of modern societies, such that various offenses against human dignity should be culturally regarded as repulsive and forbidden in law as violations of basic human rights:

> [All] offenses against life itself, such as murder, genocide, abortion, euthanasia, and willful suicide; all violations of the integrity of the human person, such as mutilation, physical and mental torture, undue psychological pressures; all offenses against human dignity, such as subhuman living conditions, arbitrary imprisonment, deportation, slavery, prostitution, the selling of women and children, degrading working conditions where men are treated as mere tools for profit rather than free and responsible persons: all these and the like are criminal; they poison civilization; and they debase the perpetrators more than the victims and militate against the honor of the Creator.[17]

Finally, the Church offered the world a model community of men and women leading coherent lives that integrated their faith and their roles as spouses, parents, consumers, and citizens: the community of the Church, the People of God living in history and society as the Mystical Body of Christ. *Gaudium et Spes* thus urged Catholics, as citizens of both the earthly and heavenly cities, to avoid any indifference to worldly affairs: "It is a mistake to think that, because we have here no lasting city, but seek the city which is to come, we are entitled to shirk our earthly responsibilities; this is to forget that by our faith, we are bound all the more to fulfill these responsibilities according to the vocation of each." There can be no bifurcation of the Christian life, the pastoral constitution taught: "One of the gravest errors of our time is the dichotomy between the faith which many profess and the practice of their daily lives." The Old Testament prophets, the Council noted, "vehemently denounced this scandal," and in the New Testament "Christ himself with greater force threatened it with severe punishment." So there should be no "pernicious opposition" between any Christian's "professional and social activity," on the one hand, and his or her "religious life," on the other—a stricture with particular application to Catholic public officials disinclined to take effective action against the grave crimes against human dignity the Council deplored.[18] Coherent Catholics, whose faith and whose understanding of the truths accessible to reason shape their public lives as citizens or public officials, are the Catholics who best help "establish and consolidate the community of men according to the law of God," honoring the inalienable dignity of the human person.[19]

By living coherent lives of Christian responsibility and solidarity, the people of the Church help Catholicism achieve its "one sole purpose—that the kingdom of God may come and the salvation of the human race may be accomplished." In doing so, the People of God embody the Church as the "universal sacrament of salvation" proclaimed by *Lumen Gentium*, "at once manifesting and actualizing the mystery of God's love for men."[20]

In Part Two of *Gaudium et Spes*, the Council addressed "Some More Urgent Problems" under five headings: "The Dignity of Marriage and the Family," "Proper Development of Culture," "Economic and Social Life," "The Political Community," and "Fostering Peace and Establishment of a Community of Nations." Theologian Matthew Levering has made a strong case that, despite the time-conditioned approach the Council took to these issues, the pastoral constitution's analysis remains in continuity with Catholic tradition, as it "applies the Catholic understanding of the nature of human beings as ordered to the end of charitable union with God . . . [through affirming] the key positions of earlier Catholic teaching."

In discussing marriage and the family, *Gaudium et Spes* taught that marriage is indissoluble and that the "ends" of marriage, which flow from the mutual self-giving and receptivity of the spouses, include both the "unitive" (love-sharing) and "procreative" (life-giving) dimensions of this unique human relationship. In the complex and variegated fields of culture, the pastoral constitution, according to Levering, taught that "Christian humanism is the measure of growth in theoretical and practical wisdom," and thus of authentic human flourishing in both the life of the mind and the application of knowledge in the world. In economic life, it reached back to Leo XIII, asserting that economies should be ordered to the well-being of the "body-soul person rather than mere profit." In the sphere of politics, *Gaudium et Spes* reiterated and amplified classic Catholic social doctrine's teaching that public authority derives its legitimacy from God and from its pursuit of the common good, not merely from autonomous individual choice. And, again consistent with traditional Catholic teaching, the pastoral constitution rejected amoral Realpolitik approaches to world affairs; insisted that international politics is a realm of moral judgment governed by the norms of justice; condemned "total war"; deplored the arms race; reaffirmed the just war tradition of assessing the proportionate and discriminate use of armed force in relation to the peace of international public order; and endorsed the use of nonviolent means of self-defense and protest when these can be deployed "without harm to the rights and duties of others and of the community."[21]

These continuities notwithstanding, it is also true that Part Two is more of a snapshot of "the modern world" in 1965 than an insightful analysis of where late modernity was heading.

The pastoral constitution implied that Marxism and existentialism were the two chief alternatives to the Christian humanism Vatican II sought to promote. Yet within two and a half decades of the Council's conclusion, Marxism was in the ash can of history, and existentialism (at least of the Sartrean variety) was of interest only to intellectual antiquarians. Moreover, *Gaudium et Spes* did not grapple with the utilitarianism that would become the default ideology of many globalized international elites in the twenty-first century. Nor did the pastoral constitution pay heed to the softer, more culturally focused forms of Marxist thought espoused by men such as Antonio Gramsci and Herbert Marcuse, which would eventually underwrite what Cardinal Joseph Ratzinger dubbed, in 2005, the "dictatorship of relativism" throughout the West. Further, *Gaudium et Spes* had virtually nothing to say about the new, late-modern Gnosticism and its insistence on the utter plasticity of the human condition. But the recrudescence of that ancient Christian cultural and intellectual antagonist, expressing itself through Marcuse's notion of "repressive tolerance," and Gramsci's strategy of a long march through the institutions of culture, would be central to what would be called, in the West, the "culture wars" of the mid-twenty-first century.

Gaudium et Spes welcomed the emergence of women in new social roles, but without anticipating the harder-edged forms of feminism that would regard abortion on demand as an essential component of women's emancipation and empowerment. Nor did it anticipate the LGBTQ movement and its impact on the very definitions of "marriage" and "family." In its discussion of the traditional nuclear family, *Gaudium et Spes* also failed to reckon with the dramatic changes in family life that would follow the emergence of the two-wage-earner family throughout the Western world.

The pastoral constitution appeared to accept the myth of "overpopulation," seemingly unaware that the term was without precise definition in the 1960s or since, and that the "carrying capacity" of the planet was far greater than that assumed by anti-natalists, eugenicists, radical environmentalists, and population control advocates.[22]

In its discussion of wealth, poverty, and international economic life, *Gaudium et Spes* did not anticipate the vast expansion of wealth that would follow the silicon revolution and the rise of a globalized, post-industrial world in which information technologies would be the drivers of economic growth. Nor did it anticipate that billions of human beings would rise above gross poverty through their incorporation into an international system of productivity and exchange in which the world became, for economic purposes, a single time zone. As for the "bottom billion" who were still mired in desperate poverty in the mid-twenty-first century, *Gaudium et Spes* did not discuss one of the principal causes of that degradation of human dignity: the corruption and incompetence of post-colonial governments in Africa and Asia, and the continuing difficulties of creating politically stable and economically prosperous societies in heavily Catholic Latin America.[23]

Gaudium et Spes was strikingly silent on what would, following Earth Day 1970, become a culturally and politically powerful environmental movement. That global movement would quickly take on several of the characteristics of an ultramundane religion, including its own divinity (Gaia) and its own apocalypticism. And in short order, leagued with radical population controllers, the new environmentalism would pose another challenge to biblical religion and its concept of humanity's relationship to the natural world.[24]

The pastoral constitution suggested that economic inequality would be the cause of future wars; yet since 1965 there have been few wars caused by economic envy or the desire to plunder resources. There have been, however, numerous wars caused by factors that *Gaudium et Spes* did not discuss in any depth, including ancient ethnic, racial, and tribal animosities and distorted religious conviction. Considering the United Nations' inability to cope with those conflicts, the pastoral constitution's confidence in that body seems misplaced.

Gaudium et Spes worried at some length about the spread of secularism but did not anticipate that the world outside of Europe and its former colonies in North America and Australasia would become more religious in the coming decades, even as the West experienced the "naked public square"—a public life shorn of religiously informed moral conviction, and indeed of any transcendent moral reference points.[25] The pastoral constitution seemed to envision a new Christian-Marxist dialogue, yet, beyond a few marginal figures, such as the French Marxist theoretician Roger Garaudy, most Marxists were unenthusiastic about any such conversation. And an even stiffer challenge would soon emerge, post–Vatican II: the crisis of spiritual and metaphysical boredom in the developed world, based on a soured indifference to the things of the spirit. *Gaudium et Spes* looked forward to a new, mutually enriching dialogue with secularists; it did not anticipate that the reaction to Catholicism's openness to such conversations would be a barely stifled yawn.[26]

In the decades since its promulgation on December 7, 1965, the Pastoral Constitution on the Church in the Modern World has often been accused of taking a naïvely optimistic view of the modern human condition—an indictment that could well be sustained by reference to this sanguine reading of the contemporary situation:

Throughout the whole world there is a mounting increase in the sense of autonomy as well as of responsibility. This is of paramount importance for the spiritual and moral maturity of the human race. This becomes more clear if we consider the unification of the world and the duty which is imposed on us, that we build a better world based upon truth and justice. Thus we are witnesses to the birth of a new humanism, one in which man is defined first of all by this responsibility to his brothers and to history.[27]

The question of how positively the signs of the times were to be read was one of many challenges faced by those drafting *Gaudium et Spes*. Aidan Nichols has noted, in addition, the "fundamental problem" of translating Catholic thinking into "social, political, economic, and cultural terms that were both realistic and intelligible to secular readers," with the Church's twin convictions concerning history—that the Kingdom of God is present in history through the Incarnation, and that the fulfillment of human destiny lies beyond history—being particularly difficult to convey. Then there was "the tension between supporters of dialogue and supporters of mission": How could Catholicism maintain a sense of evangelical and missionary urgency in a dialogical environment? A related question involved the tension between the idea of the Church as an inherently missionary enterprise and the views of some theologians that there was an "anonymous" or hidden presence of the Word of God in the unevangelized parts of the world: Would acknowledging the latter undercut the Church's efforts to preach the Gospel overtly and invite new members into the Mystical Body of Christ? And there was what Nichols described as the "conflict between what might be called post-Christendom thinkers and Christendom thinkers": Should the Church disclaim any support for her work and her institutions from political authorities, or should it seek to "revalorize what remained of historical Christendom, whenever elements of [it] could be found?" Social scientists did not agree on their analysis of the "modern world" in its economic, cultural, and political dimensions: How could a conciliar document with the weight of a "pastoral constitution" adjudicate among these conflicting views and determine the "Catholic view" (if there even was such a thing)?[28]

Judgments will differ on how well those challenges were met in the final text of *Gaudium et Spes*, as they will on the prudential judgments found in Part Two of the pastoral constitution. The development of the teaching of *Dei Verbum* and *Lumen Gentium* in Part One of *Gaudium et Spes* seems likely to stand the test of time. Less certain is the ultimate judgment on the use of social science in Part Two, which led to that part of the pastoral constitution's analysis being quickly overrun by rapid changes in culture, economics, and politics.

14

Truth, Liberty, and the Limits of State Power

The Declaration on Religious Freedom

IN THE LIGHT OF JOHN XXIII'S ORIGINAL INTENTION FOR the Second Vatican Council and the intellectual trajectory of Catholic social doctrine between Leo XIII's *Rerum Novarum* (1891) and John Paul II's *Centesimus Annus* (1991), *Dignitatis Humanae*, the Council's Declaration on Religious Freedom, comes into focus as both a major development in the tangled history of Catholicism and political modernity and a further specification of Vatican II's design for a revitalized Western humanism.

Taking its Latin *incipit* from the "human dignity" in which it grounds the right of religious freedom, the declaration boldly called for a modernity in which men and women are free to fulfill their innate desire for communion with the divine. Living out the theotropic nature of the human person and thereby meeting the human obligation to seek and adhere to the truth are essential to genuine human flourishing, the declaration taught. Concurrently, *Dignitatis Humanae* extended the analysis of the just state sketched in *Gaudium et Spes*. In doing so, it achieved a true development of Catholic social doctrine while urging the modern state to recognize the limits of its competence and the boundaries of its authority.

Dignitatis Humanae was the primary reason for the only formal fissure in the unity of the Catholic Church following the Second Vatican Council: the schism initiated in 1988 by the French archbishop Marcel Lefebvre and his followers. The Lefebrvists took offense at many of the Council's reforms and were especially critical of the implementation of the Constitution on the Sacred Liturgy. At the root of their dissent, however, was *Dignitatis Humanae*'s teaching on the inalienable right of religious freedom. This, Lefebvre insisted, was a fatal concession to political modernity and a betrayal of previous Catholic teaching on the right relationship between the Church and states. It was neither. But as similar charges continue to be made in the twenty-first century, a brief review of the struggle between Catholicism and political modernity will help set the stage for understanding what *Dignitatis Humanae* taught; why that teaching was both orthodox and necessary; and how that teaching poses a greater challenge to political modernity than anything proposed by the followers of Archbishop Lefebvre, by defenders of the *ancien régime*'s church-state arrangements, and by twenty-first-century Catholic integralists.[1]

The brutal assault on the Catholic Church during the most radical phases of the French Revolution inaugurated what Russell Hittinger aptly styled an "era of emergency" in Catholic history: one in which the political Christendom that had existed in various forms since Charlemagne was dismantled. The modern European state, during this era, often sought Catholicism's destruction or, failing that, the Church's detachment from Roman authority and its complete subordination to state power. In those attempts to break Catholicism on the wheel of the new nationalisms, dubious ecclesiologies from the past were revived as justifications for state efforts to control facets of Catholic life. Hittinger summed up the era in these terms:

Many of the [modern] European states asserted that local Churches enjoyed civil liberty only in union with the state and that the state had the power to superintend the offices and properties of the Church. The new governments born in the revolutions of the nineteenth century seized ecclesiastical properties, abolished monasteries and religious orders, liquidated or took over seminaries and parochial schools, controlled the flow of communication between Rome and dioceses, and, in many instances, asserted the right to veto, nominate, and even appoint ecclesiastical authorities. The new states used older ecclesiological [theories] of the supremacy of the local or national Church vis-à-vis Rome. In France, for instance, this was called Gallicanism; in Germany, Febronianism; in Austria, Josephetism; in Italy, Riccism.[2]

Whatever the nomenclature, these schemes aimed at turning Catholic clergy, including bishops, into functionaries of state-controlled religious agencies. The First Vatican Council addressed one issue in this "era of emergency" by declaring that the pope enjoyed universal jurisdiction throughout the Church, which meant that the bishops (who exercise their local authority because of their communion with the Bishop of Rome, the pope) were not high-ranking religious employees of "national churches" or the state. As Hittinger put it, Vatican I "rejected root and branch the ecclesiology of Gallicanism" (and, by logical extension, its cousins in Germany, Austria, and Italy).[3]

Vatican I considered the possibility of a more comprehensive teaching document on church-state relations, but was unable to formulate it before the Council's abrupt suspension in 1870. This was likely providential. Nonetheless, the draft of that never-finalized document included themes that would be taken up by Vatican II: "human rights" as attributes of the human person, rather than benefices granted by the state; the state's accountability to the moral law; the state's incompetence to judge religious matters, including doctrine and the holding of religious offices;

and the superior authority of personal conscience against the claim that whatever the state decrees is the "supreme law of conscience."[4] The Second Vatican Council amplified these themes in *Dignitatis Humanae*, *Gaudium et Spes*, and *Christus Dominus*, its Decree on the Pastoral Office of Bishops in the Church. Vatican II's teaching on church and state was thus a development of the Catholic tradition, not a break with that tradition.

In the world of quotidian politics, the Catholic Church in the nineteenth and early twentieth centuries dealt with political modernity through the concordat system: treaties signed by the Holy See* and individual states regularizing the legal position of the Church in a given country. Pope Pius VII and Napoleon agreed to a concordat in 1801 that governed Catholic life in France until 1905, when a radically secularist French government abandoned it. Several dozen other concordats had set the legal framework for church-state relations in countries as varied as Latvia, Lithuania, Romania, Yugoslavia, Portugal, Bolivia, and Colombia. The concordat system was far less successful in protecting the Church's liberty under totalitarian regimes, as the bitter experience of Italian Fascism and German National Socialism demonstrated.[5]

That experience, plus a keen sense of the political realities of the mid-twentieth century, led Pope Pius XII to look beyond the concordat system even as Vatican diplomacy continued to pursue that form of binding legal agreement with states. During the Second World War, according to Russell Hittinger, Pius XII "aban-

---

* The "Holy See" is the juridical embodiment of the ministry of the Bishop of Rome as supreme and universal pastor of the Catholic Church. As such, it has international legal personality and thus sends and receives diplomatic representatives. The Holy See existed long before the modern state, and its juridical personality was recognized in the years between the demise of the Papal States in 1870 and the creation of the Vatican City microstate by the Lateran Pacts of 1929. Conventional shorthand refers to "Vatican" diplomacy, but the diplomatic agent in question is the Holy See.

doned the old Roman policy of intransigence toward modern democratic governments and . . . began the process of making the necessary distinctions for shaping a new approach to church-state relations." Pius recognized that the revival of political Christendom was not something the Church should urgently seek, given the impossibility of its reconstruction in any foreseeable future. Pius XII also "took as normative the democratic regimes' self-understanding of the nature and scope of their authority: namely, as governments legally limited by constitutions and morally limited by a commitment to human rights."[6] Pius XII was no uncritical celebrant of the modern democratic project. In his pontificate, however, Catholicism's challenges to the democratic forms of political modernity change, and those challenges came from within an overall affirmation of the moral worthiness of the democratic project—an affirmation influenced by the prominence of Christian Democratic parties in much of Western Europe in the postwar years. Governments that were self-limiting both constitutionally and morally—that recognized the inalienable dignity of the human person, and what that recognition implied for just governance within legally defined boundaries that constrained state power—were governments the Catholic Church could not only work with, but actively support.

By the time of the Second Vatican Council, then, the church-state question that had bedeviled Catholicism for over a century and a half had evolved both politically and theologically.

Politically, the Church had to confront the challenge posed by the communist form of totalitarianism, which sought the absolute subordination of the Church to the party-state in an ultra-mundane form of the old Westphalian arrangement of *cuius regio eius religio*: the religion of the prince (or, in this case, the official atheism of the party-state) had to be affirmed by the people if they were to be full citizens. Communist regimes not only persecuted the Catholic Church with ferocity; they created puppet local churches and faux-Catholic organizations, such as Pacem in Terris in Czechoslovakia and Pax in Poland, as instruments of communist propaganda and indoctrination.[7]

The Church also had to recognize that democratic governments were both the first line of defense against the global ambitions of communism and the closest embodiments of the principles of Catholic social doctrine, as that body of teaching had evolved from Leo XIII through Pius XI and Pius XII. In 1931, for example, Pius XI cemented the anti-totalitarian principle of "subsidiarity" into the foundations of modern Catholic social doctrine in the encyclical *Quadragesimo Anno*. There, the Pope taught that natural associations, such as the family, and the voluntary associations of civil society, were crucial elements of any just society and ought not be subordinated to a putatively omnicompetent state.[8] And it was the democracies—including the American federal system and those postwar European democracies influenced by Christian Democratic political theory and parties—that embodied the principle of subsidiarity in the modern world.

The success of the Catholic Church in the United States was also a factor driving a development of Catholic thinking about church and state. Catholicism had never before experienced a democratic republic with no established Church and a constitutional guarantee of the free exercise of religion in which Catholicism flourished. That fact, and the determination of the U.S. bishops to advance a Catholic affirmation of religious freedom as a civil right, would play a significant role at Vatican II.

Finally, the Church had to get to grips with the fact that religious plurality or difference was the new normal throughout the world, including in Catholicism's European heartland. There, as in the United States, a Catholic claim to privilege in states where Catholics were a dominant majority and a Catholic claim for freedom in societies that were not Catholic was not just a public relations problem; it was, as Aidan Nichols put it, a matter of "epistemic dissonance."[9] In the practical order of things, those claims could no longer be sustained in societies in which the legal protection of human rights had become the dominant ethical template for conceiving just governance.

Twentieth-century theological developments also suggested the necessity of a development of Catholic doctrine on church and state. Maurice Blondel's efforts to heal the breach between faith and reason through his "philosophy of action" led to a theory of Catholic social initiative that sought to convert the modern world by deepening political modernity's aspirations to liberty, equality, and fraternity. Blondel's fellow Frenchman Jacques Maritain deployed a fresh reading of Thomas Aquinas to propose a Christian personalism affirming a dignitarian approach to human rights grounded in the nature of the human person, while concurrently challenging the modern tendency to reduce freedom to mere willfulness. In the United States, John Courtney Murray developed a Catholic theory of democracy and a Catholic case for religious freedom based on the encyclicals of Leo XIII.[10]

Christian personalism, the dignitarian approach to human rights, and a Catholic affirmation of religious freedom all involved a recovery of the ancient—indeed biblical—conviction that the act of faith must be freely made, or it is not a true act of faith. The gospels portray a Christ who *invites* assent; the Church, it seemed, should follow the evangelical path of its Master.[11] In doing so, the Church would also deepen the modern world's understanding of the human person's capacities. Human beings could hear a divine word spoken into history and, in full freedom of mind and will, assent to the invitation to communion with the divine contained in that word. The personalist developments in twentieth-century Catholic philosophy and theology thus positioned the Church to make an important contribution to the revitalization of Western humanism, with important implications for democratic public life.

Ecumenical developments also required a development of Catholic teaching on church and state. Pope John XXIII's great hope that Vatican II might advance the cause of Christian unity would be frustrated if, in its church-state theory, Catholicism denied to others what it claimed for itself: the *libertas ecclesiae*, the freedom of the Church, which, in contemporary political terms, meant religious freedom as a constitutionally recognized civil right of individuals and religious communities. Absent a Catholic affirmation of religious freedom in society, Catholic participation in the ecumenical movement would be virtually impossible.[12]

These developments led four groups of bishops to support a conciliar statement on religious freedom.

The first involved those bishops most committed to full Catholic participation in the quest for Christian unity, which, in their view, required disentangling Catholicism from all schemes of ecclesiastical establishment.

The second group, the bishops from the United States, wanted Vatican II to affirm that the American arrangement on church and state was something good in itself, which would be an important step beyond Leo XIII's teaching that the American arrangement could be tolerated as a prudential concession to a contingent historical circumstance.[13] The U.S. bishops did not argue that the American constitutional order was universalizable; they understood that there were different legal mechanisms for instantiating religious freedom in society. But they wanted the principle of religious freedom affirmed in itself: for ecumenical reasons, on personalist grounds, as a way to confound anti-Catholic bigots in the United States, and as a limit on the state's reach into the realm of conscience.

Defending the rights of conscience was the chief concern of the third group, the bishops from Central and Eastern Europe. Struggling for survival under constant assaults from atheistic totalitarianism, these bishops wanted another weapon in their arsenal and saw a bold Catholic affirmation of religious freedom for all as such an instrument. Some of these bishops (including Karol Wojtyła of Kraków) were sympathetic to the personalism of Maritain and its dignitarian grounding of human rights, including religious freedom; others saw in an affirmation of religious freedom a defense of civil society institutions against communist determination to bring all such free associations to heel; still others were looking for a conciliar declaration that would rebut the communist claim that Catholicism was the enemy of freedom. None of these bishops (nor any of the Americans or the ecumenists) saw a conciliar affirmation of religious freedom as a rupture with Catholic tradition or a Catholic surrender to political modernity.

Finally, there was the fourth group, the Western European bishops who hoped that Vatican II would make a decisive break with the altar-and-throne alliances and church-state arrangements of the old regimes. These bishops brought political and evangelical concerns to the Council's debate on religious freedom. French bishops, in particular, wanted to end the fratricidal war between *ancien régime* restorationists and defenders of constitutional democracy that had disfigured European Catholicism since the French Revolution. That struggle had been both enervating and embarrassing, as when it contributed to scandals such as the Dreyfus Affair and the collaborationist Vichy regime in France during World War II. As for evangelism, these bishops believed that a rapidly secularizing Europe would not rediscover Christian faith through a Catholicism backed by state power, no matter how benignly that power was deployed.

The opponents of a conciliar affirmation of religious freedom included bishops still committed to the Roman theology of the Church characteristic of the latter years of Pius XII; Iberian and Latin American bishops comfortable with the status quo of ecclesiastical establishment in their countries; and bishops such as Marcel Lefebvre who were determined to keep fighting the French Revolution. The last group would be the most vociferous in its opposition to what became the Declaration on Religious Freedom, although at the end of the day they could muster only 70 votes against *Dignitatis Humanae*, in notable contrast to the 2,308 bishops in favor.

Like *Gaudium et Spes*, *Dignitatis Humanae* was born from a complicated gestational process. An original curial draft of a constitution on the Church made references to religious tolerance and church-state issues, but, as previously noted, the Council rejected the draft of *De Ecclesia* during its first period. The Secretariat for Christian Unity then proposed that a "declaration on religious freedom" be a part of its own draft document on ecumenism. The conciliar debate on this text indicated that religious freedom was more than an ecumenical concern, and therefore should be addressed in a document specifically devoted to that subject. The Christian Unity Secretariat's material on religious freedom was then incorporated into an independent draft document that acknowledged the personalist understanding of the act of faith; recognized the modern insistence on freedom from coercion in matters of religion; insisted on the limits of state competence in religious questions; and articulated a dignitarian ground for religious freedom.

This draft was both applauded and criticized during the Council's third period in the fall of 1964. Some bishops were concerned that it would lead to "religious indifferentism": religion understood as merely a matter of lifestyle choice. There were also questions about how a conciliar affirmation of religious freedom was related to the church-state teaching of Popes Gregory XVI, Pius IX, and Leo XIII. In the judgment of Pope Paul VI, these questions were not satisfactorily resolved by the end of the Council's third period. So, in the face of considerable and somewhat raucous protests from the proponents of the draft declaration, the Pope extended the discussion (and thus a vote on the declaration) into the Council's fourth period in the fall of 1965. The protests on "Black Thursday" in November 1964 notwithstanding, this was a wise decision, for the revised draft submitted to the Council for debate in the fall of 1965 was, by virtually all reckonings, a better, tighter text. Moreover, it was a text that could garner overwhelming support when the final vote came.[14]

W hat did *Dignitatis Humanae* teach?
   The declaration began on a strong dignitarian note while tethering its teaching to Pius XII's 1944 Christmas Message and John XXIII's 1963 encyclical on peace, *Pacem in Terris*: "Contemporary man is becoming increasingly conscious of the dignity of the human person; more and more people are demanding that men should exercise fully their own judgment and a responsible freedom in their actions and should not be subjected to the pressure of coercion but be inspired by a sense of duty." Then the Council immediately noted a parallel development in public life: "At the same time [people] are demanding constitutional limitation of the powers of government to prevent excessive restriction of the rightful freedom of individuals and associations." These were "spiritual aspirations," and the Council sought to address them by searching "the sacred tradition and teaching of the Church, from which it draws forth new things that are always in harmony with the old."[15]

The declaration continued with several important affirmations that distinguished its teaching from any "indifferentism" about religious truth. The Council taught that "God himself has made known to the human race how men by serving him can be saved and reach happiness in Christ"; that the "one true religion continues to exist in the Catholic and Apostolic Church"; that "all men are bound to seek the truth, especially in what concerns God and his Church, and to embrace and hold on to it as they come to know it"; that conscience is bound to these truths; that "truth can impose itself on the mind of man only in virtue of its own truth, which wins over the mind with both gentleness and power"; and that the Council, in affirming religious freedom as "freedom from coercion in civil society," nonetheless "leaves intact the traditional Catholic teaching on the moral duty of individuals and societies towards the true religion and the one Church of Christ." Yet that teaching was not fossilized, especially regarding its practical applications, so the Council also intended "to develop the teaching of recent popes on the inviolable dignity of the human person and on the constitutional order of society."[16]

Although *Dignitatis Humanae* did not repudiate, in principle, the notion of a "Catholic state," it also recognized that any such state was highly unlikely under present historical circumstances. The declaration would thus focus on what was urgent and important now: affirming the inviolable rights of the person and insisting on the state's obligation to respect the freedom of the Church. Later, the declaration would reject *laïcité* in its most stringent forms, meaning the reduction of religion to a private lifestyle choice with no role or traction in public life. This rejection, like the previous affirmations, was intended to satisfy the concerns of the conciliar minority, to meet the objections to the 1964 draft, and to incorporate what was legitimate in those objections into the final text of the Declaration on Religious Freedom—another sign of Paul VI's skill in guiding the Council to decisions made by overwhelming consensus.

Having cleared the ground, the declaration then made its central affirmation, citing as its sources the teaching of John XXIII, Pius XII, Pius XI, and Leo XIII:

The Vatican Council declares that the human person has a right to religious freedom. Freedom of this kind means that all men should be immune from coercion on the part of individuals, social groups, and every human power, so that, within due limits, nobody is forced to act against his convictions nor is anyone to be restrained from acting in accordance with his convictions in religious matters, in private or in public, alone or in association with others. The Council further declares that the right of religious freedom is based on the very dignity of the human person as known through the revealed Word of God and by reason itself. This right of the human person to religious freedom must be given such recognition in the constitutional order of society as will make it a civil right.[17]

This personalist and dignitarian articulation of the right of religious freedom was complemented by the declaration's teaching on the social and political obligations implied by such a right. The Council thus taught that, as "the protection and promotion of the inviolable rights of man is an essential duty of every civil authority," governments must both "safeguard the religious freedom of all citizens . . . by just legislation and other appropriate means" and "help to create conditions favorable to the fostering of religious life." Listing religious freedom as a "right" in a constitution was insufficient; governments must see to it that citizens were "really in a position to exercise their religious rights and fulfill their religious duties." From that, society would "enjoy the benefits of justice and peace, which result from man's faithfulness to God and his holy will."

Moreover, if cultural and historical circumstances lead a government to "give special recognition to one religious community," that government must also recognize and respect "the right of all citizens and religious communities to religious freedom." Concurrently, governments must "see to it that the equality of the citizens before the law . . . is never violated either openly or covertly for religious reasons and that there is no discrimination among citizens." And then, as if to ensure that communist regimes did not miss the message, the Council declared that "it is wrong for a public authority to compel its citizens by force or fear or any other means to profess or repudiate any religion or to prevent anyone from joining or leaving a religious body. There is even more serious transgression of God's will and of the sacred rights of the individual person and the family of nations when force is applied to wipe out or repress religion either throughout the whole world or in a single region or in a particular community."[18]

In light of the six decades of debate that followed the promulgation of the Declaration on Religious Freedom, it is important to underscore what these core teachings of *Dignitatis Humanae* mean and what the declaration's adoption by a massive consensus signified.

In teaching that religious freedom is a fundamental human right, the Second Vatican Council was filling out its portrait of a revitalized humanism by affirming a crucial aspect of the dignity of the human person—the human capacity to seek the truth, know it, and adhere to it. Vatican II was not making concessions to liberal theories of the autonomous, unencumbered self. Indeed, the Council flatly rejected such theories, asserting that "the right to religious freedom has its foundation not in the subjective attitude of the individual but in his very nature."[19] In all this, the Council also affirmed that rights are always ordered to the fulfillment of obligations, that freedom is intrinsically ordered to truth, and that both rights and freedom find their fulfillment in the goods of justice and peace—which the Council unblushingly described as the result of "man's faithfulness to God and his holy will."

Vatican II also recognized what might be called "God's right," for God is offended when people are coerced (into either religious belief or atheism). Such coercion, the Council taught, impedes the dialogue of conscience between God and human beings that *Gaudium et Spes* recognized as "man's most secret core, and his sanctuary."[20]

In teaching that the fundamental right of religious freedom extends to communities as well as individuals, the Council insisted that the Church must be free to do its work, which includes not only those works of charity that even some laicist states approve, but the overall sanctification of society and culture.

And in teaching that the right of religious freedom should be constitutionally recognized as a civil right (and thus made legally enforceable), the Council developed modern Catholic social doctrine, declaring the Catholic Church in favor of a limited state that acknowledged constitutionally its incompetence in certain matters.

*D*ignitatis Humanae made other significant contributions to Catholic church-state theory that would exhibit a post-conciliar salience unanticipated at Vatican II.

From the days of the "enlightened despotism" of the Austrian emperor Joseph II and his concept of the Church as a department of the police, various forms of political modernity had sought to turn Catholicism into an instrument of social control. The most recent examples of what the Council called this "deplorable" practice were those regime-friendly, faux-Catholic organizations in communist states. Vatican II was having none of this. Having declared that "the freedom of the Church is the fundamental principle governing relations between the Church and public authorities and the whole social order," the Council drew out the implications of that affirmation: "As the spiritual authority appointed by Christ the Lord with the duty . . . of going into the whole world and proclaiming the Gospel to every creature, the Church claims freedom for herself in human society and before every public authority. The Church also claims freedom for herself as a society of men with the right to live in civil society in accordance with the demands of the Christian faith."[21]

In brief, Vatican II insisted that the Church cannot be an agency or instrument of the state. This was an urgent issue for the Council because of communist regimes, but a conciliar assertion of the *libertas ecclesiae* was not simply contingent on that historical circumstance; it also extended the teaching of Pope Leo XIII, who, at the time of a soft Kulturkampf in Bavaria in 1887, had vigorously defended the Church's "full freedom of action" to work for the sanctification of individuals and society. As Russell Hittinger has noted, Leo used the phrase "the freedom of the Church" more than one hundred times in his voluminous teaching, thereby setting the theological foundation for Vatican II's rejection of any modern *cuius regio eius religio* arrangement in which the state's official "faith" (including an atheistic "faith") trumped the Church's spiritual authority.

Vatican II also recognized that Church "establishment" was not the crucial issue in a post-Christendom world. Rather, the Church had to distinguish itself, and indeed defend itself, from the modern state's tendency to absorb large sectors of civil society into the state apparatus. Understanding the right of religious freedom to include the *libertas ecclesiae* said something about the Church and its nature; it also said something about the state and its nature. Here, the Council reached into the bedrock of Christian tradition and tacitly recalled Christ's injunction in Matthew 22.21 to give Caesar what Caesar is due, while giving God what God is due. If there are things of God's that are not Caesar's, then Caesar is not God or even godlike. If Caesar is not God or even godlike, then Caesar's power is limited, whether Caesar is an absolute or constitutional monarch, a president, a prime minister, or the politburo chairman of a party-state. In *Dignitatis Humanae*, then, the Catholic Church was reminding the modern world that the deepest roots of limited government lay in the Gospel's revolutionary distinction between spiritual and political authority, not in Enlightenment political theory. In doing so, the Declaration on Religious Freedom made important contributions to the conciliar project of identifying the foundational truths that must inform authentic human community in modernity.

Considering these affirmations and teachings, what is the relationship between *Dignitatis Humanae*'s defense of religious freedom for all (and its parallel teaching on the limits of state authority in religious matters) and the idea of the "social kingship of Christ," as taught by Pius XI in the 1925 encyclical *Quas Primas*, which established an annual liturgical feast of Christ the King as totalitarian shadows lengthened across Europe?[22]

The emphasis in *Dignitatis Humanae* on the relationship between religious freedom and the Church's evangelical mission suggests that, in the Council's mind, the "social kingship of Christ" is expressed in and actualized by the mission of the Catholic laity to evangelize culture, society, and public life. This was also the explicit teaching of *Gaudium et Spes*, which urged the laity to "impress the divine law on the affairs of the earthly city," as well as the teaching of the Council's Decree on the Apostolate of the Laity, which insisted that "the whole Church must work vigorously in order that men may become capable of rectifying the distortion of the temporal order and directing it to God through Christ." Three decades after the Council, the *Catechism of the Catholic Church* would make this even more explicit when it asserted that "the social duty of Christians is to awaken in each man the love of the true and the good. . . . [T]he Church [thereby] shows forth the kingship of Christ over all creation and in particular over human societies."[23] Twenty-first-century efforts to anchor a new Catholic integralism in the teaching of Vatican II, or the teaching of Pius XI which the Council developed, are thus misconceived theologically as well as incapable of application.[24]

During Vatican II's solemn closing on December 8, 1965, messages from Vatican II to different sectors of society were read by leading churchmen. In his address to political leaders, Cardinal Achille Liénart of Lille noted that, over the course of two thousand years, the Catholic Church had dealt with every imaginable form of political regime. In a given circumstance, the Church might prefer one to others. But it had no doctrinally warranted preference for any of them, because it recognized that, in the contingencies of history, no political regime is permanent, and all political regimes are evolving.

This sense of detachment, in the best sense of that term, is evident throughout *Dignitatis Humanae*. Recognizing that the Church is in the world but not of the world, and that the proclamation of the Gospel points to a fulfillment of human destiny beyond this world as we know it, the Declaration on Religious Freedom could assert that the Church is fully independent of the state, not merely different from the state. In doing so, the Catholic Church helped demystify the state, which was no small accomplishment and no small service to the human future, given the claims and pretensions of many forms of political modernity.

Dignitatis Humanae also reminded the Church that Catholicism best serves the common good, not by an alliance with state power but by being the Church: by sanctifying men and women and society so that respect for the God-given rights of all—especially the first civil right, of religious freedom, which is also the last line of defense against state-imposed skepticism and relativism—is deeply embedded in culture and sustainable over time in both custom and law.

All of this was summed up by Cardinal Liénart, who, in addressing world political leaders in the name of Vatican II, acknowledged the authority of legitimate governments, and praised just laws and those who legislated them—but also had "a sacrosanct word" to say to public officials: "Only God is great. God alone is the beginning and the end. God alone is the source of your authority and the foundation of your laws. Your task is to be in the world the promoters of order and peace among men. But never forget this: It is God, the living and true God, who is the Father of men. And it is Christ, his eternal Son, who came to make this known to us and to teach us that we are all brothers. He it is who is the great artisan of order and peace on Earth."

What did the Church ask of the modern state? "She tells you in one of the major documents of this council. She asks of you only liberty, the liberty to believe and to preach her faith, the freedom to love her God and serve him, the freedom to live and to bring men her message of life. Do not fear her. . . . Allow Christ to exercise his purifying action on society. Do not crucify him anew. This would be sacrilege, for he is the Son of God. This would be suicide, for he is the Son of man."

Dignitatis Humanae, one of the "major documents" of Vatican II, was thus another expression of the Christocentric humanism that John XXIII prayed would revitalize the Church and sanctify the world.

15

Witnesses and Missionaries

The Council's Teaching on States of Life in the Church

T HE SECOND VATICAN COUNCIL FILLED OUT ITS PORTRAIT
of the Church as a sacramentally ordered community of disciples in mission—the People of God converting and sanctifying the world—in its decrees on bishops and priests, the consecrated religious life, the lay apostolate, the Church's missionary activity, and the modern communications media, and in its declaration on Catholic education. These texts are specifications of the Council's doctrinal teaching in its four constitutions. In grasping what Vatican II taught about the various states of life in the Church, it is sufficient to highlight what these documents developed out of the authoritative teaching of the conciliar constitutions.

THE DECREE ON THE PASTORAL OFFICE
OF BISHOPS IN THE CHURCH

The heavy lifting of positioning the episcopate within the Second Vatican Council's theology of the Church was done in *Lumen Gentium*. There, the Council taught that the episcopate was established by the will of Christ; that the bishops are the successors of the apostles; that ordination to the episcopate confers the sacrament of Holy Orders in the highest degree; that every local bishop in charge of a diocese is a true vicar of Christ in that local Church; and that the bishops form a college, with and under the

Bishop of Rome, that holds supreme authority within the Catholic Church. These matters having been discussed at length and resolved by overwhelming consensus, Vatican II turned its attention to describing the ministry of bishops in more detail.

The Latin *incipit* of the Decree on the Pastoral Office of Bishops in the Church, *Christus Dominus*, "Christ the Lord," highlights once again the Christocentricity that *Dei Verbum* and *Lumen Gentium* established as the baseline of Vatican II's teaching: what bishops do, they do because "Christ the Lord, the Son of the living God, came to redeem his people from their sins, that all mankind might be sanctified." He who was sent by the Father "sent his apostles whom he sanctified by conferring on them the Holy Spirit," so that they might go out into the world to fulfill the Great Commission of universal evangelization. The starting point for any proper understanding of what bishops do is thus a firm grasp of what bishops are: they are the successors of the apostles who "perpetuate the work of Christ, the eternal Pastor."[1]

Christus Dominus, following *Dei Verbum* and *Lumen Gentium*, laid considerable stress on the bishop's role as an evangelist and teacher whose field of mission extends far beyond the Catholic flock committed to his pastoral care. Bishops are to "proclaim the Gospel to all men," proposing to them "the whole mystery of Christ," in which the truth about both God and the human person is disclosed.[2] The bishop is therefore the chief guardian of the integrity of doctrine in his diocese, his local Church's chief catechist, and a shepherd charged with animating the entire flock for mission.

The bishops are also the chief sanctifiers of their diocesan local Churches, "the principal dispensers of the mysteries of God." As such, they are responsible for the integrity of the sacraments and the decorum of the Church's liturgical worship. So bishops must "see to it that the faithful know and live the Paschal Mystery more deeply through the Eucharist," which, as part of a deepened life of prayer, is essential if the Church's people are to become "faithful witnesses to the Lord."[3]

As for governance, *Christus Dominus* emphasized the image of the bishop as a spiritual father, taking particular care for the well-being of the priests who are his co-workers and urging lay men and women to "participate in or assist the various works of the . . . apostolate." In coordinating the works of evangelization and charity in his diocese, the bishop should aim for a "close collaboration" with all the members of the Church, whose unique vocations he should encourage and support.[4]

While the decree made numerous practical proposals for the organization of dioceses and their governance, perhaps the most consequential of these was the Council's commitment to the establishment of national conferences of bishops that would "meet regularly, so that by sharing their wisdom and experience and exchanging views [the bishops of a country] may jointly formulate a program for the common good of the Church." That commitment was spelled out in some detail, as the decree specified the nature of these conferences, their membership, and their authority.

Bishops had gathered in local councils in the nineteenth century, notably in the United States; but the provincial and plenary councils of Baltimore met, legislated, and then disbanded, awaiting the approval of their work by the Holy See. Permanent national conferences of bishops had been set up in several countries since the nineteenth century, but these were coordinating bodies created to deal with specific issues of common Catholic action; the U.S. conference at the time of Vatican II, the National Catholic Welfare Conference, was an outgrowth of the National Catholic War Conference established in 1917 to coordinate Catholic activities after the United States' entrance into World War I. *Christus Dominus*, as canon lawyer Brian Ferme has noted, had something different in mind:

Christus Dominus not only recognized the reality and significance of [the meetings of bishops that had been underway for some time] but also determined their institutional structure. Meetings of bishops were transformed from what might be termed ad hoc, even if regular, meetings into a juridical institution that became part of the constitutional law of the Church. The meetings were no longer voluntary assemblies but rather became obligatory. Moreover, their clear juridical structure no longer simply wielded moral authority but also was capable of issuing juridically binding decisions.[5]

The nature, scope, and limits of the teaching authority of these conferences was not defined to any significant degree in *Christus Dominus* and would remain a subject of debate for decades. The decree also said nothing about the staffing of episcopal conferences, which in the bureaucratic ways of late modernity and post-modernity became another source of controversy.[6]

The decree made possible, while not mandating, the retirement of bishops who had reached a certain age and thus had become "less capable of fulfilling their duties properly."[7] In the long view of history, however, and keeping in mind both the ecclesiology of *Lumen Gentium* and the Council's teaching on the Church's relationship to the state in *Gaudium et Spes*, the most striking innovation of *Christus Dominus* was the decree's insistence that public authorities should not be involved in appointing bishops, a practice that had been common for centuries and that in several instances continued into the twentieth century. The Council asserted this form of the *libertas ecclesiae* in terms of the very nature of the Church and the episcopate:

Since the apostolic office of bishops was instituted by Christ the Lord and is directed to a spiritual and supernatural end, the sacred ecumenical council asserts that the competent ecclesiastical authority has the proper, special, and, as of right, exclusive power to appoint and install bishops. Therefore in order to safeguard the liberty of the Church and the better and more effectively to promote the good of the faithful, it is the desire of the sacred council that for the future no rights or privileges be conceded to the civil authorities in regard to the election, nomination, or presentation to bishoprics.[8]

Christus Dominus thereby completed the work of two conciliar constitutions in declaring the Church's independence from state power and did so at the point of maximum urgency for the integrity of Catholicism: the Church's right to order its own internal life and appoint its leadership by its own criteria.

THE DECREES ON THE MINISTRY AND LIFE OF PRIESTS AND ON PRIESTLY FORMATION

Pre-conciliar discussions of Vatican II's agenda anticipated an essentially disciplinary document on the Catholic priesthood that would legislate guidelines for the formation, ministry, and spiritual life of priests. According to theologians Guy Mansini, OSB, and Lawrence J. Welch, however, as the Council unfolded the bishops "gradually came to realize the necessity of saying something about priests comparable in dignity and fundamentality to what the Council said of bishops and laity."[9] In brief, the Second Vatican Council had to articulate a theology of the priesthood, further developing the teaching of the Council of Trent.

Given the urgency of meeting the Protestant Reformers' critique of the priesthood in the sixteenth century, Trent—in addition to mandating the seminary system as an essential instrument of reform—emphasized the cultic or sacramental character of Catholic priests. That was how Counter-Reformation Catholicism largely understood priests: above all, priests were men who "said Mass." Under the influence of *Lumen Gentium*, Vatican II's Decree on the Ministry and Life of Priests, known by its Latin *incipit* as *Presbyterorum Ordinis*, located the sacramental ministry of "the order of priests" within a broader theology of the Church's mission that also emphasized the necessity of priestly dedication to the ministry of the word (i.e., preaching and teaching) and the priest's personal union with Jesus Christ, the Church's great High Priest. *Presbyterorum Ordinis* thus synthesized "two lines of understanding" of the Catholic priesthood: "the priest as conformed to Christ and consecrated unto the service of God; [and] the priest as sharing in the apostolic mission of the bishops, itself a share in the mission of Christ, for the salvation of men."[10]

Ressourcement theologian Yves Congar played a significant role in formulating the decree's teaching that the priest, like the bishop, exercises the ministries of teaching, sanctifying, and governing. This was, in a sense, nothing new, in that post-Tridentine Catholics had ample experience of priests doing these things. The distinctive note struck here was theological and Christocentric rather than legal, in that, according to *Presbyterorum Ordinis*, the priest's exercise of these three missions (*munera*, in the technical Latin theological vocabulary) flows from both the priest's personal conversion to Christ, which is fundamental, and his unique configuration to Christ in the sacrament of Holy Orders; the missions are not simply jobs assigned by bishops to those in a lower grade of Holy Orders. As Counter-Reformation reformer St. Vincent de Paul had said, "The priest is a man called by God to share in the priesthood of Jesus Christ in order to extend the redemptive mission of Jesus Christ in doing what Jesus Christ did, in the way he did it."[11] That Christocentricity includes a call to evangelization: the mission of sanctifying the world by offering to all who will accept it the redemptive grace of friendship with Jesus Christ, through which humanity gives glory to God.[12]

While locating the Catholic priesthood's cultic aspect within a broader conception of priestly mission, Vatican II nonetheless emphasized the irreducible role of the Eucharist in a priest's life, teaching that "all ecclesiastical ministries . . . are bound up with the Eucharist and are directed towards it."[13] For the Church is born from the Paschal Mystery of Christ's passion, death, resurrection, and ascension: that Paschal Mystery is continually made present in the Eucharist, the Holy Sacrifice of the Mass, and it is from the Eucharist that the Church's mission flows and is nourished. Consecrated by the sacrament of Holy Orders, in which they are anointed by the Holy Spirit and "signed with a special character," Catholic priests, according to *Presbyterorum Ordinis*, are configured to "Christ the priest in such a way that they are able to act in the person of Christ the head [of the Mystical Body]."[14] As Christ was priest, prophet, and king, Catholic priests offer the sacrifice of the New Covenant; they preach the Gospel and teach; they govern the portion of the Church assigned by a bishop to their care.

In order to be transparent to the Christ to whom he is configured in the sacrament of Holy Orders, the priest must strive, in a special way, "to seek perfection, according to the Lord's word, 'You, therefore, must be perfect, as your heavenly Father is perfect' [Matthew 5.48]."[15] The Catholic priesthood is not, in the first instance, about power or powers; it is about holiness and pastoral charity, lived in dedicating one's life for the good of the flock entrusted to one's care.

Presbyterorum Ordinis ably integrated the two concepts of the priesthood that the world's bishops brought to the Council— Trent's concept, which emphasized the priest as the consecrated man who consecrates the Eucharist, and the more contemporary theological and pastoral emphasis on the priest as agent of the Church's evangelical mission. The linchpin the Council found to conjoin these two concepts was Christ himself: for the priest is the man who acts "in the person of Christ the head," both in the celebration of the Eucharist and across the full range of his ministry as preacher, evangelist, and shepherd. In that ministry, his holiness of life enlivens those with whom he lives and works, empowering them for the mission conferred on all Christians in Baptism.[16]

How the Church was to prepare such priests was the subject of the Second Vatican Council's Decree on Priestly Formation, *Optatam Totius*, whose Latin *incipit* links its subject matter to the "desired renewal of the whole Church." According to theologian Anthony Akinwale, OP, the decree's aim was to foster the education of "holy, intelligent, and competent" priests by reforming the seminary system mandated by the Council of Trent—a system of specialized education created to remedy the clerical corruptions of late medieval Catholicism that were contributing causes of the several Protestant Reformations.[17] That the Tridentine system of seminary formation required development in order to meet the challenges of the Church's contemporary mission seemed obvious to many bishops. As South African archbishop Denis Hurley commented later, however, Vatican II did not intend to dismantle what the sixteenth-century Catholic reformers had wrought, for "Trent had done its work well to produce the popes, bishops, and theologians of Vatican II."[18]

Optatam Totius unambiguously affirmed that "major seminaries [i.e., those in which philosophy and theology are the principal academic subjects] are necessary for priestly training." And, following *Lumen Gentium* while complementing *Presbyterorum Ordinis*, the decree taught that the whole purpose of seminaries was to form "true shepherds of souls after the example of our Lord Jesus Christ, teacher, priest, and shepherd."[19] This preparation took time: as Christ himself had called his first followers aside, inviting them to "come and see" (John 1.39), and thereby to learn from him in order to be his ministers in the world, so seminary formation meant a lengthy period of preparation that ought not be rushed. The desired outcome was the formation of men of a particular character: priests who had "no identity apart from Christ and the Church" and who were "formed to serve Christ and the Church"; who were "the sacramental presence of Christ who is prophet, priest, and king in the Church and, through the Church, to the world"; and whose identity would not be "compromised by [their] insertion in the world."[20]

The modern world posed distinctive challenges to future priests. The decree sought to meet those challenges by fostering a deeper integration of the spiritual, intellectual, and pastoral training that seminaries provided.

As holiness was the integrator of the various aspects of priestly ministry, the Council taught that spiritual formation was the integrator of the other dimensions of priestly preparation. That formation "should be conducted in such a way that the students may live in intimate and unceasing union with God the Father through his Son Jesus Christ, in the Holy Spirit." Seminarians should therefore seek and find Christ in his Paschal Mystery, "in faithful meditation on the Word of God and in active participation in the sacred mysteries of the Church, especially the Eucharist and the Divine Office."[21] As Akinwale put it, *Optatam Totius* proposed that "conformity with Christ . . . touches on training in priestly obedience, poverty, self-denial, and celibacy," so that modernity's "instinct for self-gratification" would be "tempered by a life lived in constant reference to the Paschal Mystery." And "without a deep appreciation and an internalization of the mystery of the crucified Christ, it becomes difficult, if not impossible . . . to achieve the self-control that is required for holiness."[22] Once again, Christocentricity was the hallmark of a Vatican II text.

The goal was that, through intense spiritual preparation, the priests of the future would be enabled to invite others into friendship with Christ and to deepen the discipleship of those who had already met the Lord. *Optatam Totius* completed this portrait of spiritual formation in seminaries by urging the development of a robust Marian piety in seminarians: by learning to "love and reverence the most Blessed Virgin Mary," the priests of the future would learn the true meaning of discipleship from the first of disciples.[23]

The Decree on Priestly Formation sought reform of the intellectual preparation of Catholic priests by bringing the achievements of *ressourcement* theology into seminaries as a complement to the Thomistic theology that had previously been dominant, especially in its Neo-Scholastic form. The goal was to form the priest as a man of wisdom, and Thomas Aquinas certainly was an exemplar of that: *Optatam Totius* referred to him as a privileged "teacher" of the truths of faith and their interrelatedness.[24] A broad intellectual formation was, however, a necessity for priests in the modern world.

The decree therefore taught that, before they began the study of philosophy and theology in a major seminary, students "should already have received that literary and scientific education which is a prerequisite to higher studies in their country." They should also "acquire a knowledge of Latin which will enable them to understand and make use of so many [intellectual] resources and of the documents of the Church." In major seminary studies, the "main object" of a Christocentric reform should be "a more effective coordination of philosophy and theology," so that students are equipped to grasp in ever greater depth "the Mystery of Christ, which affects the whole course of human history, exercises an unceasing influence on the Church, and operates mainly through the ministry of the priest."[25]

Philosophical studies were to be broadened so that seminarians acquired a grasp of classical, medieval, and modern philosophy, thereby gaining "a solid and consistent knowledge of man, the world, and God." Moreover, the "teaching method" ought not be rote memorization of certain philosophical postulates (a deformation in some seminary programs caused by the Modernist crisis) but should instead "stimulate in the students a love of rigorous investigation, observation, and demonstration of the truth, as well as an honest recognition of the limits of human knowledge." The decree also urged that training should pay "careful attention . . . to the bearing of philosophy on the real problems of life" while inculcating in future priests a conviction of "the connection between philosophical arguments and the mysteries of salvation which theology considers in the high light of faith."[26]

Theology, according to *Optatam Totius*, ought not be confused with religious studies, and "should be taught in the light of faith . . . in such a way that students will draw pure Catholic teaching from divine revelation, will enter deeply into its meaning, make it the nourishment of their spiritual lives, and learn to proclaim, explain, and defend it in their priestly ministry." Theological studies must be biblically rooted, grounded in "holy Scripture, which should be the soul, as it were, of all theology." In learning dogmatic or systematic theology, seminarians should begin with Scripture, continue with patristic studies drawing on "the Fathers of the Church, both of the East and West," and proceed to "the later history of dogma, including its relation to the general history of the Church." In learning the Church's theology in this integrated, multidisciplinary way, the decree, echoing *Dei Verbum*, taught that students should learn "to seek the solution to human problems in the light of revelation, to apply its eternal truths to the changing conditions of human affairs, and to express them in language which people of the modern world will understand." Moreover, the renewal of theology as a discipline ought to reflect "a more vivid contact with the Mystery of Christ and the history of salvation," and "special care should be taken to the perfecting of moral theology."[27]

In all of this, the Church's evangelical mission had to be kept in mind, so that the priests of the future could "bring the light of truth to those who are without it."[28] Pastoral formation should therefore develop in seminarians "the art of directing souls," which included inspiring "apostolic action among the laity." Pastoral skills could not be a matter of on-the-job training after ordination to the priesthood: *Optatam Totius* mandated that seminarians should be "initiated to pastoral work as a part of their course of studies, and also in holiday time, in suitable undertakings."[29]

As Akinwale pointed out, *Lumen Gentium*'s concept of the Church as a "sacrament" of authentic human community was fundamental to *Optatam Totius*. The decree thus reflected the Council's "intention to form the priest to be a servant of communion by being the sacrament of the redemptive presence of Christ, who is [the] primordial minister of communion."[30]

THE DECREE ON THE APPROPRIATE
RENEWAL OF RELIGIOUS LIFE

Lumen Gentium's teaching on the universal "call to holiness" in the Church provided the Second Vatican Council with one of its basic and recurring themes. This was particularly true of the dogmatic constitution's discussion of the consecrated religious life—life lived according to vows (or "evangelical counsels") of poverty, chastity, and obedience by men and women in religious orders, or what were known technically as "institutes." As Sisters Prudence Allen, RSM, and Judith O'Brien, RSM, noted, *Lumen Gentium* "reoriented the focus of religious life from individual perfection toward the sanctification of the Church" while encouraging the pursuit of personal sanctity and relating it to the consecrated life's "ecclesial purpose": "Let everyone who has been called to the profession of the [evangelical] counsels take earnest care to preserve and excel still more in the life to which God has called them, *for the increase of holiness in the Church* [and] to the greater glory of the one and undivided Trinity, which in Christ and through Christ is the source and origin of all holiness."[31]

Lumen Gentium emphasized that the holiness to which all Christians were called in the sacrament of Baptism should be a driver of Catholic mission. The Decree on the Appropriate Renewal of Religious Life, *Perfectae Caritatis*, applied this idea to consecrated life by mandating that each religious order, community, or institute recover its original "charism," the character and mission defined by its founder or founders.[32] For the "more fervently" those in consecrated religious life "join themselves to Christ by this gift of their whole life, the fuller does the Church's life become and the more vigorous and fruitful its apostolate."[33] In this perspective, even contemplative religious orders of men and women, who are detached from "the world" in cloistered lives of prayer and penance, contribute to the Church's mission by being a kind of spiritual reactor core within Catholicism, supporting the growth in holiness (and thus in evangelical and missionary effectiveness) of the entire Mystical Body.[34]

The decree's Latin *incipit*, by referring to the "perfect charity" that men and women seek through a vowed life marked by poverty, chastity, and obedience, helps explain why modern secular regimes sought the destruction of religious communities with singular ferocity, beginning with the French Revolution and continuing through the twentieth-century totalitarianisms. Whether the ultramundane dictator in question was a Robespierre or a Lenin, radical secularists believed sanctity was a grave threat to their enterprise. Corrupt priests, monks, and nuns could be controlled, even used; it was the men and women striving for the perfection of charity who were the gravest danger. Their very existence, premised on a kingdom not of this world, falsified the tyrants' claims to have the key to human fulfillment, while the witness of holiness contradicted the tyrants' charge that religious communities were scams for bilking the Catholic laity.

Lumen Gentium drew on this fact of modern Catholic life when, in its chapter on consecrated life, the dogmatic constitution taught that "the People of God have here no lasting city but seek the city which is to come, and the religious state of life, in bestowing greater freedom from the cares of earthly existence on those who follow it, simultaneously reveals more clearly to all believers the heavenly gifts which are already present in this age, witnessing to the new and eternal life which we have acquired through the redemptive work of Christ and preluding our future resurrection and the glory of the heavenly kingdom."[35] Being a sign of contradiction within the world, and a sign of conversion and consecration to Christ, were two reasons why those in religious life traditionally adopted a special habit or manner of dress. Those habits, according to *Perfectae Caritatis*, were to be adapted to "the requirements of health," the "needs of the time and the place," and "the needs of the apostolate"; there was no discussion in the decree of their being abandoned.[36]

Perfectae Caritatis developed this eschatological or Kingdom-oriented character of consecrated religious life when it described in moving terms the many ways in which those who have abandoned everything for Christ witness to the fact that, as *Gaudium et Spes* put it, human beings fully discover their true selves in the sincere giving of themselves to God and, through God, to others:

> Through the Gospel counsels and their perfect practice, God calls many, with many different graces, to dedicate themselves more especially to the Lord. They follow Christ. Chaste and poor, he redeemed humanity and made it holy by obedience, even unto death on a cross. Fired by that love with which the Holy Spirit fills their hearts, they live ever more intensely for Christ and the Church, his Body. The quality of their loving identification with Christ in a complete gift of self, embracing the whole of life, is the measure of the richness of the Church's life and the remarkable creativity of its mission.[37]

Each of the vows, or evangelical counsels, displayed holiness in a distinctive way, thereby making a unique contribution to the Church's mission.

Perfectae Caritatis described the vow of chastity as "freeing one to dedicate oneself with an undivided heart" to "God's service and apostolic work."[38] Living chastity as they do, those in consecrated life also make present Christ's spousal relationship to the Church, first explored by St. Paul in the Letter to the Ephesians: "That wonderful marriage made by God, which will be manifested in the future and in which the Church has Christ for her only spouse."[39]

The vow of poverty reflected the "interior surrendering of oneself" that is the perfection of charity, for living in poverty means being "poor in fact and in spirit."[40] Voluntary poverty, freely undertaken in order to live more generously for Christ, the

Church, and the Church's mission, also offered an important challenge to the materialism that often disfigures modernity.

The vow of obedience embodies the "holocaust of one's will," a phrase of Pope Paul VI's that *Perfectae Caritatis* spelled out in these terms: "Religious [men and women] trust and court God's will; they obey their superiors, therefore, in humility and under the directions of constitutions and rules. They surrender their minds and hearts, their gifts of nature and grace in doing what they are told, in living a life under obedience. They realize that the exercise of obedience develops the Body of Christ in accordance with God's plan." The decree thus posed a sharp challenge to the false humanism of personal autonomy even as it enjoined superiors to govern by discernment, not domination, in a "spirit of service."[41]

The common life lived by religious orders and institutes is another eschatological sign, according to *Perfectae Caritatis*, reminding both the Church and the world of the Wedding Feast of the Lamb, the consummation of history prophesied in the Book of Revelation.[42] At the same time, communal religious life instantiates the theology of communion taught by *Lumen Gentium* and exemplifies for the whole Church what it means to be, like the first Christians in the Acts of the Apostles, "of one heart and soul."[43]

The Decree on the Appropriate Renewal of Religious Life ended with a summary call to evangelical mission: "All religious, therefore, with undiminished faith, with charity towards God and their neighbor, with love for the cross and with the hope of future glory, should spread the good news of Christ throughout the whole world, so that their witness will be seen by all men and our Father, who is in heaven, will be glorified."[44]

THE DECREE ON THE APOSTOLATE OF THE LAITY

The theology of the laity was not well developed in pre-conciliar Catholicism, despite the emergence of "Catholic Action" movements, the prominence of Christian Democratic parties in mid-twentieth-century Europe, and the extraordinary development of Catholic associational life in the United States (exemplified by the Knights of Columbus). Yves Congar and other *ressourcement* theologians made preliminary efforts to remedy this, but when John XXIII indicated that he wanted Vatican II to develop a document on the lay apostolate, it was the first time such a task had been proposed to an ecumenical council.

By referring to the laity's apostolic activity, the *incipit* of the Decree on the Apostolate of the Laity, *Apostolicam Actuositatem*, signaled that the text would be firmly located within the Church-wide renewal of Catholicism's evangelical and missionary thrust underscored by *Lumen Gentium*. The Council was determined to "intensify" within the entire People of God an ancient feature of the Church's life (for there had never been a Catholicism that was not in mission); the laity's role in that mission now had to be emphasized, encouraged, and theologically elaborated.[45]

Doing so required locating the many forms of lay apostolate within a proper sacramental context. Early and mid-twentieth-century European "Catholic Action" was typically understood as a matter of the hierarchy assigning certain tasks to laypeople; thus the legal norms regulating that work, which emphasized the hierarchy's authorizing and directing role, tended to dominate discussion of the laity's place in the Church's mission. *Apostolicam Actuositatem* took a different approach, teaching that the apostolates of the laity were theirs because of their baptismal incorporation into Christ: "From the fact of their union with Christ the head flows the laity's right and duty to be apostles."[46] In the sacrament of Baptism, Christ himself gave laypeople the Great Commission to be agents of evangelization, so the laity did not require anyone else's authorization to be missionary disciples—although they should coordinate their efforts under the guidance of the bishops. *Apostolicam Actuositatem* thereby underscored that the Church's mission belongs to everyone, although that mission is exercised in different ways by those in different states of Christian life. The lay apostolate is not a "juridical concession of power granted by ecclesiastical authority."[47] It is an expression of the baptismal responsibility of those in the communion of the Church, which leads necessarily into mission.

Theologian Robert Oliver, BH, filled out the basic picture, stressing the sacramental ordering of the lay apostolate:

In Baptism, the faithful "are assigned" to the apostolate by Christ himself. In Confirmation, they receive from the Holy Spirit special gifts of grace for witnessing to the Gospel, gifts that are the inner force of their apostolate and the source of their "right and duty" to build up the Church and to participate in the Church's mission to the world. In the Eucharist, the Spirit consecrates the faithful to offer the spiritual sacrifices of the royal priesthood and confers upon them the gift of charity, the "true soul of the apostolate."[48]

The decree defined the lay apostolate comprehensively, including both the work of evangelization and the related work of bringing the truth of Christ into "temporal" affairs, thus sanctifying the world:

Christ's work of redemption, while of itself directed to the salvation of human beings, also embraces the renewal of the whole temporal order. Hence the mission of the Church is not only to bring the message and grace of Christ to men and women, but also to penetrate and perfect the whole order of temporal things with the spirit of the Gospel. Therefore, lay people, in carrying out this mission of the Church, exercise their apostolate in the Church and in the world both in the spiritual and temporal orders. . . . In both orders it is right for the lay person, who is both a believer and a citizen, to be guided consistently by a single Christian conscience.[49]

After discussing various ways of coordinating the lay apostolate and providing appropriate pastoral training for laypeople, *Apostolicam Actuositatem* concluded with an "exhortation," framed in the Christocentric perspective that was the hallmark of Vatican II's teaching: "It is the Lord himself . . . who is once more inviting all the laity to unite themselves to him ever more intimately, to consider his interests as their own, and to join in his mission as Savior. It is the Lord who is again sending them into every town and every place where he is to come. . . . [D]oing their full share continually in the work of the Lord, [they know] that in the Lord their labor cannot be lost."[50]

THE DECLARATION ON CHRISTIAN EDUCATION

In a commentary published in 1966, Joseph Ratzinger described the Declaration on Christian Education as a somewhat weak text and attributed that to the fact that "the Council members were tiring as they moved toward conclusion."[51] Yet while few would claim that Vatican II's reflection on "the paramount importance of education" (thus the *incipit, Gravissimum Educationis*) was one of the Council's major achievements, the declaration's teaching did contribute to the development of a revitalized Christian humanism and added important tiles to the mosaic of authentic community elaborated in *Gaudium et Spes*. The declaration also reiterated certain traditional Catholic understandings of education that would prove their salience in the decades after the Council.

In the centuries immediately preceding Vatican II, the magisterium of the Church had challenged the modern state's tendency to absorb all educational functions and institutions within itself. In 1929, Pope Pius XI's encyclical on Christian education, *Divini Illius Magistri*, summed up these concerns and the convictions about a rightly ordered society that underlay them. In the Church's view, the state ought not monopolize education, but rather should support a plurality of educational institutions. Moreover, the state should acknowledge that parents are the primary educators of their children and create the circumstances in which parents can live out that responsibility. A rightly ordered state would also recognize that the Church plays an important social role by being a moral educator of the young. *Gravissimum Educationis* assumed the perennial relevance and truth of these teachings, which were applications of Catholic social doctrine's principle of subsidiarity, while building upon them.

Throughout the declaration, the Council insisted that education is a matter of forming the whole human person in an integrated and thoroughly humanistic way, not just of teaching useful skills. As Catholic educator Don Briel put it, education has to do with truth, love, and their interrelation in forming a mature personality, as well as with the acquisition of intellectual and technical capabilities.[52] The latter were obviously important in the modern world, as *Gravissimum Educationis* recognized; yet, without citing him directly, the declaration reflected John Henry Newman's "distinction between professional instruction in which one transmits a body of knowledge and education that aims to form the human person as a whole."[53] In its own sphere, the declaration contributed to Vatican II's portrait of an integral humanism that acknowledged the many dimensions of the human person, including humanity's spiritual and moral capacities.

Gravissimum Educationis was interested in Catholic religious education as well as in the place of schools and other educational institutions in society. As Briel wrote, the decree located Catholic education and formation within Vatican II's concept of the Church as a communion of missionary disciples: Christian education must teach young people to "worship the Father in spirit and in truth," to strive for a holiness that takes its measure from Christ himself, and to become more "aware of their calling and thus to contribute to the Christian formation of the world and to the good of the whole society."[54]

The declaration stressed the educational obligations and rights of parents; described the family as "the principal school of the social virtues that are necessary to every society"; and urged that the state, "in accordance with the principle of subsidiarity," recognize parental rights and support parental obligations by its own educational institutions.[55] It also praised Catholic schools and insisted that these were truly public institutions, performing the essential social functions of educating and forming future citizens. Catholic schools should be "animated by a spirit of liberty and charity based on the Gospel," thereby contributing to "the welfare of the world . . . [and] the extension of the kingdom of God." By "living an exemplary and apostolic life," Catholic school graduates would become "a saving leaven in the community."[56]

In its discussion of Catholic higher education, the declaration acknowledged the "liberty of scientific inquiry" according to the "principles" and "methods" of the various academic disciplines, while emphasizing the importance of students understanding "the convergence of faith and reason in one truth"—a method exemplified by "the doctors of the Church and especially St. Thomas Aquinas." Higher education in colleges and universities was becoming more specialized, and the fragmentation of knowledge was one unhappy result. Catholic institutions of higher learning, and Catholic faculties within secular universities, should promote an intellectual synthesis in which faith and reason, the sciences and the humanities, were all understood to be different approaches to the truths built into the world and into the human person by the one Truth, who is God.[57]

Gravissimum Educationis did not present itself as the final word on Catholic education. The declaration's more modest intent was to set the framework for the Church's continued reflection on education and its relationship to solving modernity's dilemmas through the evolution of a deeper, nobler humanism. The declaration recognized, with Newman, that "great ideas are grown into and not learned by heart."[58] Building out from that recognition, and developing the theological anthropology summarized in *Gaudium et Spes* and its call to a Christocentric life of self-giving, Catholic education would make its appropriate contribution to "the promotion of a high culture" that infused society with the truths about the human person and human community that could be known by both reason and revelation.[59]

THE DECREE ON THE MEANS OF SOCIAL COMMUNICATION

While the *incipit* of the Decree on the Means of Social Communication celebrated the "marvelous inventions" produced by human genius "with God's help," including the technologies of the modern media, few commentators have celebrated *Inter Mirifica* itself. Not without reason, the decree has been charged with taking a defensive, minatory tone that seemed discordant in light of Vatican II's intention to open a serious conversation between Catholicism and modernity. One Protestant observer at Vatican II claimed, with less reason and even less charity, that the decree's teaching, taken to its logical conclusion, would "condone censorship, favor management of news, and promote a purely 'Catholic' religious philosophy of pre-Council isolationism."[60] The very title, with its reference to "Social Communication," also raised eyebrows: Isn't all "communication" social by nature?

Inter Mirifica would likely have been a stronger, more engaging text if it had been developed later in the Council: as theologian Richard John Neuhaus pointed out, the decree "was adopted before the Council found its distinctive voice"[61]—and, it might be added, the distinctive Christological framework of *Dei Verbum* and *Lumen Gentium*. Nonetheless, as Neuhaus also noted, the decree "bears witness to abiding truths of which we need always to be reminded."[62] Their importance has become ever more evident in the mid-twenty-first century.

Among those truths is that the various forms of modern media have to be consumed carefully. Given the state of the Catholic blogosphere and the antics of Catholic combatants in twenty-first-century social media, the decree's teaching that the Church's leaders should help the people of the Church use modern media in ways that advance "their own salvation and fulfillment, and that of the entire human family," was not misplaced.[63] From a Catholic point of view, the chief benefit of modern media is that its "instruments" can become instruments of evangelization, a theme stressed in *Inter Mirifica*. But evangelization will not be advanced if contemporary instruments of communication do not, as the decree urges, "reveal and enhance the grandeur of truth and goodness."[64]

There was no criticism of the Council's affirmation that everyone ought to be able to access "information about affairs that affect men as individuals or collectively," which was certainly a problem in communist states during the Cold War era in which the decree was formulated—and which remains a serious problem in many societies today, including some that imagine themselves replete with information. Was it naïve, though, for the Council to urge the modern media to communicate information that is both true and as "complete as charity and justice allows"?[65] Perhaps so, given that the twenty-first-century media's commitment to truth, justice, charity, and what were once called "the decencies" is not overly developed. But again, the issue was one of consumer education and formation: the Council was also addressing Catholics whose informed consciences ought to extend to a prudent consumption of what purports to be information or entertainment. As the decree puts it, "Special duties bind those readers, viewers, or listeners who personally and freely choose what these media have to communicate"[66]—and, of course, parents, who are charged with ensuring as best they can that inappropriate and humanly degrading materials "never cross the threshold of their homes and that their children do not encounter them elsewhere."[67] In light of the salaciousness evident in certain parts of the Internet, that admonition seems less defensive and scolding than wise and prudent, not least because it has become increasingly difficult to follow.

Inter Mirifica anticipated later conciliar documents in urging the Catholic laity to look upon work in the media as a potentially noble vocation, teaching that "it is the laity's particular obligation to animate these instruments [of communication] with a humane and Christian spirit."[68] As for the question of censorship, the decree does call on governments to enact and enforce laws against media abuses that would pose "serious danger to public morals and social progress."[69] As Neuhaus wrote, virtually all societies exercise some form of control over the instruments of communication, especially the broadcast media; he also noted that, as broadcast (and Internet) options expanded beyond the imagining of those who wrote and promulgated *Inter Mirifica*, such controls were "increasingly attenuated." Whether any society can survive without some form of censorship was not a question for Catholics only; social critic Irving Kristol raised the issue in a 1971 essay and defended governmental censorship of pornography and obscenity as essential to democracy.[70] The decree's intent was not to define how public authorities should meet their responsibilities in this contentious matter; it was to teach that such responsibilities exist and that Catholics must hold public officials to account to those responsibilities. Not much more could be done by a conciliar text.

The Decree on the Means of Social Communication did not envision Catholicism acting as a public censor of the media. The decree did envision a religiously formed and competent Catholic laity that, as both media consumers and workers in the media, would act as Christian witnesses and missionaries to see that these powerful instruments served the ends of truth, charity, the common good, and respect for human dignity. Despite its defects, *Inter Mirifica* thereby contributed, if modestly, to Vatican II's development of an authentic humanism in which an ennobled vision of human nature and human possibility created more humane societies.

THE DECREE ON THE CHURCH'S MISSIONARY ACTIVITY

The expansion of Catholic missions was one sign of Catholicism's vitality in the nineteenth and twentieth centuries. New missionary orders flourished. Mission schools in the colonial world prepared leaders for post-colonial nations. Native hierarchies were erected, and in 1960, Pope John XXIII created the first cardinal from sub-Saharan Africa, Laurean Rugambwa of Tanzania; Cardinal Rugambwa was one of dozens of black African bishops who attended the Second Vatican Council. Those bishops made a considerable impression on a young Polish prelate, Karol Wojtyła, who wrote a memorable poem about his conversations with them. As Pope John Paul II, he named several of these men—often first- or second-generation Christians—to senior positions in the Roman Curia.

The theology of mission developed to keep pace with this expansion of missionary activity. One of the proto-*ressourcement* theologians, Romano Guardini, would write that "the Church lives by her mission," a point amplified by modern Catholic biblical and historical studies and their exploration of the fact that the mission "to the nations" (in Latin, *ad gentes*, which became the *incipit* of Vatican II's Decree on the Church's Missionary Activity) had always been central to the Church's life. After all, the original band of Jesus's followers did not, after his ascension, settle down in Judaea as a small congregation of the elect, but immediately went out to share the gift they had been given. Popes Benedict XV, Pius XI, Pius XII, and John XXIII had all written authoritative teaching documents on the Church's missionary work. Yet there were debated questions within Catholicism's theology of mission at the time of the Council: Was "mission" a matter of converting individual non-Christians to Christ? Or did "mission" involve planting local Churches that would evangelize local cultures, such that cultures, as well as individuals, became Christian? The conciliar decree *Ad Gentes* intended to synthesize these two options in a multifaceted Catholic theology of mission that would build on and accelerate the Church's missionary activity, giving effect to *Lumen Gentium*'s clarion call to mission.[71]

The Second Vatican Council grounded the Church's theology of mission as deeply as it could, by locating "mission" within the Church's understanding of the Holy Trinity. Cardinal Francis George, OMI, described that deep relationship in these terms, referring to the teaching of *Ad Gentes* that "the Church on earth is by its very nature missionary since, according to the plan of the Father, it has its origin in the mission of the Son and the Holy Spirit":

> The relationship of communion between the Father, Son and Holy Spirit, which is the eternal being of God, overflows in the love manifested in creation and redemption to bring the Church into being as a created participation in that divine communion. In God, communion is the interplay of processions or "sendings"; in the Church, communion is a projection in time of God's mission, which makes God's inner life present in the world in a new way by drawing all who will accept it to share in that communion.

As the Son "proceeds" from and is "sent by" the Father, and as the Holy Spirit "proceeds" from and is "sent from" the Father and the Son, the Church, the Mystical Body of Christ in time and history, is sent into the world to offer everyone an opportunity to participate in the divine life of grace with which it has been blessed. Mission is not simply something the Church does, as one among many other things. Mission is what the Church *is*, because the Church is the presence within history of the dynamic communion of the Triune God.

As a Church in mission, Catholicism offers the world salvation through Jesus Christ, and *Ad Gentes* explained how "salvation" is multidimensional. Salvation history reaches its climax in three moments: the Incarnation of the Son of God, which begins the definitive revelation of God's intention to redeem the world he created; the Redemption, in which Jesus Christ, by his complete offering of self on the cross in obedience to the will of the Father, frees humanity from sin and death, and makes possible intimate friendship with God for the people of every time and place; and what the Eastern Fathers of the Church called "deification," by which, through the outpouring of the Holy Spirit, human nature is enabled to participate in the communion, the divine life of gift and reception, of the Trinity.[72]

In offering friendship with Jesus Christ to everyone, the Church, while making salvation available to all who accept the offer, also "reveals to men their true situation and calling, since Christ is the head and exemplar of that renewed humanity, imbued with that brotherly love, sincerity, and spirit of peace, to which all men aspire."[73] So in its missionary proclamation of Jesus Christ as Lord and Savior, the Church is doing its utmost to advance the renewal of an ennobled humanism.

"Mission" and "evangelization" are thus intrinsically connected, such that the Church's mission cannot be reduced to its embodiment of human decency or its works of charity.[74] *Ad Gentes* made the appropriate distinctions and clarifications:

> "Mission" is the term usually given to those particular undertakings by which the heralds of the Gospel are sent by the Church and go forth into the whole world to carry out the task of preaching and planting the Church among people and groups who do not yet believe in Christ. . . . The special purpose of this missionary activity is evangelization. . . . [Evangelization] is that activity through which, in obedience to Christ's command and moved by the grace and love of the Holy Spirit, the Church makes herself fully present to all persons and peoples in order to lead them to faith, freedom, and the peace of Christ by the example of her life and teaching and also by the sacraments and other means of grace.[75]

In all of this, *Ad Gentes* echoed and amplified the teaching of *Gaudium et Spes* that the Church engages the modern world in order that Jesus Christ may be known and loved as "the hope of the nations and their Savior."[76] So the Church's mission has "a spiritual and transcendent" character that "cannot be reduced to a socioeconomic or political agenda," although conversion to Christ has implications for the right ordering of society.[77]

The decree also clarified that the work of evangelization and of converting men and women to friendship with Jesus Christ is not proselytism:

> Conversion, as *Ad Gentes* describes it, is . . . first of all the action of God, whose grace [of which the evangelizer is an instrument] brings a person to faith. . . . This conversion has to be followed by a real change in the life of the person freed from sin into a life marked by the liberty of God's children . . . [in which they] entrust themselves to Christ, who renews them in the depth of their being. To seek to make converts is not proselytism, since the faith is offered freely in order to offer union with God, salvation in Jesus Christ, and participation in the blessings and tasks of God's kingdom.[78]

The decree urged all those doing the work of evangelization to seek out whatever among the unevangelized could lead to their conversion. *Ad Gentes* instructed missionaries to "establish relationships of respect" with those to whom they wished to bring the Gospel, sharing in their "social and cultural life" so as to discover those "seeds of the Word which lie hidden among [them]."[79] Though this admonition was directed in 1965 to the Church's work in Third World countries, it nonetheless has twenty-first-century implications in post-Christian Western societies. Whom Christians would offer friendship with Jesus Christ, they must first know and love. That is why, as *Ad Gentes* put it, "the Church strictly forbids that anyone should be forced to accept the faith or be induced or enticed by unworthy devices."[80]

16

From Plurality to Pluralism

*The Council's Teaching on the Eastern
Catholic Churches, on Ecumenism,
and on Non-Christian Religions*

I N ITS EFFORTS TO PROMOTE AN INTEGRAL HUMANISM THAT
would enliven fraternity, solidarity, and community under the
social, cultural, and political conditions of modernity, the Second
Vatican Council had to wrestle with the fact of plurality: that modernity's natural condition was what sociologist Peter L. Berger
has described as the coexistence of different worldviews and value
systems within the same society.[1] That was obviously true of an
increasingly interdependent and imperiled world "society"; it was
also true of life within most modern nations. The fact of plurality was another signal that Christendom was over, and that fact
posed new challenges for the Church's mission.

One of those was the challenge of helping to transform plurality into pluralism.

The words are often used as if they were synonymous, but
they are not. Plurality denotes the facts of difference noted by
Berger. Pluralism, according to American theologian John Courtney Murray, is something different. Pluralism is a considerable social achievement, for a truly pluralistic society (or world) is one
in which the bare fact of plurality has been transformed into a
distinctive type of community. Murray described that community
as one in which different "creeds"—Berger's term for different

worldviews and value systems—were "intelligibly" in conflict, because they had found a grammar by which to turn cacophony into conversation.[2]

In the first phases of its encounter with modernity, the Catholic Church resisted the fact of plurality. The Second Vatican Council accepted that plurality had been written into the script of history and judged it useless to rail against it in a fruitless quest for a uniformity unlikely to be achieved except by means of draconian social control. The signs of the times demanded something else, and so did the Church's evangelical mission. Historical reality and the Great Commission demanded that the Catholic Church help transform the fact of plurality into the social and spiritual accomplishment of pluralism. That, in turn, meant a serious conversation about the human future structured by common intellectual and moral reference points, animated by goodwill, and characterized by a commitment to understanding the deepest sources of the convictions of the "other."

That was the kind of world envisioned by *Gaudium et Spes*: a world of genuine pluralism, in Murray's sense of the term. The Church could only make its proper contribution to building such a world if it demonstrated, within the household of faith and in Catholicism's relationship to other religious communities and belief systems, a commitment to the transformation of plurality into pluralism. Defining that commitment and how it might best function within the Catholic Church, between the Catholic Church and other Christian communities, and between the Catholic Church and other world religions, was the task taken up by three conciliar documents that, like others, should be read through the prism of *Dei Verbum* and *Lumen Gentium*.

THE DECREE ON THE EASTERN CATHOLIC CHURCHES

The ubiquitous use of the phrase "Roman Catholic Church" tends to obscure the fact that the Catholic Church includes numerous

Churches that are "Eastern" or Byzantine in their liturgy, structure, internal governance, disciplines, and theological outlook. There are almost two dozen of these Catholic communities that, retaining their own distinctiveness, are nonetheless in full communion with the Bishop of Rome. Some are large, such as the Ukrainian Greek Catholic Church; others are quite small. Many celebrate the Divine Liturgy of St. John Chrysostom; the Maronites, for their part, use the Syriac Liturgy of St. James. Some of these Eastern Catholic Churches have always been in communion with the Bishop of Rome, notwithstanding the division between Rome and Constantinople formalized in 1054; most entered into full communion with Rome through a variety of historical circumstances during the second half of the second millennium.[3]

Painfully aware of their minority status within the Catholic Church, ever conscious of their often testy relations with Orthodox Churches not in full communion with Rome, and deeply suspicious of a Roman habit of centralization that led them to be treated (in their view) as fractious stepchildren, the bishops of the Eastern Catholic Churches were "not always reasonable men" at Vatican II, as Aidan Nichols delicately put it. The Melkite patriarch of Antioch, Maximos IV Saigh, insisted on addressing the Council in French rather than what he regarded as a hegemonic Latin (a practice for which he was occasionally applauded in the *Aula*). The patriarch also objected that the first sentence of the Decree on the Eastern Catholic Churches—"The Catholic Church values highly the institutions of the Eastern Churches, their liturgical rites, ecclesiastical tradition, and their ordering of Christian life"—was arrogant and smacked of Latin paternalism: Could anyone imagine a conciliar decree beginning with the phrase, "The Catholic Church values highly the institutions of the Latin Church . . . ?"[4] Some bishops suggested that the idea of a separate document on these distinctive Catholic communities was misbegotten; on this view, whatever the Council had to say about the Eastern Catholic Churches should be incorporated into *Lumen Gentium*. That argument was not without merit. But by standing alone as an independent conciliar decree, *Orientalium Ecclesiarum* (the decree's title, taken from the *incipit* that Patriarch Maximos IV found offensive) did make three important doctrinal and disciplinary points that advanced the cause of demonstrating that pluralism had been created from plurality within the Catholic Church.

The first point was embedded in that controversial first sentence. Pre-conciliar Roman theology described the Eastern Churches as different "rites," defined by their distinctive way of celebrating the liturgy. *Orientalium Ecclesiarum* took a different tack from the start, teaching that these ancient communities had their own distinct and valuable spiritualities and disciplines as well as their own liturgies, and because of that were unique Churches. The implication was that the communion of the Catholic Church was a communion of ecclesial communities as well as a communion of individuals—and thus an example of genuine pluralism.

By stressing the many gifts of grace in the spiritual traditions of the Eastern Churches, which the Council said it "insists on viewing as the heritage of the whole Church of Christ," the decree set the stage for Pope John Paul II's later teaching on the necessity of the Church breathing with both her lungs, the Eastern as well as the Western (an image the Pope adopted from Yves Congar).[5] That imagery, and the conviction about the perennial value of the theology and spirituality of the Christian East that undergirded it, was also intended to build bridges to those Orthodox Churches not in full communion with Rome, opening a path to healing the breach of 1054 (another of Pope John XXIII's major concerns).[6]

Orientalium Ecclesiarum paid tribute to the Eastern tradition of the patriarchate (as the heads of some Eastern Catholic Churches were known), teaching that "special honor" was to be accorded these leaders.[7] How this role of the patriarchs was to be understood within *Lumen Gentium*'s teaching on episcopal collegiality (which implied the equality of all bishops within the episcopal college) was not worked out.[8] The decree also reaffirmed

226

the distinctive practice by which the Eastern Catholic Churches' standing synods of bishops selected new bishops for those communities, subject to the final approval of the pope—another signal that pluralism in the Church was an operational reality, not merely an aspiration.

Theologian Khaled Anatolios noted that earlier Church documents on the Eastern Catholic Churches tended to "depict the Roman Church as beautified by the 'jewel' or 'ornament' of the Eastern Church and in turn to be its guardian and benefactor." In *Orientalium Ecclesiarum*, however, "the Roman Church stands alongside the Eastern Churches as corecipients of an integral divine revelation."[9] In doing so, the decree grounded its teaching in the Council's most basic text, *Dei Verbum*, while demonstrating that the catholicity, or universality, of the Catholic Church is not just a matter of geography, but of legitimate and mutually enriching spiritual traditions, living in communion for the sake of the same evangelical mission and offering a witness of unity in diversity to a fragmented world.

THE DECREE ON ECUMENISM

John XXIII's determination that the pursuit of Christian unity be among the primary tasks of the Second Vatican Council markedly accelerated the Catholic Church's engagement with the modern ecumenical movement—a Protestant-initiated enterprise about which Pope Pius XI had expressed considerable reservations in a 1928 encyclical, *Mortalium Animos*. His successor, Pius XII, opened the door to a more active Catholic involvement in the quest for Christian unity by acknowledging that such efforts might well be considered a work of the Holy Spirit. And while cautioning against concessions that would weaken the Catholic Church's claims to be uniquely the true Church of Christ, Pius XII also taught that in ecumenical conversations Catholics should participate as equals who did not assert special privileges.[10] The bridge that linked these modest openings to Vatican II's Decree on Ecumenism and its call for the "restoration of unity among all Christians" (reflected in the decree's *incipit*, and thus its title, *Unitatis Redintegratio*) was largely a personal one. For it was Pius XII's confessor and confidant, Augustin Bea, who, named cardinal by John XXIII, became the head of the Council's Secretariat for Christian Unity and the driving force behind the preparation of the decree.[11]

While the modern ecumenical movement was largely a Western Christian enterprise, the conciliar Decree on Ecumenism painted on a broad ecclesiastical canvas, stressing the importance of ecclesial reconciliation with the Orthodox Churches of the Christian East as well as Catholic ecumenical engagement with Protestant ecclesial communities in the fractured Christian West. *Unitatis Redintegratio* did not attempt a fully elaborated theology of the Church; that had already been done in *Lumen Gentium*. Rather, it addressed itself to healing Christian division, a sad fact that "openly contradicts the will of Christ, scandalizes the world, and damages that most holy cause, the preaching of the Gospel to every creature."[12] From the outset, then, *Unitatis Redintegratio* linked the ecumenical cause to the revitalization of Christian mission.

Fruitful ecumenism, the decree insisted, begins with sound ecumenical theology rooted in salvation history. *Unitatis Redintegratio* therefore taught that the Triune God's self-revelation to humanity, which reaches its decisive moment in the Paschal Mystery of Jesus Christ, has as its purpose both the redemptive sanctification of the world and the unification of the human race. The Holy Spirit, given to the Church at Pentecost so that the Church might live out the Great Commission, is therefore the chief agent of the quest for Christian unity. For the unity worth recomposing in the Church is unity in the truth that Christ bequeathed to the Church, which the abiding presence of the Holy Spirit guarantees over time.[13]

Unitatis Redintegratio then made its most creative contribution to extending the ecclesiology of *Lumen Gentium*:

[Those] who believe in Christ and have been truly baptized are in communion with the Catholic Church even though this communion is imperfect. The differences that exist in varying degrees between them and the Catholic Church—whether in doctrine and sometimes in discipline, or concerning the structure of the Church—do indeed create many obstacles, sometimes serious ones, to full ecclesiastical communion. . . . But even in spite of them it remains true that all who have been justified by faith in Baptism are members of Christ's body, and have a right to be called Christian, and so are correctly accepted as brothers by the children of the Catholic Church.

Moreover . . . many of the significant elements and endowments which together go to build up and give life to the Church itself can exist outside the visible boundaries of the Catholic Church: the written word of God; the life of grace; faith, hope and charity, with the other interior gifts of the Holy Spirit, and visible elements too. All of these, coming from Christ and leading back to Christ, properly belong to the one Church of Christ.[14]

In sum: There is one Church of Christ, and the fractures within it cannot be blamed on any one party. That one Church of Christ subsists in a unique way in the Catholic Church. There are, however, "degrees of communion" within the one Church of Christ, such that all those who profess Jesus Christ and are baptized properly are in various degrees of imperfect communion with the Catholic Church. The ecumenical journey, then, is one in which imperfect communion is transformed into ever more perfect communion, until the unity of the Church is fully recomposed. While this teaching certainly marked a development in Catholic ecumenical theology, it was also deeply rooted in Church tradition, reflecting as it did St. Augustine's theology of the sacrament of

Baptism as amplified by St. Thomas Aquinas and interpreted for the Council by Augustin Bea and Yves Congar.[15]

This "imperfect" but real communion among all the baptized makes ecumenical prayer, ecumenical works of charity, and ecumenical dialogue on contested doctrinal, theological, and disciplinary issues possible: all the baptized are brethren and should acknowledge each other accordingly (a teaching and admonition with application not only to Catholics, in their understanding of Protestant and Orthodox Christians, but to Orthodox and Protestant Christians, in their understanding of Catholics).

The recomposition of the Church's unity would necessarily involve serious theological dialogue, the contours of which were outlined in *Unitatis Redintegratio*. Catholic ecumenists were enjoined to clarity, charity, and precision; they should present Catholic belief "in such a way and in such terms that our separated brethren can . . . really understand it." Concurrently, that doctrine must be "clearly presented in its entirety," avoiding an ecumenically damaging and "false irenicism which harms the purity of Catholic doctrine and obscures its genuine and certain meaning." That being said, Catholic ecumenists ought to bear in mind that "in Catholic doctrine there exists an order or 'hierarchy' of truths, since they vary in their relation to the foundation of the Christian faith."[16] This did not mean that some of the truths of Catholic faith were, so to speak, truer than others, the latter being somehow less important, even disposable. It did mean that, to take two examples, the Nicene doctrine of the Trinity and the Chalcedonian doctrine of the Incarnation, being more fundamental to the *regula fidei*, or rule of faith, ought to be the primary focus of ecumenical theological dialogue. For it was only when there was agreement on the meaning of those foundational truths of the faith that the truths involved in later developments of doctrine could be grasped.[17]

Unitatis Redintegratio was realistic in its understanding that the recomposition of Christian unity between Rome and the "Churches" of the Christian East was likely to be easier than with the Protestant "ecclesial communities" of the West. The decree may, however, have misunderstood the degree to which an anti-Roman conviction had entered into the self-consciousness of many Orthodox Christians. There are few Catholics for whom the idea "I am not in full communion with the Ecumenical Patriarch of Constantinople" is integral to their Catholic identity; for many Orthodox, however, the conviction that "I am not in communion with the Bishop of Rome" is an essential component of their Orthodox identity. That human reality notwithstanding, Vatican II's acknowledgment that Orthodoxy may well have "come nearer to a full appreciation" of "some aspects" of divine revelation than Catholicism was both true and generous.[18] In this acknowledgment, as well as in *Unitatis Redintegratio*'s expression of admiration for Protestants' "love and reverence" for Scripture and recognition of the "sacramental bond of unity" already existing between Catholics and Protestants through their common practice of baptism, Vatican II committed the Catholic Church to the development of a unified Christian witness amid a genuine pluralism, however difficult in practice that might be to achieve.[19]

THE DECLARATION ON THE RELATIONSHIP OF THE CHURCH TO NON-CHRISTIAN RELIGIONS

Although its opening weeks coincided with the Cuban Missile Crisis, the Second Vatican Council was not significantly affected by the world politics swirling around it. The exception to this rule was its Declaration on the Relationship of the Church to Non-Christian Religions, in which events of the moment (which also gave the declaration its *incipit*, *Nostra Aetate*, "In Our Age") helped ensure that the Council's briefest document was also one of its most contentious.

Pope John XXIII, having made clear during the Council's preparatory phase that he wanted Vatican II to consider a statement on Catholicism's relationship to Judaism and the Jewish people,

had entrusted Cardinal Augustin Bea and the newly created Secretariat for Christian Unity with the job of drafting a document
on that subject. Angelo Roncalli had been a Vatican diplomat in
the Balkans during the Second World War; he knew the agony
of European Jewry in those years firsthand, and had done what
he could to rescue Jews threatened by Nazi racial mania. On assuming the papacy, he took several steps to open a new dialogue
with Jewish leaders. In a meeting with a French Jewish proponent of Jewish-Catholic dialogue, Jules Isaac, the Pope received
a petition urging that the forthcoming Council address the false
claims—never Catholic doctrine but certainly believed by some
Catholics—that the Jews were "deicides" (a theologically absurd
notion), and that the dispersion of the Jews was divine punishment for Jewish rejection of Jesus as the Messiah: a claim that
had been rejected by the Catechism of the Council of Trent, which
taught that Christ's death was caused by sinners of all times and
places. Thus, in addition to his passionate concern for advancing
the cause of Christian unity, John XXIII's original intention for
Vatican II included forging a new solidarity between Catholics
and Jews.

When the Arab press, intensely hostile to the State of Israel,
learned in 1961 that a draft conciliar document on Judaism was
being prepared, it became aggressive. From that point on, as Aidan
Nichols noted, "politicians in the Arab nations and, in due course,
bishops from those nations at the Council were determined at all
costs to prevent a conciliar statement 'in favor of the Jews.'" The
politicians' ire was enough to bring the Vatican's Secretariat of
State (historically unsympathetic to the Zionist cause) into play
as a cautionary force. Jewish indiscretions and Arab passions continually roiled the process, and by the time Vatican II opened it
was unclear whether there would be any conciliar statement on
Catholicism and Judaism at all, either as an independent document or as a feature of some other conciliar text—perhaps, Bea
suggested, the conciliar text on ecumenism.

In his 1964 inaugural encyclical on Christ's Church, *Ecclesiam Suam*, Pope Paul VI wrote of Catholicism's relationship to concentric circles of people, "groups . . . who were more or less close to her, or more or less distant from her, by virtue in each case of religious or moral inheritance or choice." That imagery came to life when, on a December 1964 papal visit to Bombay for a Eucharistic Congress, the Pope found himself in conversation with representatives of a variety of world religions, including Muslims, Hindus, and different communities of Christians. The encyclical and the papal pilgrimage to the subcontinent seemed to suggest a path forward: the Council could enfold a statement on Catholic-Jewish relations within a broader statement on the Church's relationship with other world religions. Any hopes that that would take the politics out of the development of what became *Nostra Aetate* were soon dashed. But despite the often unedifying politics, the declaration was debated and adopted with strong support from a German episcopate that had been enthusiastic about Bea's work from the outset.[20]

What, then, did the Declaration on the Relationship of the Church to Non-Christian Religions teach?

It taught that the Church has a "duty to foster unity and charity among individuals, and even among nations." It taught that the human race is "but one community," thus taking a firm stand against the racial and eugenic theories that had caused such lethal havoc in modernity. In treating the Church's relationship to Hinduism, Buddhism, and "other" faiths, *Nostra Aetate* taught that "the Catholic Church rejects nothing of what is true and holy in these religions. She has a high regard for the manner of life and conduct, the precepts and doctrines which, although differing in many ways from her own teaching, nevertheless reflect a ray of that truth which enlightens all men." At the same time, the declaration insisted that the Church "proclaims and is in duty bound to proclaim without fail, Christ who is the way, the truth, and the life," and in whom all "find the fullness of their religious life."[21]

These affirmations may seem difficult to reconcile. Yet, as theologian Arthur Kennedy has noted, "the theological motivation of the Church in its outreach and care for other religions is . . . grounded in her awareness of the fullness of life and love in Christ alone."[22] In the teaching of *Nostra Aetate*, interreligious dialogue is not a matter of good manners, though showing respect for the human dignity of others is important. Rather, serious interreligious dialogue for the Catholic is a matter of speaking the truth in that charity and solidarity that are born from the love of Christ constantly poured into the Church by the Holy Spirit. Catholics are therefore called to work for unity and authentic human community across the religious, sectarian, ethnic, racial, and political divides that separate people by rejecting prejudice and discrimination and by being mediators of those encounters that make possible the transformation of difference into dialogue and plurality into pluralism.

The declaration went on to state that "the Church has a high regard for the Muslims," although its Latin text on Islam's faith in the God who is "living and subsistent, merciful and almighty, the Creator of heaven and earth," suffered from an ambiguity, as noted by Aidan Nichols: Should the words *unicum Deum adorant* be translated as affirming that Muslims worship the "one God" (which is to say, the God worshipped by Jews and Christians), or as stating that the Muslims worship "the God who is one"? Nichols argued that the latter translation "better reflects the conciliar discussion," while pointing out that this is a distinction that makes a considerable difference. A rejection of the Trinitarian notion of God is bedrock Islamic doctrine, and acknowledging that raises serious questions about the notion of there being "three Abrahamic faiths." For as Nichols noted, from a Christian point of view, "Judaism is a pre-trinitarian—or, as some would prefer, proto-trinitarian—religion and in either case (pre- or proto-) is not founded on repudiation of belief in the Trinity."[23]

In contrast to the relative brevity of its statement on Islam and the Church's relationship to Muslims, *Nostra Aetate* then recalled and discussed at much greater length "the spiritual ties which link the people of the New Covenant to the stock of Abraham": the Jewish people, who are described within the same salvation history in which the Church believes herself to be embedded. Christian faith, the declaration insists, begins with "the patriarchs, Moses, and the prophets," and the salvation proclaimed by the Church is "mysteriously prefigured in the exodus of God's chosen people from the land of bondage." With St. Paul (in Romans 11.28–29), and reaffirming the teaching of *Lumen Gentium*, *Nostra Aetate* taught that "God does not take back the gifts he bestowed or the choice he made" when adopting the Jewish people as his own. The declaration taught that "neither all Jews indiscriminately" at the time of Christ, "nor all Jews today, can be charged with the crimes committed during [Christ's] passion." The decree also insisted that, even as the Church is "the new people of God, yet the Jews should not be spoken of as rejected or accursed as if this followed from holy Scripture." The Council deplored "all hatreds, persecutions, [and] displays of antisemitism leveled at any time or from any source against the Jews." Such behavior was an offense against "Christian charity," and an offense against the God who is love.

As to how and when the "common spiritual heritage" of Christians and Jews would resolve itself in unity, the Catholic Church, while urging an intensified Jewish-Catholic dialogue, would leave the timing of that ultimate reconciliation to a higher authority: "Together with the prophets and [St. Paul], the Church awaits the day, known to God alone, when all peoples will call on God with one voice" and serve him together.[24]

Despite its rough passage through the Council, *Nostra Aetate* made every affirmation that Cardinal Bea's proposed Decree on the Church's Affinity with the Jewish People wished to make, except for a call to commemorate the saintly figures of the Old Testament in the Church's liturgical calendar.[25]

The declaration's opening statement—"In this age of ours . . . men are drawing more closely together and the bonds of friendship between different peoples are being strengthened"—may fairly be judged as rather naïve in light of such post-conciliar phenomena as jihadist Islam, "Hindu nationalism," and the Buddhist persecution of Rohingya Muslims in Myanmar. Notwithstanding that lapse into an excessively optimistic reading of the signs of the times, *Nostra Aetate* taught important truths that extended the dogmatic affirmations of *Dei Verbum* and *Lumen Gentium*. And by affirming the theotropic nature of the human person, it contributed to Vatican II's efforts to define a humanism capable of building authentic human community.

Part III

THE KEYS TO VATICAN II

17

Jacques Maritain's Lament

DURING VATICAN II'S CLOSING CEREMONIES ON DECEMBER 8, 1965, the Council fathers sent messages, read aloud in the *Aula*, to various audiences to whom the bishops wished to say a special word: rulers; artists; women; the poor, sick, and suffering; workers; young people. The conciliar message to intellectuals was read by Cardinal Paul-Émile Léger, PSS, of Montréal. Pope Paul VI then gave the text to the man he had personally invited to represent the world of learning at this solemn moment, Jacques Maritain. Handing him the document, the Pope said, "The Church is grateful to you for the work of your whole life." Maritain was overwhelmed with emotion.[1]

Giovanni Battista Montini and Jacques Maritain had been friends for years; even after Montini became pope, he referred to Maritain in their conversations as "my *maestro* [teacher]." More than personal affection prompted this papal gesture at the end of the Council, however. For while Maritain, then in his early eighties, did not have a formal role at Vatican II, his philosophical explorations of Christian humanism, as well as his writings on democracy, human rights, the laity, and Christian-Jewish relations, had all left their mark on the Council's texts. At two points, moreover, Maritain had intervened privately with his papal friend, urging the strongest possible conciliar condemnation of anti-Semitism and a robust conciliar affirmation of religious freedom.

That Maritain would play an influential (if indirect) role in an ecumenical council would have come as a shock to many, including him, a decade earlier.

Maritain's 1936 book, *Humanisme intégrale* (*Integral Humanism*), was written as a Catholic response to the crisis of political modernity that had become unmistakable with the rise of the totalitarian powers; the book had an immense influence in reformist Catholic circles and shaped the Christian Democratic movement in European politics during and after World War II. Yet Maritain's reading of Thomas Aquinas came under critical Roman scrutiny in the days when the Neo-Scholasticism of Réginald Garrigou-Lagrange was often deemed the only acceptable school of Thomistic thought. In 1956, the Jesuit journal *La Civiltà Cattolica*, editorially vetted in the Vatican Secretariat of State, launched a harsh public campaign against the French thinker in an article that specifically attacked Maritain's understanding of Christian humanism. A second article (which, like the first, was aimed at preparing the ground for a Roman condemnation of Maritain's work) was only spiked when Pius XII intervened to forbid its publication.[2]

Given this history, no lay Catholic intellectual of international repute had more reason than Maritain to celebrate Vatican II. His Thomistic personalism had shaped the Council's Christocentric anthropology. He had been vindicated in his defense of lay initiative in the Church's mission, in his promotion of religious freedom, in his concept of the constitutionally limited state, and in his insistence that Catholicism forge a new human and spiritual relationship with living Judaism. The Pope, his friend, had recognized him at the Council's closing ceremonies because he regarded Maritain as the embodiment of the intellectual life lived nobly in service to Christ, the Church, and humanity.

Thus Maritain's lament for the state of the post-conciliar Church, published in English in 1968 as *The Peasant of the Garonne: An Old Layman Questions Himself About the Present Time*, sent shock waves throughout Anglophone Catholicism—as

it had throughout Francophone Catholicism when it was first published two years earlier.

Maritain began by praising John XXIII's intention to increase
the Church's "evangelical awareness" and Vatican II's many accomplishments: its teaching of "the true idea of the human person" and "the true idea of freedom"; its insistence that Catholics
"treat as brothers all those whom we know [who are] more or less
distant from the Truth"; its teaching that "anti-Semitism is an anti-
Christian aberration"; its recognition of "the value, beauty, and
dignity of the world . . . with all those goods of nature which bear
the mark of their Creator's generosity"; its blessing of "the temporal mission of the Christian" to convert culture, society, politics,
and economics; and its teaching that the laity are not second-class
members of the Mystical Body but are "called to the perfection of
charity . . . and to the labors through which the Kingdom of God
is expanded." In all of this, Maritain saw the Church coming "to
defend the human" in an age of degraded humanisms. Moreover,
the Council had recognized that "an immense spiritual ferment"
was at work in the world, a stirring that was like "a nostalgia for
the Gospel and for Jesus."

All that should be affirmed. At the same time, Maritain bluntly
criticized "advanced Catholic thinkers" who, in the name of "the
spirit of the Council" or "the spirit of John XXIII," were headed
for an apostasy in which virtually every Christian doctrine rooted
in a historical claim was considered a "myth," Christ's cross and
resurrection being "great and stirring symbols." In this, he saw
Catholic scholars falling prey to a notion first articulated by Auguste Comte, a progenitor of atheistic humanism: "Everything is
relative, that is the only absolute principle."

Maritain noted that, in his address to the Council's last working session on December 7, 1965, Pope Paul VI had made clear
that the *aggiornamento*, the "updating" of the Church, "was in no
way an adaptation of the Church to the world, as if the latter were
supposed to establish norms for the former."[3] That papal counsel

was not heeded. What Maritain now saw was a "kind of *kneeling before the world*," a "complete *temporalization of Christianity*," in which "*there is no kingdom of God distinct from the world*." This is what the "prophets of the avant-garde," who imagined that Christ's call to convert the world had been somehow repealed, were essentially promoting. In doing so, they were, consciously or not, replicating the claim of Ludwig Feuerbach (another founding father of atheistic humanism) that Christian faith was just "a simple sublimating aspiration": the projection of human longings onto an imaginary supernatural scrim rather than a response to God's self-revelation in history.[4]

According to another of Paul VI's French friends, Jean Guitton, the Pope found Maritain's book "a bit too somber."[5] But that was in 1966, before widespread theological dissent, unauthorized and sometimes sacrilegious liturgical experimentation, and the breakdown of clerical discipline reached gale force in Catholicism. By the early 1970s, when the Church seemed to be coming apart at the seams—thanks to vast defections from the priesthood and consecrated religious life, open disdain for papal teaching among theologians and some bishops, and a rapid dissolution of Catholic practice at the grass roots—Maritain, that great influence on the Second Vatican Council and defender of its achievements, was looking less like a cranky old man and more like someone who had presciently discerned a vast, post-conciliar confusion that was impeding the evangelical springtime for which John XXIII, Paul VI, and Maritain himself had hoped.

That confusion had much to do with one of Vatican II's distinctive characteristics.

18

The Council Without Keys

A LL TWENTY-ONE ECUMENICAL COUNCILS WERE BORN OF controversy; all were conducted in controversy; and all resulted in controversy. In this respect, there was nothing new about the fact of controversy before, during, and after the Second Vatican Council. Indeed, the struggle in twenty-first-century Catholicism to define Vatican II's meaning and to implement its teaching properly might put some in mind of St. Basil the Great's fourth-century description of the Church after the First Council of Nicaea: "To what, then, shall I liken our present condition? It may be compared, I think, to some naval battle which has arisen out of time old quarrels, and is fought by men who cherish a deadly hate against one another . . . and [are] eager for the fight. . . . The disorder and confusion [are] tremendous."[1] Taken as a whole, that would be an exaggerated view of the post-conciliar Catholic situation between 1966 and the mid-twenty-first century. It would, however, aptly describe various moments in the six decades since Pope John XXIII, in *Gaudet Mater Ecclesia*, summoned Catholicism to a new Pentecost and a new evangelical fervor that would revitalize world civilization.

If the fact of controversy before, during, and after Vatican II does not distinguish the Council from its predecessors, something else does, however. For unlike previous councils, the Second Ecumenical Council of the Vatican did not provide authoritative keys by which its meaning could be fixed, and thus its teaching properly implemented.

Nicaea I provided such a key in its Creed, still recited in Christian communities today. Ephesus and Chalcedon provided keys to their proper interpretation in their dogmatic definitions: Ephesus defined Mary as *Theotokos*, and Chalcedon definitively taught that there are two natures in the one person of Christ. The Third Council of Constantinople provided an authoritative key to its meaning by condemning the heresy of Monotheletism, which claimed that there was only one will in Christ. The Third and Fourth Lateran Councils provided keys to their proper interpretation by legislating new canons into the Church's legal system. The Council of Trent condemned heresies, affirmed doctrines, and legislated new canons; it also gave the Church a catechism that was both a key to the Council's meaning and an important instrument in the Tridentine reform of the Church.

Vatican II did none of this. It wrote no creed, defined no doctrines, anathematized no heresies, legislated no canons, and commissioned no catechism. It promulgated sixteen documents of different magisterial weight, but it did not provide an authoritative key or keys to their interpretation or to the documents' inner relationship. This lack of keys helps explain why the renewal of Catholic faith, piety, and evangelical fervor for which John XXIII hoped was not quickly realized in a Pentecostal experience that intensified missionary energy throughout world Catholicism.

The "Council without keys" ended just as the cultural revolutions of the 1960s were exploding. The vast social, political, and cultural upheavals of that decade were another factor in the bitter contest over what the Council meant, and those contentions sapped the vitality of many local Churches. Yet Vatican II also provided the Church with the tools, and nurtured the leadership, by which Catholicism played a significant role in the collapse of European communism. And although Catholic practice was withering in what for centuries had been its Western European heartland, the Council energized evangelization in sub-Saharan Africa and led to explosive Catholic growth there. It seems that this is a recurring historical pattern. As patristics scholar Joseph Carola, SJ, once put it, "The ecclesial golden ages of sanctity—the fourth and sixteenth centuries, for example—have also been ages of great turmoil in the life of the Church."[2] That pattern of sanctity amid turmoil began in the fifteenth chapter of the Acts of the Apostles and has continued ever since.

The debate over Vatican II's meaning began as soon as the Council opened, as the assembled bishops wrested control of the proceedings from the curial bureaucracy and, with the exception of the texts on the liturgy and on social communication, demanded an overhaul of what the Curia-dominated conciliar drafting committees had proposed. The debate intensified and became more complex throughout the four periods of Vatican II, and by the fourth working period, in the fall of 1965, a major rift had opened within the group of reformist theologians who had been so influential in the Council's first three periods. A theological War of the Conciliar Succession was then fought for decades in two theological journals, *Concilium* and *Communio*.[3]

In its opening phases, this struggle for the Council was defined by the question of what might be called the Church's "voice": the division between those comfortable with the abstract intellectual style and vocabulary of Neo-Scholasticism in expressing what *Gaudet Mater Ecclesia* called the "deposit of faith," on one side, and, on the other, those who favored a Catholic "voice" that was more biblical, more evocative of the Fathers of the Church, and more expressive of salvation history. In the decades before Vatican II, this phase of the struggle was presaged in the polemics between Neo-Scholastic theologians (and the Roman authorities with whom they were leagued) and the theologians of a Catholic *ressourcement*. The Council decisively opted for the *ressourcement* "voice," perhaps influenced in part by the positive reception that John XXIII's personalistic approach to magisterial teaching in the 1963 encyclical *Pacem in Terris* had received.[4]

The achievements made possible by the decision to adopt a different kind of Catholic voice were considerable, especially in Vatican II's two principal texts, *Dei Verbum* and *Lumen Gentium*. There, the deposit of faith that John XXIII sought to defend and bring anew to the modern world came alive as a fresh invitation to communion with God, in which humanity would discover anew the truths about the nobility of the human person, genuine human community, and the majesty of human destiny. This choice of voice also contributed to the post-conciliar confusion, however. For the imagery and vocabulary adopted by the Council were more susceptible to a variety of interpretations (some contentious, others bizarre) than the precise vocabulary, finely honed distinctions, and tight logic characteristic of Neo-Scholasticism.

Neither party to this conflict was blameless. The pre-conciliar Neo-Scholastic polemic asserting that virtually every form of *ressourcement* theology was an opening wedge to Modernism was badly overstated. Moreover, the conviction among some Neo-Scholastics that the deposit of faith could be fixed for all time within a certain conceptuality and vocabulary was neither sustainable as a historical matter (for it would have sidelined many of the great Church Fathers) nor an appropriate response to the intellectual challenges of post-Cartesian and post-Kantian modernity. For their part, the *ressourcement* theologians were too confident that they had the decisive Christian answer to overcoming late modernity's skepticism and nihilism, and the ferocity of their anti-Scholastic polemic blinded some of those dedicated to a "return to the sources" to Neo-Scholasticism's genuine achievements. Decades after Vatican II, it would become clear to the intellectual heirs of the mid-twentieth-century Neo-Scholastics and *ressourcement* theologians that they needed each other. Indeed, the Church needed them both, because each played an important role in helping the Church articulate a comprehensive presentation of the deposit of faith, especially in the sphere of moral life.[5]

That Vatican II was a council without keys also reinforced the media imagery of a post-conciliar, pan-Catholic struggle between open-minded liberals or progressives and narrow-minded conservatives or traditionalists. That ubiquitous portrayal made it even more difficult to achieve agreement on what the Council intended. The liberal/conservative taxonomy quickly evolved beyond questions of theological attitude and approach and became a matter of dividing the Church—between those in tune with the "spirit of Vatican II" (never precisely defined, and often resembling the *Zeitgeist* of the moment) and those out of touch with or hostile to that "spirit." Over time, the terms of reference would shift again. Some argued that Vatican II stood for renewal within tradition, or reform through the development of doctrine. Others insisted that the Council marked a fundamental paradigm shift in Catholic self-understanding.[6]

These debates continue six decades after the Council opened. They are often more acrimonious than fraternal.

A ny serious wrestling with the legacy of the Second Vatican Council will avoid the fallacy of *post Concilium ergo propter Concilium*: "What happened after the Council happened because of the Council." This is particularly important in assessing the role of Pope Paul VI in and after Vatican II. As Cardinal Giovanni Battista Montini, he was a significant behind-the-scenes figure in the Council's first period. He was likely John XXIII's preferred successor. At the opening of Vatican II's second period, Paul VI, recalling the Christocentricity of *Gaudet Mater Ecclesia*, reminded the bishops that "the starting point and goal [of the Council] is that here and at this very hour we should proclaim Christ to ourselves and to the world around us: Christ our beginning, Christ our life and our guide, Christ our hope and our end."[7] He reconfigured

conciliar procedures so that the Council could work more effi-
ciently, and he skillfully guided a sometimes fractious assembly
to consensus decisions.[8] Then he presided over thirteen turbulent
years of conciliar implementation continually marked by controversy. The man who was initially worried about the "hornet's nest"
that John XXIII was stirring up by summoning a council must
have had many occasions to reflect on that remark as he caught the
full blast of the nest's eruption during his pontificate.

Paul VI's intellectuality—Cardinal Franz König of Vienna once
described him as so intelligent that he could see every side of a
question, and thus found decisions difficult to make[9]—and his essential kindliness are often blamed for the post-conciliar breakdown of Catholic discipline, especially his willingness to dispense
tens of thousands of priests and those in consecrated religious life
from their vows. Yet the mass exodus from the priesthood and
consecrated religious life that took place in the years immediately
following Vatican II—the greatest since the sixteenth-century Reformations—certainly was influenced by the ethos of the 1960s
and 1970s throughout the Western world. The tsunami of the sexual revolution left no institution untouched or unshaken; neither
did the rebellion against all forms of traditional authority in what
Europeans still call, simply, "1968"; and it is unclear what a firmer
papal disciplinary hand would have achieved in the face of all that.
As for the claim that these defections and disciplinary breakdowns
were the fault of the Council per se, it might be asked why, if pre–
Vatican II programs of priestly and religious formation were so
sound, those recently formed in those programs were most susceptible to the siren songs of the Sixties, abandoning their vocational
commitments so quickly in the years after the Council.[10]

In assessing Paul VI and Vatican II, it should also be remembered
that the Pope showed considerable skill in guiding the Council:
a council in which, as Aidan Nichols wrote, "the conciliar minority—guarded, prudent, and concerned for explicit continuity
with the preceding tradition—played a beneficial role in steadying

the conciliar majority—enthused by movements of biblical, patristic, and liturgical *ressourcement* and a desire to reach out to the world . . . in generosity of heart." Thanks to Paul VI's several critical interventions in the drama of Vatican II, the Council's documents were firmly anchored in the Catholic tradition even as they developed that tradition, so that what emerged from the Council's often-impassioned debates would "remain susceptible to a reading of a classically Christian kind."[11] That was a considerable achievement. It took no little skill, no little patience, and, one imagines, no little suffering.

Initially skeptical about a council, Giovanni Battista Montini seems to have been persuaded by John XXIII's vision of an evangelically revitalized Church. His character, and the contributions to the Council that flowed from that character, mirror those of another influential Vatican II figure, Cardinal Josef Frings, as described by Cardinal Joseph Ratzinger:

[He led and acted] not as a conservative or a progressive but as a believer [who] was certainly no liberal in the ideological sense. . . . [Being] blown hither and thither by every wind and making ideas dependent on the way the dice of opinion fell was deeply abhorrent to him. [His] "Catholic liberality" . . . was in radical contradiction to ideological liberalism. He wanted to go beyond all outward obedience to authority, to a faithfulness whose power source lay in the insight of the believing conscience. . . . [He] was God-fearing and therefore wise. For him, God was the real standard he had to keep to. That was the viewpoint from which he acted.[12]

Toward the end of his pontificate, Paul VI sought to recover that animating vision of vibrant, Christocentric conviction and apostolic possibility in the 1975 post-synodal apostolic exhortation *Evangelii Nuntiandi*. There, the Pope reminded the

Church that its very essence was Christ-centered and evangelical, as he taught that "there is no true evangelization if the name, the teaching, the life, the promises, the kingdom, and the mystery of Jesus of Nazareth, the Son of God, are not proclaimed." Pope Paul also wrote that "modern man listens more willingly to witnesses than to teachers, and if he does listen to teachers, it is because they are witnesses."[13] The Church's proclamation of Christ and the Church's way of life had to be seamless. Proposal and witness were one.

Evangelii Nuntiandi sounded several other themes that would shape the contest for the legacy of Vatican II in the decades after Paul VI: that to meet Christ was to meet the Church; that to be "in" the Church was to be a member of a community formed by the sacraments, those fonts of grace that nourished faith, hope, and charity; and that to live "in" this Church most fully, those who had been evangelized had to become evangelizers. By "announcing the Gospel" (as Pope Paul styled his apostolic exhortation), Catholics would also become renovators of culture, as they offered the world a humanism in which the demands of truth and the privileges of conscience met, as truth was freely accepted and lived in a reconciled world that had learned the nature of authentic human community.

His close collaborator, Cardinal Lucas Moreira Neves, OP, once described *Evangelii Nuntiandi* as Pope Paul VI's "pastoral testament to the Church."[14] It was more than that, however: *Evangelii Nuntiandi* was one of the missing "keys" to the proper interpretation of Vatican II. As *Gaudet Mater Ecclesia* had been John XXIII's prescription for the Council, *Evangelii Nuntiandi* was Paul VI's recapitulation of the Council's achievement and purpose, which was "to make the Church of the twentieth century ever better fitted for proclaiming the Gospel to the people of the twentieth century."[15]

And for the twenty-first century and beyond.

Giovanni Battista Montini was arguably the only papal candidate in the conclave of 1963 who would have continued the work of Vatican II as conceived by John XXIII. Some prominent *papabili* in 1963 (Cardinal Giuseppe Siri of Genoa, for example) would have quietly buried the Council. Others (such as Cardinal Giacomo Lercaro of Bologna) might have led a reconvened Vatican II in a direction that could have caused serious ruptures in the Church's unity.[16] That the Council reached consensus across a broad range of contested questions and ended on a note of hope is much to Paul VI's credit. Whether the particular cast of mind and the set of skills that were essential in Pope Paul's guiding Vatican II to a united conclusion were the approach and the methods needed to implement the Council while maintaining a measure of order within the Church is another matter.

That the Church was in considerable disarray when Paul VI died on August 15, 1978, cannot be disputed. Paul VI seems to have lost control of certain facets of conciliar implementation (notably with regard to *Sacrosanctum Concilium* and the reform of the liturgy), and his essential gentility of spirit translated into a reluctance to enforce discipline in the immediate post–Vatican II years. His defense of priestly celibacy in an eponymous 1967 encyclical *Sacerdotalis Caelibatus* took courage. He displayed even more grit—and an acute sense of the issues at stake—when, in his 1968 encyclical on the transmission of human life, *Humanae Vitae*, he reaffirmed the Church's teaching that the natural rhythms of biology are the most appropriate means of regulating fertility, especially in terms of the dignity of human love and the dignity of women. In the latter case, though, his gentility led him to resist calls to push back against bishops' conferences and theologians who overtly rejected his authoritative teaching, even as that teaching prevented a deconstructive view of Catholic moral theology from achieving official status. This reticence led to serious problems in the future.[17]

Whether a firmer papal hand on the tiller would have led to a less convulsed Church will be debated long into the future. What seems clear in retrospect is that much of the contention in the post-conciliar years of Paul VI was miscast because it assumed that Vatican II had been a council of rupture with the Church's tradition. Traditionalists, following the lead of Archbishop Marcel Lefebvre, continued to ask why the Council had abandoned the tradition. Progressives asked why "the tradition" should be a constraint on the evolving "spirit of Vatican II." Both traditionalists and progressives made the same error: they failed to see that the Second Vatican Council was "in fundamental continuity with the past," as Cardinal Joseph Ratzinger insisted, an assertion with which Cardinal Avery Dulles agreed.[18]

Evangelii Nuntiandi made a start at re-centering the post-conciliar Catholic conversation on Christ and the Church's mission to convert the world. Yet a more comprehensive and authoritative interpretation of the Council that would energize the Christocentric, evangelical renewal of the Church envisioned by John XXIII in *Gaudet Mater Ecclesia* was required. Vatican II, the Council without keys, needed more keys. They would be provided by two men whose understanding of the Church and its possibilities in the late modern and postmodern worlds was decisively shaped by their experience of the Second Vatican Council.

19

Keys to the Council: John Paul II

T HE FIRST CONCLAVE OF 1978, HELD AFTER THE DEATH OF
Pope Paul VI, took place during the stifling heat of a late
Roman summer. Sequestered in the hothouse of the Vatican's Ap-
ostolic Palace, two younger cardinal-electors decided to get some
fresh air one evening by taking a walk in the palace's Cortile San
Damaso. During their conversation, Cardinal Karol Wojtyła of
Kraków and Cardinal Joseph Ratzinger of Munich discovered
that they shared a common analysis of the Catholic Church's situation thirteen years after the conclusion of the Second Vatican
Council, to which they had both made significant contributions.
Vatican II, they agreed, was both necessary and fruitful, having
given the Church and the world a body of teaching rooted in the
Church's tradition and well suited to the needs of the age. What
was missing was an authoritative interpretation of that teaching:
a set of interpretive keys by which the Church would regain the
evangelical initiative it was losing, thanks to the unresolved debate over what the Council actually meant.[1]

This was the first lengthy conversation between these two men,
but it would not be their last. For over the next three and a half
decades, between Wojtyła's election as pope in October 1978 and
Ratzinger's abdication of the papacy in February 2013, they gave
the Church those authoritative keys, in two pontificates marked
by an exceptional richness of papal teaching. As men of the

Council, both Wojtyła and Ratzinger wanted to reclaim Vatican II for John XXIII's original intention. Both would have regarded as ludicrous, even sinister, the claims heard in the mid-twenty-first century that Vatican II was the work of diabolical conspiracies aimed at destroying Catholicism.[2] They had been there; they knew the dynamics in play; and they understood how those dynamics had shaped the world Church during the decade and a half after the Council. There was great truth in Vatican II, they believed. That truth should be re-proposed, explained, and implemented.

The pontificates of John Paul II and Benedict XVI were one continuous moment in contemporary Catholic history in which two men of genius gave the Council without keys what it lacked: an authoritative interpretation, a set of keys capable of unlocking the evangelical renewal of the Church that Pope John XXIII intended for the Second Ecumenical Council of the Vatican.

As archbishop of Kraków, Karol Wojtyła led one of the most thorough implementations of Vatican II in the world, involving thousands of clergy and laity in a nine-year process of prayer, reading, reflection, and pastoral planning. At the center of that process was a careful reading of the Council's documents guided by a *vademecum* prepared by the archbishop himself: a digest of the Council's teaching that Wojtyła organized according to his understanding of Vatican II's teaching on Christocentric humanism.[3] Thus he brought to the papacy a thorough understanding of the theological architecture of Vatican II and extensive pastoral experience in implementing its teaching.

The day after his election, John Paul II pledged to the cardinals who had just chosen him that his pontificate would be dedicated to the full implementation of Vatican II. That was his "definitive duty," because the Council had been an "event of utmost importance" in the Church's two-thousand-year history. Fulfilling that duty required that the Church's leaders "take once again into our hands the 'Magna Carta' of the Council, the Dogmatic Constitution *Lumen Gentium*," so that its Christocentric meditation on the Church's "way of being and acting" could be received throughout Catholicism "with renewed and invigorating zeal."[4] Over the ensuing twenty-six years, John Paul II fulfilled that "definitive duty" and kept that pledge of a full implementation of Vatican II through his papal magisterium, through the mechanism of the Synod of Bishops, and in his conduct of the papacy.

His 1979 inaugural encyclical, *Redemptor Hominis*, was the first papal encyclical ever devoted to Christian anthropology—and, it can be argued, his authoritative interpretation of Vatican II's Dogmatic Constitution on Divine Revelation, *Dei Verbum*. In the encyclical, John Paul filled out the portrait of the Christocentric humanism for which he had called in his 1959 letter to the Council's Ante-Preparatory Commission. Affirming *Dei Verbum*'s robust defense of the reality of divine revelation, *Redemptor Hominis* placed Jesus Christ, the "Redeemer of Man," at the center of the Church's proclamation, for, as the Council taught, in Jesus Christ men and women meet both the truth about God and the deepest truths about themselves. As J. Michael Miller, CSB, has observed, in *Redemptor Hominis* John Paul explained how, in drawing near to Christ, "individuals can plumb the depths of their identity in light of their creation in God's image and likeness . . . but most especially in light of their redemption by Christ's blood." The true "journey of self-discovery ends not in oneself, but in Christ."[5] True humanism is not solipsistic or narcissistic; true humanism is ordered to the crucified and risen Son of God, who in himself reveals the full dignity and destiny of the human person.

Having eloquently underscored the Christocentricity of Vatican II in an encyclical whose title and theme evoked John XXIII's solemn convocation of the Council in *Humanae Salutis*, John Paul added two other encyclicals to produce a Trinitarian triptych: *Dives in Misericordia*, on God the Father, and *Dominum et Vivificantem*, on the Holy Spirit.[6] These encyclicals further developed the Catholic vision of the God who speaks into the silence of late modernity and reveals essential truths about humanity. As its name suggests, *Dives in Misericordia*, issued in 1980, stressed the richness of the divine mercy that God the Father offers a prodigal world, while *Dominum et Vivificantem*, issued in 1986, was a powerful reaffirmation to Catholics concerned by post-conciliar ecclesiastical turbulence that the "Lord and Giver of Life" had not, and would not, abandon the Church. John Paul II's 1998 encyclical *Fides et Ratio* offered another key to the proper understanding of *Dei Verbum*, robustly affirming the mutually beneficial relationship of religious faith and the life of the mind: faith—in the divine word manifested in history—and reason—the innate quest for the truth of things—needed each other. They always had and they always would.

John Paul provided keys for the authoritative interpretation of *Lumen Gentium*, the Dogmatic Constitution on the Church, in several ways.

He used the mechanism of the Synod of Bishops to deepen the Church's reflection on the different states of life among the People of God, and then issued post-synodal apostolic exhortations as keys to understanding those vocations as the Council wished them to be understood. Thus the 1988 apostolic exhortation *Christifideles Laici* (Christ's Faithful Laity), which completed the 1987 Synod on the Laity, deepened the analysis of the lay vocation to evangelical mission offered in the Decree on the Apostolate of the Laity, *Apostolicam Actuositatem*, and proposed an authoritative key for understanding chapter four of *Lumen Gentium*. The 1992 apostolic exhortation *Pastores Dabo Vobis* (I Shall Give You Shepherds) completed the 1990 Synod on the reform of the priesthood and seminary formation (both urgent post-conciliar issues) while providing keys to the proper interpretation of *Lumen Gentium*'s discussion of the ordained priesthood as well as the conciliar decrees on priestly ministry (*Presbyterorum Ordinis*) and priestly formation (*Optatam Totius*). Those keys were further refined in

John Paul's annual letters to the world's priests on Holy Thursday of each year.[7] Consecrated religious life had experienced serious disturbances in the post-conciliar years. These were addressed in the 1994 Synod and in the 1996 apostolic exhortation *Vita Consecrata* (The Consecrated Life); *Vita Consecrata* was also a key to the interpretation of chapter six of *Lumen Gentium* and of the conciliar decree *Perfectae Caritatis*. The 2001 Synod on the ministry of bishops in the third millennium led to the 2003 apostolic exhortation *Pastores Gregis* (The Shepherds of the Flock), which provided keys to chapter three of *Lumen Gentium* and to the conciliar decree *Christus Dominus*.

John Paul II also proposed keys to the interpretation and implementation of *Lumen Gentium* in the apostolic exhortations that completed the work of the continental synods on Africa, the Americas, Asia, Oceania, and Europe, held in preparation for the Great Jubilee of 2000: *Ecclesia in Africa*, issued in 1995; *Ecclesia in America* and *Ecclesia in Asia*, both issued in 1999; *Ecclesia in Oceania*, issued in 2001; and *Ecclesia in Europa*, issued in 2003.[8] The 1985 encyclical on Saints Cyril and Methodius, *Slavorum Apostoli* (The Apostles of the Slavs), deepened *Lumen Gentium*'s teaching on the universality of the Church and offered a key to the proper interpretation of the conciliar decree *Orientalium Ecclesiarum*, underscoring what John Paul understood to be Vatican II's intention that the Church breathe again with both its lungs: the Eastern or Byzantine lung and the Western or Latin lung. For its part, the 1987 encyclical *Redemptoris Mater* offered an authoritative key to the Council's teaching on the Blessed Virgin Mary, the "Mother of the Redeemer," in chapter eight of *Lumen Gentium*.[9]

Karol Wojtyła did not have direct experience of the liturgical crisis that unfolded in many parts of the Church in the decade and a half immediately following Vatican II. Around the world, implementation of the reforms mandated by the Constitution on the Sacred Liturgy (and specified by Paul VI in several post-conciliar documents) was often haphazard, and sometimes zany. This was not the case in Poland, where ecclesiastical discipline remained firm, liturgical experiments were not welcome, and the translation of the revised liturgical texts into a fine, literary Polish did not replicate the callowness that beset other translations into the vernacular, notably the English and French. Wojtyła's personal experience of the post-conciliar liturgy was positive.

He was, however, one of the most experienced churchmen in the world when he was elected pope, so John Paul II was certainly aware of the many challenges that had arisen to a proper understanding and implementation of *Sacrosanctum Concilium*. He also knew that the constitution itself had mandated the criteria by which liturgical reform should be implemented: *Sacrosanctum Concilium* had insisted that "sound tradition be retained" even as "the way remain open to legitimate progress," and had taught that "there must be no innovations unless the good of the Church genuinely and urgently requires them." Moreover, the constitution continued, "care must be taken that any new forms adopted should in some way grow organically from forms already existing."[10] It is not easy, however, to see how these criteria were observed during the five years in which the dramatic revision of the Mass, embodied in the new Roman Missal promulgated in 1969, was undertaken.

John Paul II's approach to what would be called the "reform of the reform" of the liturgy was to offer authoritative keys to *Sacrosanctum Concilium* by deepening the Church's theological understanding of its public worship. Thus, the Pope's last encyclical, *Ecclesia de Eucharistia* (The Church from the Eucharist), issued in 2003, echoed themes in his first apostolic letter, *Dominicae Cenae* (The Lord's Supper), issued in 1980, and his last, *Mane Nobiscum Domine* (Remain with Us, Lord), issued in 2004. The Church, he stressed, should recover a sense of "eucharistic amazement," for in the celebration of the Eucharist Christ is truly and "substantially" present in his Paschal Mystery, which the Eucharist extends throughout history. To reduce the Eucharist to "simply a fraternal banquet" was to deprive it of its "enormous capacity" to bring alive in the world "the grace of the redemption." So Catholics must understand that, in the sacrifice of the Mass, they are incorporated into Christ's uniquely redemptive gift of himself to the Father, and thereby into the very life of the Holy Trinity. If all involved in the Church's public worship grasped that extraordinary truth, questions of the proper implementation of liturgical reform would be more readily answered.[11]

While that truth was being worked into the texture of Catholic life by a "reform of the reform," discipline had to be restored and maintained. In 2001, the Congregation for Divine Worship issued, with the Pope's authority, the Instruction *Liturgiam Authenticam*, which was intended to correct the inadequate vernacular translations of the Mass and other sacramental actions that had plagued the Church for decades. And in 2004, John Paul personally approved an instruction from the Congregation for Divine Worship, *Redemptionis Sacramentum*, that identified and proscribed numerous post-conciliar liturgical abuses.[12]

In many sectors of the world Church, Catholic devotional life deteriorated in the immediate post-conciliar years, in part because of misunderstandings of liturgical reform in general (and *Sacrosanctum Concilium* in particular), which held that a liturgically renewed Church had no need of non-liturgical experiences of prayer. John Paul II's efforts to bring the Divine Mercy devotion to the attention of the world Church, and his 2002 apostolic letter *Rosarium Virginis Mariae*, corrected that misunderstanding and provided other keys to the twenty-first-century development of Catholic piety. By adding the "Luminous Mysteries" of Christ's public life to the Rosary, *Rosarium Virginis Mariae* also implemented the teaching of *Sacrosanctum Concilium* and *Lumen Gentium* on the fuller integration of Scripture into the Church's life of prayer.[13]

As a priest with extensive experience as a confessor and spiritual director, Karol Wojtyła had long known the importance of the sacrament of Penance (or Reconciliation). He came to the papacy convinced that the collapse of sacramental confession in post-conciliar Catholicism was a grave misunderstanding of the Council's teaching in *Sacrosanctum Concilium* and an impediment to a revitalized Church in mission. For it was in the sacrament of Penance that missionary disciples bring the difficulties and failures of their respective evangelical vocations to the Lord and, by receiving Christ's forgiveness through the priest-confessor, are re-energized for mission. He therefore led the 1983 Synod of Bishops in a month-long reflection on "Penance and Reconciliation in the Mission of the Church Today," and then issued the 1984 apostolic exhortation *Reconciliatio et Paenitentia*. Characteristically, John Paul linked the practice of confession to the Church's mission of proclaiming a nobler humanism to the world: to take freedom seriously is to take sin seriously; to take sin seriously is to take moral responsibility seriously; confessing one's sins and asking for the assistance of divine grace in leading an upright life adds to human dignity, as the penitent acknowledges that taking responsibility is a measure of human maturity.[14]

During the conciliar intersession between Vatican II's third and fourth periods, Archbishop Karol Wojtyła worked hard to refine the draft text of *Gaudium et Spes*, the Pastoral Constitution on the Church in the Modern World; its definition of an ennobled, Christocentric humanism in sections 22 and 24 would become the two most cited conciliar texts in the papal magisterium of John Paul II. John Paul also understood that *Gaudium et Spes* had too often been detached from Vatican II's more fundamental teaching in *Lumen Gentium*, and throughout his pontificate he would insist that *Gaudium et Spes* could only be properly read "through" the Dogmatic Constitution on the Church.

The Polish pope was also aware that the pastoral constitution had in many respects been overtaken by the rapid flow of history, and in his social magisterium he sought to develop the themes in *Gaudium et Spes* that were of enduring value. His first social encyclical, *Laborem Exercens*, issued in 1981, offered the Church and the world a rich phenomenology of work, emphasizing that human labor is an expression of human creativity and thus has spiritual and moral dimensions: work is about "being more," not just "having more."[15] In discussing the Church's "social concern" in his second social encyclical, *Sollicitudo Rei Socialis*, which was issued in 1987, he refined the discussion of post-colonial societies found in *Gaudium et Spes*, emphasizing the human and cultural dimensions of the development of poor countries and teaching that governments and international aid should facilitate the economic creativity of Third World peoples.[16] His most developed social encyclical, *Centesimus Annus*, was, as its *incipit* indicated, issued for the 1991 centenary of Leo XIII's *Rerum Novarum*, although its primary focus was a look forward into the post–Cold War world through the lens of Catholic social doctrine. *Centesimus Annus* adopted from *Gaudium et Spes* a tripartite understanding of the free and virtuous society of the future—a democratic polity, a free or market-oriented economy, and a vibrant public moral culture—while insisting that the cultural sector's capacity to form men and women capable of living freedom nobly was the key to democracy and the free economy facilitating genuine human flourishing and social solidarity.[17] John Paul II's 1995 encyclical on the gospel of life, *Evangelium Vitae*, forcefully underscored the condemnation of abortion and euthanasia in *Gaudium et Spes* (issues that had become more urgent since 1965) and warned that a state in which grave moral wrongs were defined as "rights" risked the incoherence that eventually led to one form or another of tyranny.[18]

Throughout the quarter-century of his pontificate, John Paul II's magisterium provided further keys to *Gaudium et Spes* and its sketch of the contours of a new Christian humanism by addressing perennial issues of human dignity and social solidarity. The 1984 apostolic letter on salvific suffering, *Salvifici Doloris*, deepened the pastoral constitution's reflection on the unavoidable human realities of pain and death while teaching that these seeming absurdities find ennobling meaning in the passion, death, and resurrection of Christ. The 1981 post-synodal apostolic exhortation on the family, *Familiaris Consortio*, and the 1988 apostolic letter on the dignity of women, *Mulieris Dignitatem*, addressed the sexual revolution in far greater depth than *Gaudium et Spes*, as did John Paul's innovative Theology of the Body, which he developed between 1979 and 1984 in a series of 133 general audience addresses on the meaning of human love and its place in a genuinely ennobling humanism.[19]

At Vatican II, Karol Wojtyła was a strong proponent of the Declaration on Religious Freedom while insisting, during the Council's fourth period, that the right of religious freedom must always be tethered to the responsibility to seek and adhere to the truth, including the truth about God. As pope, John Paul deployed *Dignitatis Humanae* as a powerful weapon against various tyrannies, especially communism. His two addresses to the United Nations General Assembly, in 1979 and 1995, were keys to the declaration and to the interpretation of *Gaudium et Spes*, its portrait of Christian humanism, and its ideas on world politics.

At the beginning of his 1979 U.N. address, John Paul II struck the dignitarian note prominent in *Dignitatis Humanae* and *Gaudium et Spes* by insisting that politics, whether national or international, was an exercise of moral responsibility and therefore ordered to the whole human person, "in all the fullness and manifold riches of his spiritual and material existence." That was why peace could only be built upon "the recognition of, and respect for, the inalienable rights of individuals and communities of peoples."

That was why Vatican II had taught that denying anyone the freedom to search for the truth and adhere to it dehumanized individuals and distorted society. Religious freedom was not a sectarian matter; it was about respect for our common humanity, and was thus something on which people of faith, agnostics, and atheists alike ought to be able to agree.

In 1995, John Paul returned to the issue of human rights in his second U.N. address. There, reflecting on the "global acceleration of that quest for freedom which is one of the great dynamics of human history," the Pope proposed that the universality of that aspiration confirmed the reality of a universal human nature and a universal moral law. The world needed dialogue, but that dialogue had to be structured: and the "universal moral law written on the human heart" was "precisely [the] kind of 'grammar'" the world needed if it was to engage in a serious discussion about the human future. In that conversation, the world ought to ponder more deeply the relationship between freedom and truth, for "the truth about the human person . . . is, in fact, the guarantor of freedom's future."[20]

O ther teachings of John Paul II's papal magisterium sought to correct false interpretations of the documents of Vatican II while offering course corrections in the Council's implementation.

The Decree on Priestly Formation, *Optatam Totius*, had called for a renewal of Catholic moral theology. What too often followed was a deconstruction of Catholic moral theology. John Paul's 1993 encyclical, *Veritatis Splendor* (The Splendor of Truth), directly addressed that crisis by deepening three classic Catholic convictions: that there are moral truths built into the world and into the human person; that those truths can be known by both reason and revelation; and that grasping those truths discloses our moral responsibilities. Certain post-conciliar schools of Catholic moral theology denied, for example, that there were intrinsically evil acts: actions that were always and everywhere gravely wrong, irrespective of intentions or circumstances. *Veritatis Splendor* strongly reaffirmed the reality of intrinsically evil acts while concurrently teaching that human beings aspire to goodness and excellence. Thus against caricatures common in both the Church and the world, the encyclical taught that every "no" the Catholic Church believes it must pronounce is based on a higher "yes": a "yes" to the inalienable dignity and value of every human life; a "yes" to the human capacity to distinguish freedom from willfulness; a "yes" to the human equality that is rooted in our equal responsibility before the moral law; a "yes" to personal flourishing and social solidarity. *Veritatis Splendor* also offered the Church an example of how the fine-grained distinctions of Thomistic philosophy could work together with a *ressourcement*-influenced approach to biblical interpretation and theology.[21]

Vatican II's Decree on Ecumenism, *Unitatis Redintegratio*, led to an initial wave of optimism about the possibilities of Christian unity. That wave soon crested. Centuries-long psychological and cultural obstacles still impeded the restoration of full communion between the Catholic Church and the Eastern Orthodox Churches. Bilateral dialogues between Catholics and various Protestant communities demonstrated that issues far beyond those raised in the sixteenth-century Reformations—issues involving the reality and binding force of divine revelation—were creating further barriers to Christian unity within a divided Christian West. The ecumenical temperature had certainly improved since Vatican II; intra-Christian polemics were, with rare exceptions, a thing of the past, and that was no small achievement. But the one Church of Christ was no closer to being recomposed in unity than it had been when the Council overwhelmingly endorsed full Catholic engagement in the ecumenical movement.

John Paul II sought to address those disappointments, to correct the excessive optimism characteristic of certain readings of *Unitatis Redintegratio*, and to remind the Church that ecumenical dialogue was not a zero-sum negotiation with *Ut Unum Sint*, the first papal encyclical on ecumenism, issued in 1995, which took its *incipit*, "That They May Be One," from Christ's prayer at the Last Supper. In that text, John Paul deepened the Council's teaching that the Christian unity worth seeking was a unity in truth and reaffirmed that the quest for unity in moral truth (as well as dogmatic truth) was part of any worthy ecumenical endeavor. At the same time, the Pope insisted that the Catholic Church's commitment to the quest for Christian unity was irreversible, because Christianity's fragmentation impeded the proclamation of the Gospel. And in an unprecedented gesture that dramatically implemented the Council's teaching in *Lumen Gentium* and *Unitatis Redintegratio* about "degrees of communion" with the Catholic Church, John Paul asked Orthodox and Protestant Christians to work with him and the Catholic Church in thinking through a papacy that could serve Orthodox and Protestant needs in the future: "Could not the real but imperfect communion existing [between divided Christians]" form the basis of a discussion about the kind of papacy that would serve all Christians?[22] The invitation was not immediately answered, but the fact that it was made set a standard for future ecumenical discussion about a crucial issue dividing Christianity.

The renewal of Catholic education at all levels envisioned in the Declaration on Christian Education was not realized in the immediate post-conciliar years. Religious education at the elementary and secondary levels too often fell into content-free disarray, while many Catholic institutions of higher education sought to cut any tether to the authority of the Church. These were serious misreadings of the Council's intention and teaching in *Gravissimum Educationis*.

John Paul II tried to end the free-fall of catechetics or elementary and secondary Catholic religious education and provide a charter for catechetical renewal with the 1979 post-synodal apostolic exhortation *Catechesi Tradendae* (Catechesis in Our Time).

In it, he taught that all authentic catechesis is Christocentric; that Christian learning is lifelong; that catechesis at any level must nourish the heart and soul as well as the mind; and that authentic catechetical reform cannot avoid the most challenging of Christian truths, but must find ways to make those truths come alive in contemporary circumstances.[23]*

The crisis in Catholic higher learning was addressed in two apostolic constitutions, *Sapientia Christiana* (Christian Wisdom), issued in 1979, on the renewal of pontifically chartered Catholic institutions, and *Ex Corde Ecclesiae* (From the Heart of the Church), which in 1990 described in detail the character of all Catholic colleges and universities as they ought to be renewed according to the teaching of Vatican II. These institutions, John Paul taught, were part of the Church's mission and ought to understand themselves in those terms: a genuinely Catholic college or university existed to help convert the culture, not supinely reflect it.[24]

I n tandem with *Redemptor Hominis*, John Paul II's 1990 encyclical *Redemptoris Missio* (The Mission of the Redeemer) can be considered a special "key" to Vatican II. *Redemptor Hominis* defined the Christocentric core of the Church's proclamation to the world and the Catholic proposal for a revitalized humanism. *Redemptoris Missio* built on Paul VI's *Evangelium Nuntiandi* in calling the post-conciliar Church to live John XXIII's original, evangelical intention for the Council, for, as John Paul II wrote, "the Church is missionary by her very nature." The two encyclicals thus complemented each other, and once again, the center is Christ. A sense of evangelical urgency was necessary for the Church's renewal, for faith in Christ is "strengthened when it

---

* The catechetical crisis in the post-conciliar Church was also addressed in a decisive way by the development of the *Catechism of the Catholic Church*, to be discussed below.

is given to others." Catholics claim to have been saved by Jesus Christ; their willingness to share his Gospel with others is an important measure of how deeply they have been converted.

Redemptoris Missio also offered interpretive keys to *Lumen Gentium* and *Gaudium et Spes*. In the encyclical, John Paul II taught that *Lumen Gentium*'s universal call to holiness is a universal call to mission: every Catholic is baptized into a missionary vocation, and every place is mission territory. Those places include the fields of culture, politics, science, the media, and the arts, where lay Catholic witness is the Church's point of evangelical entry. *Gaudium et Spes* sought to insert the Church into the many critical issues of contemporary life; *Redemptioris Missio* was a powerful reminder that the greatest service the Church does the world is to tell the world its true story, which is the story of its creation, redemption, and sanctification by a God who ennobles humanity as, through the People of Israel and through his incarnate Son, he charts the path toward the fulfillment of human destiny, which is communion with the divine.[25]

John Paul II's evangelical or missionary "keys" to Vatican II were also embodied in his conduct of the papacy and his papal pilgrimages throughout the world, each of which was intended to strengthen a local Church for mission. During those pilgrimages, as in Rome, the Pope frequently conducted beatification or canonization ceremonies, lifting up new exemplars of the universal call to holiness. Thus the 482 saints canonized by John Paul II and the 1,338 men and women he beatified were another key to his authoritative interpretation of the Council: here were examples, often within living memory, of men and women who answered their baptismal call to mission, even to the point of martyrdom.

The implementation of the Second Vatican Council in the pontificate of John Paul II reached its apogee during the Great Jubilee of 2000. Within hours of John Paul's election as pope, the Polish primate, Cardinal Stefan Wyszyński, had pointed out that it would be his task to lead the Church into the third millennium of Christian history. In John Paul II's mind, the turn into the new millennium was less a matter of looking back and marking an anniversary about the distant past than of looking forward. So the 1998 Bull of Indiction formally announcing the Great Jubilee of 2000, *Incarnationis Mysterium*, struck a Christocentric and evangelical note, by evoking the "Mystery of the Incarnation" in its *incipit*, while linking the renewal of Catholic mission to Vatican II and the call to proclaim a new humanism:

> The coming of the Third Millennium prompts the Christian community to embrace new horizons in proclaiming the Kingdom of God. It is imperative therefore at this special time to return more faithfully than ever to the teaching of the Second Vatican Council, which shed new light upon *the missionary task of the Church* in view of the demands of evangelization today. . . .
>
> The journey of believers towards the Third Millennium is in no way weighted down by the weariness which the burden of two thousand years of history could bring with it. Rather, Christians feel invigorated, in the knowledge that they bring to the world the true light, Christ the Lord. Proclaiming Jesus of Nazareth, true God and perfect Man, the Church opens to all people the prospect of being "divinized" and thus of becoming more human.[26]

John Paul II's epic pilgrimage to the Holy Land in March 2000 was a week-long effort to embody this kerygmatic, evangelical, future-oriented approach to the Great Jubilee of 2000. The Pope, who had long wanted to go on pilgrimage to the holy places, was fulfilling a desire of his Christian heart; but he was doing much more. He was reminding the entire Church, indeed the entire world, that Christianity is not based on pious stories or myths. Christianity is rooted in real lives, lived in real places that can be touched, seen, heard, and smelled today. And at a precise moment in history, in those very specific places, men and women encountered someone they knew first as an itinerant rabbi, Jesus of Nazareth, and later met as the Risen Lord Jesus, after what seemed to have been the disaster of his degrading and violent death. Those men and women, in turn, went and told what they had seen and heard throughout the Mediterranean world and beyond. "This is Christianity," John Paul was saying with Vatican II as he walked where Jesus and the first disciples had walked: Christianity is an encounter with the incarnate Son of God, which so transforms men and women that their lives are spent in mission, offering others the gift they have received through the communion of the Church.

That point was underscored in the January 6, 2001, apostolic letter *Novo Millennio Ineunte,* in which John Paul II reflected on the Great Jubilee of 2000 as a preparation for the Church "entering the new millennium." The biblical story the Pope chose to summarize the meaning of the jubilee year was taken from the fifth chapter of Luke's gospel. Simon and his partners, after a frustrating night of failing to catch any fish on the Lake of Galilee, nonetheless heed Jesus's instruction to "put out into the deep for a catch [Luke 5.4]"—and, after hauling in a miraculous drought of fish, they become the first disciples. That dominical command, "Put out into the deep," was John Paul II's biblical metaphor for the Catholic Church in the third millennium, and it explicitly evoked the original evangelical intention of Vatican II defined by Pope John XXIII in *Gaudet Mater Ecclesia:* the Church must leave the shallow waters of institutional maintenance, transforming its institutions into platforms from which to launch new missions out on the roiling, tempestuous seas of the late modern and postmodern worlds. As in the biblical story, the goal of putting out "into the deep" was to make a great catch: in this instance, to convert others to friendship with the Lord Jesus Christ. Mission, the Pope insisted, "cannot be left to a group of 'specialists' but must involve the responsibility of all the members of the People of God." That responsibility was exercised by a Church in which no one was permitted to be mediocre, for holiness was and is the *"standard of ordinary Christian life."* Living holy lives transparent to the truth of the human person revealed in Christ, the people of the Church would build a "communion of love" that would embody "the destiny of human beings and the future of civilization."

If the Church's pilgrimage through the Great Jubilee of 2000 had been a true walk with God, John Paul wrote, "it will have stretched our legs for the journey still ahead." That journey, as defined by the Second Vatican Council, was both evangelical and humanistic: for if Christ is the key to the truth of the human person, human community, and human history, then a deepened encounter with Christ, through a Church in which all had become "proclaimers and heralds," would serve the world in its deepest need.[27]

20

Keys to the Council: Benedict XVI

JOSEPH RATZINGER'S INFLUENCE ON THE SECOND VATICAN Council antedated its formal opening, as a pre-conciliar speech he drafted for Cardinal Joseph Frings of Cologne (which Frings delivered in Genoa on November 20, 1961) made a great impression on Pope John XXIII. Three months later, the Pope called Frings out of a meeting of the Council's Central Preparatory Commission, embraced him, and said, "Eminence, I must thank you. Last night I read your speech. . . . You have said everything that I've thought and wanted to say but was unable to say myself." Themes from that Genoa speech (which Frings told John XXIII had been written by "a young professor") would be prominent in Pope John's opening address to Vatican II, especially the radical Christocentricity of *Gaudet Mater Ecclesia* and its summons to the Church to bear a deeper witness to Christ in the world, offering a positive alternative to humanity's Promethean self-deification.[1]

During the Council's four periods and its intersessions, Ratzinger, with Yves Congar and Gérard Philips, was one of Vatican II's most influential and productive theologians. The "young professor" made important contributions to several conciliar documents, above all the Council's fundamental text, the Dogmatic Constitution on Divine Revelation. As his biographer Peter Seewald noted, in *Dei Verbum* Ratzinger sought to "radicalize" Christian faith for the contemporary world by returning to Christianity's biblical roots. This was not just a question of moving beyond the abstract Neo-Scholastic theology Ratzinger found uninspiring during his seminary studies. It was a matter of animating Vatican II so that it would "be seen as the beginning of a new evangelization of the world." *Dei Verbum*, then, was more than a charter for the theologians, making Scripture "the soul of Catholic theology"; it was a charter for the entire Church, calling it into mission.[2]

Joseph Ratzinger's role in the struggle to define Vatican II's meaning and legacy began during the Council itself, when the reformist camp of theological advisers, of which the Bavarian was a principal member, began to experience tensions that would eventually create a serious rift.

During the Council's second period, two prominent *periti*, Karl Rahner and Edward Schillebeeckx, began planning a new theological journal, *Concilium*. They were eager to have fellow conciliar theologians join the project, especially the most venerable of the *ressourcement* theologians, Henri de Lubac. De Lubac originally agreed, but a year later, in 1964, he wrote Rahner about the editorial direction the new journal might take. His concerns had been triggered by a lecture Schillebeeckx gave during the Council's third period at the Dutch Documentation Center, a center of progressive fervor in Rome. There, the Flemish Dominican had suggested that the world had always been "Christian" in some sense and that divine revelation made explicit what was already implicit in the world. De Lubac wrote in his journal that this was a "betrayal of the Gospel" and told fellow Jesuit Rahner that, if this were the editorial direction *Concilium* would take, he would have none of it.[3] Rahner said that Schillebeeckx's view was one of the many that would be debated in the new journal. De Lubac was temporarily reassured. A few months later, however, during the intersession between the Council's third and fourth periods, de Lubac wrote Rahner again, saying that *Concilium*'s first issues had taken a line that he regarded as "propaganda" in service to an "extremist school" that was not "in line with the Council" while pretending to be just that. The Frenchman resigned quietly from the journal's editorial committee.[4]

This was the first significant skirmish in the theologians' War of the Conciliar Succession, which broke out in earnest when a group of former conciliar *periti*, including Ratzinger, met on the sidelines of a 1969 assembly of the International Theological Commission and planned another journal, *Communio*, which would read Vatican II through the prism of the entire Catholic tradition. Their new journal would challenge the notion, implicit in *Concilium* (and sometimes quite explicit), that the Council marked a rupture with the past and a new starting point for Catholicism. *Communio* would stress the Christocentricity of the Council and would emphasize the Church's evangelical mission in a world thirsting for the divine but attempting to quench that thirst at the wrong wells.

The *Concilium/Communio* division among the reformist theologians at Vatican II was far more than a scrap among intellectuals; it was a battle over the proper interpretation of Vatican II. Were the keys to the Council without keys to be found in the Council's "spirit" or in its texts, read as a development of the Church's tradition and doctrine? Ratzinger was firmly on the side of understanding Vatican II through the texts he had helped develop, especially *Dei Verbum* and its bold assertion of the reality and enduring authority of divine revelation. That was the conviction animating his leadership of the Congregation of the Doctrine of the Faith under Pope John Paul II, as the Bavarian theologian worked in close harness with the Polish pope to give the Church authoritative keys to Vatican II.

There were two paradigmatic moments in the collaboration between Joseph Ratzinger and John Paul II by which the

Council was given an authoritative interpretation: paradigmatic, because they corrected distorted readings of *Gaudium et Spes* and other conciliar texts by a proper reading of Vatican II's two defining documents, *Dei Verbum* and *Lumen Gentium*.

Among the distortions of *Gaudium et Spes* that resulted from reading the pastoral constitution through an amorphous "spirit of Vatican II," none were more consequential in the late twentieth century than those promoted by the various theologies of liberation. Mistakenly presented in much of the world media as an indigenous Latin American development, the theologies of liberation were the by-product of a misguided fascination with Marxist theory by European Catholic theologians, whose work was then refracted back into Central and South America by Latin Americans who took advanced degrees under the direction of those Europeans.

There were different types of liberation theology, but they shared certain family characteristics.

The differing forms of liberation theology agreed that Vatican II had been insufficiently radical, its teaching dulled by the compromises necessary to achieve consensus. Liberation theologies thus sought to go beyond the reformism of *Gaudium et Spes*, which presumed Christian humanism's dialogue with modernity, to adopt a more revolutionary approach to social change that drew explicitly on Marxist categories and concepts. In the theologies of liberation, the "class struggle" was understood to be the vehicle for overcoming the "sinful social structures" of contemporary Latin American social, economic, and political life. In this struggle, the Church, exercising a "preferential option for the poor," would create "base communities" where the poor would be taught to grasp their victimhood. Then, inspired by the image of Jesus the Liberator, they would build a new society from the ground up. If this necessitated violence, then the "second violence" of the revolutionary poor should be judged an act of self-defense against the "first violence" of the "dominant" social structures. Far from

disentangling the Church from political power, the various liberation theologies were eager to embrace a new alliance with power
through a "partisan" Church that would act on behalf of some
people and against others in the name of justice.

The social and economic displacements the theologies of liberation wanted to redress were real enough; it was scandalous that
they had been so inadequately addressed by a Catholicism present
in Latin America for five centuries. But the Christ taught by the
theologies of liberation was not the Christ of *Dei Verbum*. And the
Church proposed by the theologies of liberation as an instrument
of liberation from systemic "immiseration" was not the Church
envisioned by *Lumen Gentium* and *Gaudium et Spes*. John Paul II
sought to correct some of these distortions while challenging Latin
America to the deep reform the continent needed when he addressed the bishops of Latin America and the Caribbean at Puebla,
Mexico, on January 28, 1979.[5] The more developed magisterial
response to the theologies of liberation came in two Instructions
from the Congregation for the Doctrine of the Faith, developed
after Cardinal Joseph Ratzinger became the congregation's pre-
fect in early 1982. The first Instruction, issued in 1984, identified
the principal errors in various theologies of liberation. The second
Instruction, issued in 1986, laid the foundations for a more profound and Christocentric theology of liberation. Both were issued
with the personal endorsement of John Paul II, and both are keys
to the proper interpretation of Vatican II.

The 1984 *Instruction on Certain Aspects of the Theology of
Liberation* took many themes from John Paul's Puebla address
of 1979. The liberation of humanity was indeed a key part of a
biblically based Christian proclamation, and the Church had a responsibility to address injustice and exercise a special care for the
poor. But certain teachings prominent in the theologies of liberation were not congruent with the Church's faith. The great biblical
image of the Exodus and the liberation from bondage it embodied
could not be translated into merely political terms. Sin was not

primarily located in social structures but in human hearts. Class struggle was not the driver of history as the Church understood history; any attempt to translate salvation history into the history of the Marxist class struggle was a grave distortion of revelation. The "poor in spirit" of Matthew 5.3 were not the proletariat of Marx and Engels; Jesus was not a political messiah; his atoning and redemptive death on the cross could not be given an exclusively political meaning; Catholicism was not a partisan Church identified with any one social class or political faction; and the Eucharist was not the community's celebration of its own liberation struggle. In sum, Christians had a greater freedom to proclaim than the freedom promised by "the revolution."

The character of that greater freedom was spelled out in the 1986 *Instruction on Christian Freedom and Liberation*. The Church proclaimed the liberation of humanity in its deepest sense: liberation, through Christ's redeeming work, "from the most radical evil, namely, sin and the power of death."[6] God wished to be adored by people who are free to make the act of faith, and by entering into communion with God, human beings learned the true meaning of their freedom. The Church's love, like Christ's, excluded no one, and while the Church did have a "love of preference" for the poor, Catholicism also taught the God-given dignity of every human person—and the responsibility of all to live in solidarity.[7]

The second paradigmatic moment in Joseph Ratzinger's collaboration with John Paul II in providing keys for the Council without keys came during the Great Jubilee of 2000, when the Congregation for the Doctrine of the Faith issued the Christological declaration *Dominus Iesus*, on "The Unicity and Salvific Universality of Jesus Christ and the Church."[8] That Jesus Christ is the one, unique, and universal savior was unambiguously taught by Vatican II in *Dei Verbum*, *Lumen Gentium*, *Nostra Aetate*, and

Dignitatis Humanae. That Jesus Christ uniquely reveals to humanity both the truth about the human person and the truth about God was taught by *Gaudium et Spes.* That the one Church established by Christ exists in its most complete form in the Catholic Church was taught by *Lumen Gentium* and *Unitatis Redintegratio.* Yet some theologians were misinterpreting *Nostra Aetate* to suggest that there was supernatural and revelatory value, as well as moral and spiritual value, in religions such as Buddhism and Hinduism. Others were misinterpreting *Lumen Gentium*'s declaration that the one Church of Christ "subsists in" the Catholic Church to suggest an ecclesiological equivalence among Christian communities. Both distortions suggested that Catholicism was simply one option in a supermarket of religious possibilities. That was not the Church's faith, nor was it the teaching of Vatican II. A correction of those distortions was needed, not least as the Church prepared to enter its third millennium with a renewed faith and a more urgent sense of missionary fervor.

That *Dominus Iesus* was issued amid the interreligious good feeling evoked by the Great Jubilee of 2000 made its reception difficult, and there was press speculation that the declaration indicated a rift between John Paul II and Joseph Ratzinger. There was nothing of the sort, and John Paul vigorously defended the declaration during his October 1, 2000, Sunday Angelus address. In fact, the declaration was a reiteration of the integral Catholic faith proclaimed by Vatican II, which John Paul was eager to underscore during the jubilee year because that faith was the substantive core of the Church's mission. As *Dominus Iesus* reminded the Church and the world, Catholicism holds that there is one true God and thus one history of salvation; that if Jesus is Lord, he is Lord of all, whether his lordship is recognized or not; that God does not deny anyone the grace needed for salvation; that all who are saved are saved through the redemption wrought by Jesus Christ, even those who have never heard of Christ; that there is only one Church of Christ, for the Church is the Body of Christ in history, and Christ does not have multiple bodies; that the Catholic Church, which gratefully acknowledges the workings of divine grace outside itself, nonetheless understands itself to be the fullest expression of the one Church of Christ; and that the Church has an ongoing responsibility—indeed, a divine mandate—to proclaim Christ through its work of evangelization, for making that proclamation is what the Church is.[9]

Despite the caterwauling that surrounded it at the time, *Dominus Iesus* reiterated the authentic teaching of Vatican II in the context of the Great Jubilee and its summons to mission.[10]

E lected as John Paul II's successor on April 19, 2005, Joseph Ratzinger, having taken the regnal name of Benedict XVI, continued to provide keys for the authoritative interpretation of the Second Vatican Council throughout an eight-year pontificate.

He developed the Church's reflection on the "deposit of faith" that, in *Gaudet Mater Ecclesia*, John XXIII had asked the Church to offer the world in a fresh and compelling way. Thus Pope Benedict's triptych of encyclicals on the theological virtues—*Deus Caritas Est* (God Is Love), issued in 2005; *Spe Salvi* (Saved by Hope), issued in 2007; and *Lumen Fidei* (The Light of Faith), issued in 2013 by Pope Francis, who acknowledged Benedict's authorship of most of the text—paralleled John Paul II's trinitarian triptych of *Redemptor Hominis*, *Dives in Misericordia*, and *Dominum et Vivificantem* in deepening the content of the Church's evangelical proclamation according to the teaching of *Dei Verbum* and *Lumen Gentium*, and the missionary mandate taught by those two basic conciliar texts and the decree *Ad Gentes*.

In *Verbum Domini* (The Word of the Lord), a 2010 apostolic exhortation completing the 2008 Synod of Bishops' discussion of the Bible in the life of the Church, Benedict XVI provided further keys to the authentic interpretation of the Dogmatic Constitution on Divine Revelation. Perhaps even more decisive for the future of the Church's encounter with the written Word of God, however, was the publication of Pope Benedict's three-volume study *Jesus of Nazareth*. While noting that these books were "in no way an exercise of the [papal] magisterium," but rather the reflections of a scholar who, like the Psalmist, was searching "for the face of the Lord," Benedict also emphasized that he was seeking to extend the "decisive step forward" in Catholic biblical studies made by *Dei Verbum*.

Benedict acknowledged the achievements of the historical-critical study of ancient texts while asserting that the essential fruits of that method had been reaped and the time had come for a more rounded approach to biblical interpretation: one that "read individual [biblical] texts within the totality of the one Scripture, which then sheds light on the individual texts"; that took into account "the living tradition of the whole Church"; and that read the Bible within the context of the Church's faith and the inter-locking truths within that faith.[11] In the three volumes of the trip-tych, Ratzinger offered the Church and the world a lucid model of what *Dei Verbum* had taught on the nature of the Bible and the Bible's importance for the mission of the Church while giving Catholic teachers and preachers many examples of how biblical texts can become invitations to encounter God in Christ.

J oseph Ratzinger brought to the papacy sixty years of experi-ence in the work of liturgical reform—and the conviction that, if the truths taught by *Sancrosantum Concilium*, the Council's Constitution on the Sacred Liturgy, were to be fully embodied, a reform of the implementation of the Council's liturgical reform was necessary, so that the Church's liturgy would become a deeper experience of divine grace, animating an intensification of mission and evangelization.

To put that deeper reform on a secure theological foundation and link liturgy to mission, Benedict XVI issued the 2007 apostolic exhortation *Sacramentum Caritatis* (The Sacrament of Charity), which completed the 2005 Synod of Bishops on the Eucharist. There, he taught that "the love that we celebrate in the [Eucharist] is not something we can keep to ourselves. By its very nature it demands to be shared with all. What the world needs is God's love; it needs to encounter Christ and to believe in him. The Eucharist is thus the source and summit not only of the Church's life, but also of her mission: 'an authentically eucharistic Church is a missionary Church' [as the Synod Fathers had stated]."[12] He also sought to give a new dynamism to the "reform of the reform" with the 2007 apostolic letter *Summorum Pontificum*, which authorized the more widespread use of the pre-conciliar Order of Mass. That experience, he hoped, would help the reform of the post-conciliar liturgical reform advance in a direction that re-emphasized the sacred and the sacrificial in the Church's celebration of the Eucharist.

These initiatives were important in the ongoing process of providing keys for the Council without keys. The proper implementation of the Council required something more, however: an understanding of just what the Council had been as an ecclesial *event*. So at the very outset of his pontificate, and to establish a baseline for what he would do during his papacy, Benedict XVI gave a decisive answer to the question of how the Church should understand the contending interpretations of the Second Vatican Council. Eight months after his election and two weeks after the fortieth anniversary of Vatican II's closing ceremony, he masterfully summarized the problems of conciliar interpretation that had beset the Church since 1965 in a historic address to the Roman Curia. Here, he forthrightly explored the question of why the post-conciliar years had been so challenging and then proposed a way forward that was congruent with the teaching of the Council itself—as well as with the deepening of that teaching by John Paul II, in which he had cooperated for more than two decades.

"In vast areas of the Church," Benedict admitted, "the implementation of the Council has been somewhat difficult." He did not think things were as bad as those described after the First Council of Nicaea by St. Basil—who had bemoaned the "confused din of uninterrupted clamoring"—but the question still had to be faced: "Why has the implementation of the Council, in large parts of the Church, thus far been so difficult?"[13]

The answer, he said bluntly, was that two "contrary" interpretations of Vatican II "came face to face and quarreled with each other." One, the "hermeneutic of discontinuity and rupture," had "caused confusion." The other, the "hermeneutic of reform," which reflected *Gaudet Mater Ecclesia* and Paul VI's closing address to Vatican II, "bore and is bearing fruit."

The hermeneutic of rupture reflected certain trends in contemporary theology and "the sympathies of the mass media." It sundered the post-conciliar Church from the pre-conciliar Church, as if Catholicism had been reinvented at Vatican II. Like various liberation theologies, it demeaned the actual texts of the Council, because they were thought to reflect "compromises" necessary to reach consensus and so retained "many old things that are now pointless." The true Council, on this reading, can be found in the "spirit of the Council" and in the "impulses toward the new that are contained in the text."

The problem with this hermeneutic was that it left open the question of how this "spirit of Vatican II" should be defined and thereby made room "for every whim."

This, Benedict continued, was a fundamental misunderstanding of the nature of an ecumenical council. A council was not a "constituent assembly" called to write a new constitution. No council ever had such a mandate, and Vatican II certainly didn't, "because the essential constitution of the Church comes from the Lord and was given to us so that we might attain eternal life and . . . be able to illuminate life in time and time itself."

By contrast, the "hermeneutic of reform," taking seriously John XXIII's original intention for Vatican II, gratefully accepted as a living heritage the abiding and constituting truths that Christ had given the Church. It sought to find a "new and vital relationship" to those truths in a synthesis of fidelity and dynamism that would help resolve the "great dispute" about the human person that "marks the modern epoch." That way of understanding the Council was, in 2005, much "livelier" than it had been in "the turbulent years around 1968." In light of the keys to the Council given the Church by Paul VI in *Evangelii Nuntiandi* and then by John Paul II in his extensive magisterium, Benedict said, "we see that although the good seed developed slowly, it is nonetheless growing, and our deep gratitude for the work done by the Council is likewise growing."

The modern world had indeed set new challenges before the Church: "the relationship between faith and science"; the relationship "between the Church and the modern state"; the "problem of religious tolerance" in a plural world, which "required a new definition of the relationship between the Christian faith and the world religions"; and the challenge of articulating "in a new way the relationship between the Church and the faith of Israel," in light of a "long and difficult history" and the "crimes of the Nazi regime." The Second Vatican Council had met those challenges without abandoning a "continuity of principles." The Declaration on Religious Freedom, for example, had "recovered the deepest patrimony of the Church"—the conviction that the act of faith must be freely made to be a true act of faith—and thereby underscored that "a missionary Church known for proclaiming her message to all peoples must necessarily work" for religious freedom, even as the Church works to "transmit the gift of the truth that exists for one and all." In doing so, the Church gave one of political modernity's aspirations a more secure foundation, for authentic freedom cannot be sustained by "the canonization of relativism."

Yes, some Catholics had been overly optimistic about the way modernity would respond to the Church's openness. And that, Benedict suggested, was due to a misunderstanding of the tensions within the modern project, a misunderstanding of history, and a misunderstanding of the nature of the Church. The Church would always be a sign of contradiction, but that did not prevent the Church from engaging different cultures and drawing from them elements that helped it proclaim the Gospel. That was what had happened in the Christian encounter with classical culture, which was not without challenges but which also led to the dogmatic definitions of the first ecumenical councils. That was what had happened in the thirteenth century, when Thomas Aquinas had "mediated the new encounter between faith and Aristotelian philosophy, thereby setting faith in a positive relationship with the form of reason prevalent at the time."

And that was what Vatican II had attempted in and for the modern world. So the contemporary "dialogue between faith and reason" would find its "bearings on the basis of the Second Vatican Council." Interpreted correctly according to the hermeneutic of reform, the Council would become an "increasingly powerful" force for the "ever necessary renewal of the Church" and the revitalization of its evangelical mission: "The Church, both before and after Vatican II, was and is the same Church, one, holy, catholic, and apostolic, journeying on through time."

Those who did not grasp that truth of Vatican II—whether progressives or radical traditionalists, both of them mired in the hermeneutic of rupture—understood neither the Church nor the Council.

21

The Master Key

IN ADDITION TO GIVING THE CHURCH MANY SPECIFIC KEYS for interpreting the sixteen documents of Vatican II, the Wojtyła-Ratzinger collaboration gave the Church the master key to the Council's teaching: the key that helps the other keys function properly. That master key was forged at the Extraordinary Synod of 1985, summoned on the twentieth anniversary of Vatican II's conclusion so that bishops from all over the world could together assess what had gone right—and what had gone wrong—in the Council's reception. Cardinal Joseph Ratzinger played a defining role at that Synod, shaping its crucial final report and guiding the development of its most consequential product.

Styled an "Extraordinary Synod" because it fell outside the triennial pattern of "Ordinary Synods," Synod-1985 was also extraordinary in its dynamics. As the bishops met in Rome in November and December 1985, the familiar categories shaping media commentary on all things Catholic suddenly became obsolete. Those whom the press called the "progressives" or "liberals" were now the party of the status quo; the pseudonymous "Xavier Rynne" was heard to ask, "Why does there have to be a change? What's wrong with the way things have been going?" Conversely, those whom the media dubbed "conservatives" or "traditionalists" were those pressing for deeper Catholic reform. Their agenda was defined in part by a book-length interview Cardinal

Ratzinger gave an Italian journalist, Vittorio Messori, which was published as *The Ratzinger Report* some months before the Synod convened.[1]

T he Synod's Final Report began by affirming the Second Vatican Council as "a grace of God and a gift of the Holy Spirit, from which have come forth many spiritual fruits for the universal Church and the particular Churches, as well as for the men of our time." As for those who either celebrated or deplored Vatican II as a rupture with the Catholic past, the Synod's bishops bluntly rejected their claim: "Unanimously and joyfully, we also verify that the Council is a legitimate and valid expression and interpretation of the deposit of faith as it is found in Sacred Scripture and in the living tradition of the Church." Nonetheless, there were "lights and shadows" in the way the Council had been received throughout the world Church.

Why had *Lumen Gentium*'s teaching on the Christocentric and evangelical nature of the Church not been thoroughly worked into the texture of Catholic life? Why had the Council's noble vision of the human person not moved the hearts and minds of those committed to a materialistic concept of life, whether Marxist or consumerist? Why did some sectors of the world Church indulge in a "partial and selective reading of the Council, as well as a superficial interpretation of its doctrine"? Why were there still so many battles over power and authority in the Church, when Vatican II had called Catholicism beyond a primarily institutional self-understanding to a deeper understanding of the Church as a sacramentally ordered community animated by the abiding presence of the Triune God? Yet notwithstanding the turbulence in the Church and the challenges of an ever more assertive secularism, the bishops of Synod-1985 also discerned "signs of a return to the sacred . . . of a new hunger and thirst for the transcendent and the divine."

The Synod then reminded the Church of the reason for its existence: "The primary mission of the Church, under the impulse of the Holy Spirit, is to preach and witness to the good and joyful news of the election, the mercy and charity of God which manifest themselves in salvation history, which through Jesus Christ reach their culmination in the fullness of time and which communicate and offer salvation to man by virtue of the Holy Spirit." If the Council's promise had been frustrated in parts of the world Church, that likely reflected a failure to put Christ, who reveals both the truth about God and the truth about humanity, at the center of the Church's life and work.

Because Christ is ever present to the Church, the Church is a mystery—a reality comprehended in love, an ongoing encounter between God and humanity—before it is a hierarchically structured organization or a voluntary association of members. Because Christ is ever present in and to the Church, the Church, which is always in need of purification, is also holy and must lift up the saints in its midst as a reminder that holiness is every Christian's vocation. And because Christ is ever present in the Church, the Church is a communion: a communion of disciples in mission. This idea of communion, Synod-1985 taught, "is the central and fundamental idea of the Council's documents," and is ultimately rooted in the Triune God's will to divinize humanity through the redemptive work of Christ and the gift of the Holy Spirit, by which men and women come to know the Father.[2]

As a communion of disciples in mission, Catholicism begins with friendship with Jesus Christ: a personal encounter between the individual believer and the incarnate Son of God, present through the sacraments and the written Word of God. To meet, choose, and embrace Christ is not a nobler form of individualism, however; it is to be enfolded within the Mystical Body of Christ, the Church. And the Church, the Synod taught, is best understood as a "communion." Although it can be experienced as such, the Church is not a family, because it is not biologically generated.

The Church has a public life, but it is not a political party or a state. The Church has an economic life, but it is neither a corporation nor a trade union. Sociologically speaking, the Church is a voluntary association, in that no one is compelled to join it and everyone in it is free to leave; but to speak of the Church in sociological terms is to empty it of its supernatural, religious essence. Thus Synod-1985 chose the Latin term *communio* as the most apt description of the Church: the Church-as-communion is a living organism in which the baptized relate to each other as the cells in a living body.

And, the Synod insisted, that communion of disciples exists to share with others the gift that its members have received, friendship with Jesus Christ. In doing so, the Church actualizes in history its nature as a "sacrament for the salvation of the world."

At the end of Synod-1985's Final Report, the bishops thanked God "for the greatest grace of this century, that is, the Second Vatican Council." And they prayed that there may come "in our day that 'new Pentecost' of which Pope John XXIII had . . . spoken." That "new Pentecost," the Synod taught, would be one in which the Church lived fully the truth about itself as a communion of disciples in mission. That self-understanding was the master key to Vatican II and to the Catholic future.[3]

O ne other product of Synod-1985 should be noted. In an echo of the Council of Trent, that product—a new universal catechism—became a key chest containing many of the keys to the Council.

The Synod's Final Report noted that many bishops had called for "a catechism or compendium of all Catholic doctrine regarding both faith and morals." John Paul II accepted this proposal, put Cardinal Joseph Ratzinger in charge of a commission assigned to prepare a new catechism, and then issued the *Catechism of the Catholic Church*, along with the 1992 apostolic constitution

Fidei Depositum (The Deposit of Faith). There, the Pope explicitly linked the new *Catechism* to the Second Vatican Council, which "had as its intention and purpose to highlight the Church's apostolic and pastoral mission and, by making the truth of the Gospel shine forth, to lead all people to seek and receive Christ's love, which surpasses all knowledge."[4] The *Catechism* thus became the most visible and influential product of the Extraordinary Synod of 1985, and in several ways.

Written in a narrative style and drawing extensively on the documents of Vatican II, the *Catechism* established an authoritative template for catechetical materials throughout the world Church. It thus reinforced the "reform of the reform" of catechetics, which had been a major issue in the post-conciliar period.

The *Catechism* was also something of a populist text. As John Paul II wrote in *Fidei Depositum*, the *Catechism* is "a statement of the Church's faith . . . [and] a sure norm for teaching the faith."[5] The *Catechism* gave the people of the Church an authoritative source by which to challenge doctrinally dubious preaching and similarly dubious teaching in Catholic schools and parish programs of sacramental preparation.

The *Catechism* also demonstrated, in its four parts, the spiritual richness of the Catholic tradition, which was being obscured in some sectors of the world Church because of self-referential institutional squabbles over authority and power. It begins with an explication of the Apostles Creed, the ancient baptismal creed of the Church of Rome that gives an architectonic form to the profession of Christian faith. The *Catechism* then lays out the Church's sevenfold sacramental system, the sources of grace by which Christ is present to his people and their faith is nourished. In the *Catechism*'s third part, which is structured around the Ten Commandments, the moral life is described as a pilgrimage toward the goal of human existence, beatitude or happiness with God forever. Finally, the fourth and most lyrical part of the *Catechism* explores the Christian life of prayer, using the three professions and seven petitions of the Lord's Prayer as a biblical and spiritual framework. Throughout its seven hundred pages, the *Catechism* draws heavily on Scripture while citing the writings of the saints over the centuries. The *Catechism* is structured in small, numbered paragraphs, and reading through it, one experiences the symphonic character of Catholic truth, in which the Church's teachings work together in a coherent and harmonious way.

Because the *Catechism* was one product of a Synod aimed at recovering Vatican II's central idea of the Church as a communion of disciples in mission, it also pointed the Church into that twenty-first century and third millennium that John XXIII hoped would be an era of vibrant evangelization. At the end of two millennia, and with an eye on the third that lay just ahead, the Catholic Church could humbly but confidently say to the world, through the *Catechism*, "Here is what we believe; here is how we worship; this is what we think makes for righteous living; and this is how we pray." No other Christian community made such a comprehensive confession of its faith and its way of life on the edge of the talismanic year, 2000. That the Catholic Church could, and did, was a result of the Extraordinary Synod of 1985, which gave the Church the master key to the proper, Christocentric, and evangelical interpretation of the Second Vatican Council.[6]

22

Christ at the Center

Pope John XXIII's purposes in summoning the Second Vatican Council are often encapsulated by the Italian word *aggiornamento*, typically understood as "updating" or even "keeping up with the times." As a close reading of *Gaudet Mater Ecclesia*, the Pope's crucial opening address to the Council, should make clear, that is too shallow an understanding of *aggiornamento*. John XXIII knew full well (and the post-conciliar decades have amply confirmed) that *aggiornamento* undertaken without a profound appreciation of the riches of the deposit of faith—the revealed truths on which Catholicism rests—inevitably leads to the deconstruction and dissolution of the deposit of faith. And that is what the Church offers the world for its sanctification and salvation: it offers the truths about humanity, its origin and its destiny, as revealed in Jesus Christ, the Redeemer promised to the People of Israel.

In his September 29, 1963, opening address to the second period of Vatican II, Pope Paul VI proposed that any true *aggiornamento* of the Church would be a continual deepening of the Church's "imitation of Christ" and its "mystical union with him," which was made possible by the abiding presence of the Holy Spirit which Christ had sent into the Church. The path of sanctity was thus the path of authentic reform, and that path ran through a deeper appropriation of the Church's tradition, not a "rupture" with it.[1] Or, as Pope Paul's friend Jean Guitton wrote in 1965, of the Pope's vision for the Council and for the Catholic future, *aggiornamento* must always be a process of *approfondimento continuo*—"constant deepening."[2]

The essential character of that deepening was embodied in the ceremony that began each working session of the Second Vatican Council. Every day before the Council began its debates, the Book of the Gospels was solemnly enthroned before the papal altar in the Basilica of St. Peter. Positioned beneath Bernini's great bronze *baldacchino*, that altar also stands over what modern archaeological research has confirmed (insofar as archaeology and forensics can provide confirmation) is the resting place of Simon Bar-Jonah, whom Jesus renamed "Peter" (Matthew 16.18).

Every day, then, the Council—which asserted in its fundamental text that the New Testament gospels tell the world "the honest truth about Jesus"[3]—was reminded of the bonds linking it to the very origins of the Church: the transformation of ordinary and sometimes timid men into courageous apostles through their experience of the Risen Lord Jesus. As the encounter with Christ is the origin of the Church, so the encounter with Christ must always be the center of the Church's renewal. If the teaching of Vatican II could be summed up in a single sentence, it would be this: *Christ is the center*—of history, of the cosmos, and of the quest for an authentic humanism that creates human community in freedom and solidarity.

Joseph Ratzinger's concerns about the Council began during Vatican II and continued for decades afterward. For that reason, his summary of the "unambiguously positive effects" of Vatican II deserves special attention. Writing a decade after the Council's conclusion, he listed Vatican II's "more important theological results," which addressed certain imbalances in pre-conciliar Catholicism's self-understanding that required correction:

> [The] Council reinserted into the Church as a whole a doctrine of [papal] primacy that was dangerously isolated; it integrated into the one *mysterium* of the Body of Christ a too-isolated conception of the hierarchy; it restored to the ordered unity of faith an isolated Mariology; it gave the biblical word its full due; it made the liturgy once more accessible; and, in addition, it made a courageous step forward toward the unity of all Christians.[4]

That Vatican II should have been followed by contention, even crisis, should not have surprised anyone familiar with the history of ecumenical councils. In this case, the contentiousness was amplified by divergent readings within the Church of what Ratzinger described as "the global spiritual crisis of humanity itself, or, at least, of the Western world"[5]—precisely the crisis that John XXIII summoned the Council to address. From that perspective, perhaps the various crises of the Catholic Church in the decades since Vatican II should be understood as a form of penance: a purification of the Church essential to the revitalization of its evangelical mission in the world.

In the Christian understanding of the term, penance is not a matter of self-flagellation or self-rejection, but rather, as Ratzinger put it, of "self-discovery."[6] In discovering the imperative of *aggiornamento* through *approfondimento continuo*—in renewing its capacity to reach the Gospel through a deeper encounter with Christ and the Gospel—the Catholic Church was not and is not being called to start over again from zero. An honest reckoning with the ecclesiastical failures of the past was not (and is not) intended to create a rupture with that past, as if everything in the past were unclean and a re-start in innocence were necessary. To suggest any such thing was, and is, to suggest the impossible. It is also to deny that Christ has kept his promise to "be with you always" (Matthew 28.20).

And on this point, as on so many others, Joseph Ratzinger provided the Church of the twenty-first century with a key to unlocking the promise of the Second Vatican Council:

> It was both necessary and good for the Council to put an end to the false forms of the Church's glorification of self on earth, and by suppressing her compulsive tendency to defend her past history, to eliminate her false justification of self. But it is time . . . to reawaken our joy in the reality of an unbroken community of faith in Jesus Christ. We must rediscover that luminous trail that is the history of the saints and of the beautiful—a history in which the joy of the Gospel has been irrefutably expressed throughout the centuries.[7]

To bring the Second Vatican Council to fruition, the Catholic Church of the twenty-first century and beyond must recover its nerve, which is less a psychological than a spiritual matter: a matter of deeper conversion to Christ. Over two millennia of history, Catholicism has been confronted by "the world" in some of the world's most aggressive, demonic, and lethal forms. But it has endured, and it has continued to bring men and women to Christ, particularly whenever it has remembered the assurance the Lord Jesus gave his friends at the Last Supper: "In the world you have tribulation; but be of good cheer, I have overcome the world" (John 16.33).

Pope John XXIII's summons to the Church to sanctify the world through Christocentric evangelism and mission is as urgent in the twenty-first century as it was when the Pope issued that challenge in *Gaudet Mater Ecclesia* on October 11, 1962. For the crisis of world civilization that the most insightful Catholic minds of the late nineteenth and early twentieth centuries all believed the Catholic Church must address, not merely condemn, has intensified since 1962. That intensification is displayed in a cultural force that has gained considerable political power in the West: the new Gnosticism.

Gnosticism, a protean cast of mind, has taken many forms over the past two millennia. Wherever and whenever Gnosticism has appeared, however, it has deprecated the material world, the givenness of things. In its twenty-first-century form, the new Gnosticism is built on the conviction that there are no Things-As-They-Are, no givens in the human condition. Everything about us as individuals and communities is plastic and malleable. Everything can and ought to be bent to human willfulness and human desire. And because there are no Things-As-They-Are—and therefore no stable guides to righteous living and human flourishing—all those desires are morally commensurable. In the world of the new Gnosticism, it is literally impossible to say that some desires are wicked because they are humanly degrading and thus impede the quest for happiness that is intrinsic to the human person. If there is no human nature, nothing given in our lives, how can anyone say that this or that desire is dehumanizing or wrong?

The new Gnosticism, which is one cultural by-product of nineteenth-century atheistic humanism, has had profound public, political, and legal impacts. For if there are no stable truths to guide our public life, what happens when different conceptions of the truth—call them "my truth" and "your truth"—collide? What almost inevitably happens is what Joseph Ratzinger dubbed, in 2005, the "dictatorship of relativism": the use of coercive state power to enforce a relativistic ethic on all of society. A distorted concept of the human person and an equally distorted concept of freedom-as-willfulness combine to erode the freedom that modernity claims as one of its great aspirations and to make the achievement of genuine human community in solidarity even more difficult.[8]

Given the challenges posed by this severe deformation of the humanistic project, the implementation of the Second Vatican

Council in a global program of evangelization—one that proposes the truth of the human person through an encounter with Jesus Christ—is even more essential in the mid-twenty-first century than when the Council was convened. And while there is much to be criticized in postmodern culture and postmodern society, the Church's efforts at civilizational rescue cannot be carried out in terms of the anathema or the strategic retreat. As Ratzinger put it more than a decade after Vatican II, "there can be no return to the *Syllabus*, which may have marked the first stage in the confrontation with [the ideologies of modernity] but cannot be the last stage." Neither a Church uncritically embracing modernity nor a Church content to live in a religious ghetto of its own construction could solve for Christians the problem of the modern world. "The fact is, as Hans Urs von Balthasar pointed out as early as 1952, that the 'demolition of the bastions' [of a fortress Catholicism] is a long-overdue task."[9]

What, then, is the post-conciliar Church of the twenty-first century to do? It must learn what the Second Vatican Council actually taught, by reading its texts in their proper sequence and interrelationship, using the keys provided by John Paul II and Benedict XVI. In doing so, the Church will find the inspiration and the means to teach and embody the truths about the human person, authentic human community, and genuine human liberation that Vatican II proposed. Amid the many contentions and trials the Catholic Church faces, it should be an encouragement to realize that this kind of reception of the Council is already happening. For the living parts of the world Church know that Catholicism is a communion of disciples in mission and live that understanding with joy—even in the face of scorn and persecution.

In them—in the Church that has received the Council according to the original intention of John XXIII and the authoritative keys provided by John Paul II and Benedict XVI—the struggle for Vatican II that began at the Council itself has been essentially resolved, and the Council is being properly and fruitfully implemented. In them, the great promise of the Second Vatican Council is being realized in worship, in charity, and above all in the proclamation of Jesus Christ as the answer to humanity's deepest longings, in every time, place, and culture.

For no other foundation can anyone lay than that which is laid, which is Jesus Christ.

—1 Corinthians 3.11

Acknowledgments

My FIRST ENCOUNTER WITH THE SECOND VATICAN COUN-
cil took place in July 1964, when I visited St. Peter's Basilica during the intersession between Vatican II's second and
third periods and was stunned by the long rows of upholstered
bleachers stretching the length of the nave. I had no idea then of
the drama that would unfold in that conciliar *Aula* four months
later, as the Council wrestled with finalizing *Lumen Gentium* and
sharply debated religious freedom—debates that would resonate
in my own thought and work for decades. But a seed seems to
have been planted, and so my first word of thanks must be to my
parents, George and Betsy Weigel, for taking my brother and me
on a parish tour of Europe when we were boys.

Many friends and colleagues responded generously to my
questions about what was misunderstood about Vatican II today,
especially among younger Catholics. Others drew my attention
to particular texts and commentaries that I found helpful. I thank
them all for their insights and encouragement: Ryan Anderson;
Fr. Daniel Barnett; Bishop Robert Barron; Joseph Capizzi; Ann
Carey; Fr. Joseph Carola, SJ; Jeff Cavins; Larry Chapp; Msgr.
Paul Cook; William Doino Jr.; Douglas Farrow; Robert Fas-
tiggi; Fr. Kevin Flannery, SJ; Msgr. Anthony Frontiero; Fr. Mauro
Gagliardi; Fr. John Gavin, SJ; Tim Gray; Fr. Carter Griffin; Msgr.

Thomas Guarino; Susan Hanssen; Fr. Peter Harman; Mary Healy; Nina Heereman; Peter Herbeck; Fr. Richard Hermes, SJ; Russell Hittinger; Joshua Hochschild; Sr. Clare Hunter, FSE; Fr. Christian Irdi; Christa Klein; Al Kresta; Matthew Levering; Bruce Marshall; Ralph Martin; Fr. Wilson Miscamble, CSC; Anna Moreland; Francesca Aran Murphy; Hugh O'Donnell; Timothy O'Donnell; Fr. John W. O'Malley, SJ; Jonathan Reyes; Fr. Ross Romero, SJ; Matthew Schmitz; Alan Schreck; Fr. Bryce Sibley; Anna Silvas; Msgr. K. Bartholomew Smith; Bishop David Toups; Margaret Turek; Fr. Thomas Weinandy, OFMCap; Stephen White; Fr. Thomas Joseph White, OP; and Julia Yost. Fr. Christopher Seiler helped me track down an important text. Daniel B. Gallagher was helpful with a tricky translation.

I am also grateful to Fr. Robert Imbelli and Fr. Jay Scott Newman for their close reading of a draft of the text and for their counsel.

My colleagues at the Ethics and Public Policy Center, my professional home for over three decades, continue to be all that anyone living the vocation of ideas could hope for. Special thanks are due the EPPC board; to its two presidents while this book was being prepared, Ed Whelan and Ryan Anderson; and to the William E. Simon Foundation for its generous support of my EPPC chair. The manuscript benefited greatly from a close reading by Ella Sullivan Ramsay, and my work on the entire book in its early stages of gestation was facilitated by Natalie Robertson.

This is the sixth book that Lara Heimert and I have brought to the public together, and I remain deeply grateful for her friendship, encouragement, wise editorial counsel, and leadership of Basic Books. Marissa Koors's editorial insights made this a better, more tightly argued study. On the production side of the project, I would like to thank old friends Kathy Streckfus, the best copy editor in the trade, and Michelle Welsh-Horst, a consummately professional production manager, for their exemplary work.

My wife, Joan, guided our family through the pandemic during which the book was written, for which I am most grateful.

It is a privilege to dedicate this book to my brother, John H. Weigel, and my late sister-in-law, Linda Bauer Weigel.

GW

North Bethesda, Maryland

October 22, 2021, Memorial of Pope St. John Paul II

Notes

All biblical citations are from the
Revised Standard Version, Catholic Edition.

Introduction: Reimagining Vatican II

1. On the conclave of 1963, see George Weigel, *The Irony of Modern Catholic History: How the Church Rediscovered Itself and Challenged the Modern World to Reform* (New York: Basic Books, 2019), 111. The somewhat imaginative reconstruction of the conclave proposed by Francis A. Burkle-Young, in *Passing the Keys: Modern Cardinals, Conclaves, and the Election of the Next Pope* (Lanham, MD: Madison Books, 1999), 149–180, nonetheless captures the conclave's crosscurrents and tensions, which centered on Vatican II. See also Peter Hebblethwaite, *Paul VI: The First Modern Pope* (New York: Paulist Press, 1993), 318–332, for some useful detail.

2. See Taylor Marshall, *Infiltration: The Plot to Destroy the Church from Within* (Manchester, NH: Crisis Publications, 2019).

3. Cardinal Blase Cupich has been prominently identified with this point of view. See "Cardinal Cupich Delivers the 2018 Von Hügel Lecture on 'Amoris Laetita as a New Paradigm of Catholicity,'" Von Hügel Institute, February 2018: www.vhi.st-edmunds.cam.ac.uk/copy_of_news/cupich -von-hugel-lecture-9-february-2018.

4. See John W. O'Malley, SJ, *Trent: What Happened at the Council* (Cambridge, MA: Belknap Press of Harvard University Press, 2013), 248–275; Hubert Jedin and John Dolan, eds., *History of the Church*, volume 5, *Reformation and Counter Reformation* (New York: Crossroad, 1986), 499–567.

5. See John R. Cihak, "Introduction: Reform from Within," in Charles Borromeo, *Charles Borromeo: Selected Orations, Homilies, and Writings*, ed. John R. Cihak (London: Bloomsbury T&T Clark, 2017), 1–21.

PART I: WHY VATICAN II WAS NECESSARY

1: Crisis? What Crisis?

1. Cited in Joseph Ratzinger, *Principles of Catholic Theology: Building Stones for a Fundamental Theology* (San Francisco: Ignatius Press, 1987), 368.

2. Jaroslav Pelikan explains the theological importance of the Iconoclast Controversy and its orthodox resolution in *Jesus Through the Centuries: His Place in the History of Culture* (New Haven, CT: Yale University Press, 1985), 83–94.

3. The complex reasons for Lateran V's failure are discussed in Hubert Jedin, *A History of the Council of Trent*, volume 1, *The Struggle for the Council* (Edinburgh: Thomas Nelson, 1957), 117–138.

4. As Carlos M. N. Eire demonstrates in *Reformations: The Early Modern World, 1450–1650* (New Haven, CT: Yale University Press, 2016), the multiplicity of reform movements in sixteenth-century Western Christianity and the contradictions among them privileges the use of the plural "Reformations" rather than the more familiar singular. For a provocative view of how those Reformations shaped the issues with which Vatican II would have to contend, see Brad S. Gregory, *The Unintended Reformation: How a Religious Revolution Secularized Society* (Cambridge, MA: Belknap Press of Harvard University Press, 2012).

5. John Henry Newman, "Sermon 9: The Infidelity of the Future," Opening of St. Bernard's Seminary, October 2, 1873: www.newmanreader.org/works/ninesermons/sermon9.html (emphasis added).

6. Christopher Dawson, "The Modern Dilemma," in Christopher Dawson, *Christianity and European Culture: Selections from the Work of Christopher Dawson*, ed. Gerald Russello (Washington, DC: Catholic University of America Press, 1998), 118.

7. Newman, "Sermon 9."

2: Modernity as Ideology

1. John W. O'Malley, SJ, *What Happened at Vatican II* (Cambridge, MA: Belknap Press of Harvard University Press, 2008), 54–55.

2. Michael Allen Gillespie offers an intriguing intellectual taxonomy of modernity in *The Theological Origins of Modernity* (Chicago: University of Chicago Press, 2008).

3. Wojciech Chudy, *Rozwój Filosofowania a Pułapka Refeleksji* (Lublin: Wydawnictwo Katolickiego Uniwersytetu Lubelskiego, 1994).

4. See Henri de Lubac, SJ, *The Drama of Atheist Humanism* (San Francisco: Ignatius Press, 1995).

5. Social historian Philipp Blom notes that, in the early twentieth century, Britain's social elites, across the spectrum of political opinion and party affiliation, were enthusiastic proponents of eugenic ideas:

> In Britain, the Galton Institute, named after the nineteenth-century eugenicist Francis Galton, counted among its members economist John Maynard Keynes, future prime minister Arthur Neville Chamberlain and former prime minister Arthur Balfour, Charles Darwin's son Leonard and his grandson Charles Galton Darwin, the sexologist Havelock Ellis, and American doctor and cereal magnate John Harvey Kellogg, and the birth control activists Margaret Sanger and Marie Stopes. Other prominent supporters were George Bernard Shaw, Virginia Woolf, philosopher Bertrand Russell, and novelist H. G. Wells; the list goes on to form a virtual who's who of British intellectual life. (Philipp Blom, *Fracture: Life & Culture in the West, 1918–1938* [New York: Basic Books, 2015], 164)

Daniel Okrent describes the effects of the eugenics movement on the other side of the Atlantic in *The Guarded Gate: Bigotry, Eugenics, and the Law That Kept Two Generations of Jews, Italians, and Other European Immigrants Out of America* (New York: Scribner's, 2019).

3: The New Thirty Years War

1. De Lubac, *The Drama of Atheist Humanism*, 12, 14.

2. Blom, *Fracture*, 7.

3. Blom, *Fracture*, 29.

4. Aleksandr Solzhenitsyn, "Men Have Forgotten God," *National Review*, July 2, 1983, 872–876.

5. On this and related questions of why the Great War continued, see George Weigel, "The Great War Revisited," in *The Fragility of Order: Catholic Reflections on Turbulent Times* (San Francisco: Ignatius Press, 2018), 17–31.

6. Benedict XV, *Ad Beatissimi Apostolorum*: www.vatican.va/content/benedict-xv/en/encyclicals/documents/hf_ben-xv_enc_01111914_ad-beatissimi-apostolorum.html. On Benedict XV, see John F. Pollard, *The Unknown Pope: Benedict XV (1914–1922) and the Pursuit of Peace* (London: Geoffrey Chapman, 1999). A promising opportunity in 1916–1917 to secure a rational peace, which was stymied by the machinations of David Lloyd George in Great Britain and the incompetence of U.S. president

Woodrow Wilson and his counselor Edward House, is described in Philip Zelikow, *The Road Less Traveled: The Secret Battle to End the Great War, 1916–1917* (New York: PublicAffairs, 2021).

7. Blom describes the significance of the Hubble's findings:

Hubble's discovery . . . revolutionized humanity's conception of its place in the world, and it is difficult to overestimate its long-term effect. Over three millennia, from an essentially local idea of Earth as a disc, the planet had become round and had been dislodged from its place at the center of the universe to be a mere satellite of a sun, which in turn had been found to be one of many in a galaxy of suns, the Milky Way. Now this galaxy was no longer a universe— the only universe—but merely one among countless galaxies in the immense, fathomless, and expanding darkness of space, and Earth had become an infinitesimal dot in a world of unimaginable magnitude. . . . Humanity was not at the center, and not even prominently placed in the periphery; it appeared to be lost, cast into the darkness and void of deep space as a tiny speck inside the vast apparent emptiness of the universe. (Blom, *Fracture*, 17)

8. See Blom, *Fracture*, 117–121.

9. Wilfred Owen, *The Collected Poems of Wilfred Owen* (London: Chatto & Windus, 1963), 55. The "old lie" was that it was "sweet and fitting to die for one's native land."

10. See Blom, *Fracture*, 128–130.

11. See Blom, *Fracture*, 97–122 (on jazz), 131ff. (on Dada).

12. See Richard J. Evans, *The Coming of the Third Reich* (New York: Penguin, 2005).

13. On the distinctiveness of the totalitarian enterprise, see Hannah Arendt's three-volume study, *The Origins of Totalitarianism*, and especially volume 3, *Totalitarianism* (New York: Harcourt, Brace & World, 1968).

14. Cited in Michael Scammell, "The Eerily Prescient Lessons of *Darkness at Noon*," Lit Hub, September 12, 2019, https://lithub.com/the-eerily -prescient-lessons-of-darkness-at-noon.

15. Cited in Winston S. Churchill, *The Gathering Storm* (London: Cassell, 1948), 6.

16. Churchill, *The Gathering Storm*, x.

17. On the Versailles Treaty, see Margaret Macmillan, *Paris 1919: Six Months That Changed the World* (New York: Random House, 2003). Churchill's verdict on what he termed the "follies" of the victors was unsparing:

The economic clauses of the Treaty were malignant and silly to an extent that made them obviously futile. . . . The triumphant Allies continued to assert that they would squeeze Germany "until the pips squeaked." All this had a potent bearing on the prosperity of the world and the mood of the German race . . . [and was] a sad story of complicated idiocy in the making of which much toil and virtue was consumed. . . . A democratic constitution, in accordance with all the latest improvements, was established at Weimar. Emperors having been driven out, nonentities were elected. . . . The Weimar Republic, with all its liberal trappings and blessings, was regarded as an imposition of the enemy. It could not hold the loyalty of the German people. For a spell they sought to cling as in desperation to the aged Marshal Hindenburg. Thereafter mighty forces were adrift, the void was open, and into that void after a pause there strode a maniac of ferocious genius, the repository and expression of the most virulent hatreds that have ever corroded the human breast—Corporal Hitler. (*The Gathering Storm*, 6–10)

18. See Gerhard L. Weinberg, *A World at Arms: A Global History of World War II* (New York: Cambridge University Press, 1994), 894.

19. Dwight D. Eisenhower, *At Ease: Stories I Tell to Friends* (Garden City, NY: Doubleday, 1967), 251.

4: The End of Christendom

1. See Owen Chadwick, *The Secularization of the European Mind in the Nineteenth Century* (Cambridge: Cambridge University Press, 1990).

2. Joseph Ratzinger, "The New Pagans and the Church: A 1958 Lecture by Joseph Ratzinger (Pope Benedict XVI)," trans. Kenneth Baker, SJ, *Homiletic and Pastoral Review*, January 30, 2017: www.hprweb.com/2017/01/the-new-pagans-and-the-church.

3. Six years earlier, in 1952, Hans Urs von Balthasar had expressed serious concerns about the Church's seeming inertness when confronting the postwar situation in *Schleifung der Bastionen: Von der Kirche in Dieser Zeit*, which was later published in English as *Razing the Bastions: On the Church in This Age* (San Francisco: Ignatius Press, 1993).

5: The Renewal of the Catholic Mind

1. On Pius VII, see Weigel, *The Irony of Modern Catholic History*, 25–29.

2. See Mike Rapport, *1848: Year of Revolution* (New York: Basic Books, 2010).

3. See Pius IX, *Quanta Cura*: www.papalencyclicals.net/pius09 /p9quanta.htm; Pius IX, *The Syllabus of Errors*: www.papalencyclicals .net/pius09/p9syll.htm.

4. See John R. Page, *What Will Dr. Newman Do? John Henry Newman and Papal Infallibility, 1865–1875* (Collegeville, MN: Liturgical Press, 1994), and the text of Newman's *Letter to the Duke of Norfolk*, his riposte to Gladstone, originally published in 1874 and reprinted in *Certain Difficulties Felt by Anglicans in Catholic Teaching Considered*, volume 2 (London: Longmans, Green, 1900), online at Newman Reader: www.newmanreader .org/works/anglicans/volume2/gladstone/index.html.

5. See Michael B. Gross, *The War Against Catholicism: Liberalism and the Anti-Catholic Imagination in Nineteenth-Century Germany* (Ann Arbor, MI: University of Michigan Press, 2005).

6. See Weigel, *The Irony of Modern Catholic History*, 34–35, 42–46.

7. Russell Hittinger, "The Spirit of Vatican I," *First Things*, October 2018: www.firstthings.com/article/2018/10/the-spirit-of-vatican-i.

8. On Scheeben, see Cyril Vollert, SJ, "Matthias Joseph Scheeben and the Revival of Theology," *Theological Studies* 6, no. 4 (December 1, 1945): 453–488.

9. See Newman's "Biglietto Speech," on reception of the formal announcement (*biglietto*) of his elevation to the cardinalate, May 12, 1879, at the Newman Reader: www.newmanreader.org/works/addresses/file2 .html.

10. These nineteenth-century theological developments are discussed in greater detail in Weigel, *The Irony of Modern Catholic History*, 53–65. For Newman on development, see John Henry Newman, *An Essay on the Development of Christian Doctrine* (Notre Dame, IN: University of Notre Dame Press, 1989).

11. Leo XIII, *Aeterni Patris*: www.vatican.va/content/leo-xiii/en/ency clicals/documents/hf_l-xiii_enc_04081879_aeterni-patris.html.

12. Gertrude Himmelfarb usefully distinguished between distinct forms of "the Enlightenment" in *The Roads to Modernity: The British, French and American Enlightenments* (New York: Alfred A. Knopf, 2004). The anti-Enlightenment critique by nineteenth- and early twentieth-century Roman authorities was aimed almost entirely at what Himmelfarb dubbed the "ideology of reason" in the French Enlightenment.

13. Leo XIII, *Providentissimus Deus*: www.vatican.va/content/leo-xiii /en/encyclicals/documents/hf_l-xiii_enc_18111893_providentissimus-deus .html.

14. Leo XIII, *Rerum Novarum*: www.vatican.va/content/leo-xiii/en
/encyclicals/documents/hf_l-xiii_enc_15051891_rerum-novarum.html.

15. On this point, see Russell Hittinger, "Pope Leo XIII," in John Witte Jr. and Frank S. Alexander, eds., *The Teachings of Modern Roman Catholicism on Law, Politics, and Human Nature* (New York: Columbia University Press, 2007), 39–75.

16. These points are explored in more depth in Weigel, *The Irony of Modern Catholic History*, 77–81.

17. For more on Leo XIII, see Weigel, *The Irony of Modern Catholic History*, 71–77, 81–84.

18. Pius X, *Lamentabili*: www.papalencyclicals.net/pius10/p10lamen .htm; Pius X, *Pascendi Dominici Gregis*: www.vatican.va/content/pius-x /en/encyclicals/documents/hf_p-x_enc_19070908_pascendi-dominici-gregis .html. See also Russell Hittinger, "*Pascendi Dominici Gregis* at 100—Two Modernisms, Two Thomisms: Reflections on the Centenary of Pius X's Letter Against the Modernists," *Nova et Vetera* 5, no. 4 (2007): 843–880, and Russell Hittinger, "Two Thomisms, Two Modernities," *First Things* 184 (June/July 2008), 33–38.

19. O'Malley, *What Happened at Vatican II*, 68.

20. Yves M.-J. Congar, OP, *A History of Theology* (Garden City, NY: Doubleday, 1968), 191.

21. On Blondel, see J. M. Somerville, "Blondel, Maurice," in *New Catholic Encyclopedia*, volume 5 (New York: McGraw-Hill, 1967), 617–618, and William L. Portier, "Twentieth-Century Catholic Theology and the Triumph of Maurice Blondel," *Communio* 38, no. 1 (May 2010): 103–137.

22. The Anti-Modernist Oath may be found in Fergus Kerr, *Twentieth-Century Catholic Theologians* (Oxford: Blackwell, 2007), 223–225.

23. See, for example, Gerald P. Fogarty, SJ, *American Catholic Biblical Scholarship: A History from the Early Republic to Vatican II* (New York: Harper & Row, 1989), 96–119.

24. See Kerr, *Twentieth-Century Catholic Theologians*, 1–16.

25. Taylor Marshall's *Infiltration* is a prime example of this tendency to ill-informed calumny.

26. Hans Urs von Balthasar, *The Glory of the Lord: A Theologica Aesthetics*, volume 2, *Studies in Theological Style: Clerical Styles* (San Francisco: Ignatius Press; New York: Crossroad, 1984), and volume 3, *Studies in Theological Styles: Lay Styles* (San Francisco: Ignatius Press, 1984).

27. See Robert P. Imbelli, *Rekindling the Christic Imagination: Theological Meditations for the New Evangelization* (Collegeville, MN: Liturgical Press, 2014), especially chapter 4, "*Ecclesia* as Call to Holiness."

28. Balthasar's 1952 book, *Schleifung der Bastionen: Von der Kirche in Dieser Zeit*, was published in 1993 by Ignatius Press as *Razing the Bastions: On the Church in This Age*.

29. Cited in Weigel, *The Irony of Modern Catholic History*, 117. See also Karl Adam's *The Spirit of Catholicism* (New York: Crossroad, 1997), and *Christ Our Brother* (New York: Macmillan, 1931).

30. See Weigel, *The Irony of Modern Catholic History*, 117–118. See also Romano Guardini's *The End of the Modern World* (Wilmington, DE: ISI Books, 1998), *The Lord* (Chicago: Henry Regnery, 1954), and Romano Guardini, *The Essential Guardini: An Anthology of the Writings of Romano Guardini*, ed. Heinz R. Kuehn (Chicago: Liturgical Training Publications, 1997).

31. O'Malley, *What Happened at Vatican II*, 75.

32. Henri de Lubac, SJ, *The Mystery of the Supernatural* (New York: Herder and Herder, 1988). See also the chapter on de Lubac in Kerr, *Twentieth-Century Catholic Theologians*, 67–86. De Lubac ponders his stormy ecclesiastical career in *At the Service of the Church: Henri de Lubac Reflects on the Circumstances That Occasioned His Writings* (San Francisco: Ignatius Press, 1993). On the shabby treatment de Lubac received from his French Jesuit colleagues when Pope John Paul II named him a cardinal—a nasty episode that captures the brutality of some forms of progressive authoritarianism in the post-conciliar Church—see George Weigel, *Witness to Hope: The Biography of Pope John Paul II* (New York: HarperCollins, 1999), 446.

33. On Chenu, see Kerr, *Twentieth-Century Catholic Theologians*, 17–33.

34. On Garrigou and Wojtyła, see Weigel, *Witness to Hope*, 85–86.

35. On Garrigou and his school, see Helen James John, SND, *The Thomist Spectrum* (New York: Fordham University Press, 1966), 3–16. See also Richard Peddicord, OP, *The Sacred Monster of Thomism: An Introduction to the Life and Legacy of Réginald Garrigou-Lagrange, OP* (South Bend, IN: St. Augustine Press, 2015).

36. Karl Rahner, SJ, *Hearers of the Word* (New York: Herder and Herder, 1969).

37. See Karl Rahner, "On the Theology of the Incarnation," in *Theological Investigations IV* (London: Darton, Longman and Todd, 1966), and Rahner, "'I Believe in Jesus Christ': Interpreting an Article of Faith," in *Theological Investigations IX* (New York: Herder and Herder, 1972), 167.

38. Cited in Peter Seewald, *Benedict XVI: A Life*, volume 1, *Youth in Nazi Germany to the Second Vatican Council, 1927–1965* (London: Bloomsbury Continuum, 2020), 324. On Rahner's work and legacy, see Herbert Vorgrimler, *Understanding Karl Rahner: An Introduction to His*

Life and Thought (New York: Crossroad, 1986); Leo J. O'Donovan, SJ, ed., *A World of Grace: An Introduction to the Themes and Foundations of Karl Rahner's Theology* (New York: Seabury Press, 1980); and Patrick Burke, *Reinterpreting Rahner: A Critical Study of His Major Themes* (New York: Fordham University Press, 2002).

39. See John, *The Thomist Spectrum*, 16–31.

40. See John, *The Thomist Spectrum*, 32–51.

41. Yves M.-J. Congar, OP, *True and False Reform in the Church*, revised edition (Collegeville, MN: Liturgical Press, 2010).

42. Avery Dulles, SJ, "Foreword," in Yves M.-J. Congar, OP, *The Meaning of Tradition* (San Francisco: Ignatius Press, 2004), viii.

43. See Dulles, "Foreword," ix–x.

44. Congar, *The Meaning of Tradition*, 2–3.

45. Other works by Congar that would influence the Council (most of which were translated into English after Vatican II) include *The Revelation of God* (New York: Herder and Herder, 1968); *Jesus Christ* (New York: Herder and Herder, 1966); *Christians Active in the World* (New York: Herder and Herder, 1968); *Lay People in the Church: A Study for a Theology of the Laity* (Westminster, MD: Newman Press, 1956); and *I Believe in the Holy Spirit* (New York: Crossroad, 1997). See also Kerr, *Twentieth-Century Catholic Theologians*, 34–51.

46. Hubert Jedin, *Ecumenical Councils of the Catholic Church: An Historical Survey* (New York: Herder and Herder, 1960).

47. For an overview of the back and forth between Catholic exegetes and Roman authorities, see Thomas Aquinas Collins, OP, and Raymond E. Brown, SS, "Church Pronouncements," in Raymond E. Brown, SS, Joseph A. Fitzmyer, SJ, and Roland E. Murphy, OCarm, eds., *The Jerome Biblical Commentary* (Englewood Cliffs, NJ: Prentice-Hall, 1968), 624–632. The dedication of the book is instructive: "To the Memory of Pope Pius XII, Whose Promotion of Biblical Studies Bore Fruit in the Second Vatican Council."

48. See M. Ducey, "Guéranger, Prosper," in *New Catholic Encyclopedia*, volume 6, 832–832.

49. O'Malley, *What Happened at Vatican II*, 74.

50. See R. W. Franklin and Robert L. Spaeth, *Virgil Michel: American Catholic* (Collegeville, MN: Liturgical Press, 1988).

51. "To 'A,'" January 17, 1956, in Flannery O'Connor, *The Habit of Being: Letters of Flannery O'Connor*, ed. Sally Fitzgerald (New York: Farrar, Straus, & Giroux, 1979), 131. O'Connor exempts one of the precursors of *ressourcement* theology from this indictment: "One reason Guardini is a relief is that he has nothing of it [smugness]" (p. 131).

52. Cited in Seewald, *Benedict XVI*, 203–204.

53. Quoted in Seewald, *Benedict XVI*, 227.

54. See "The Unbeliever and Christians," in Albert Camus, *Resistance, Rebellion, and Death* (New York: Vintage Books, 1974), 67–74.

6: What Kind of Church?

1. On Lamennais, a tragic figure and the prototype of a certain kind of Catholic intellectual who would become prominent in the post–Vatican II Church, see Weigel, *The Irony of Modern Catholic History*, 33–37.

2. *Non Abbiamo Bisogno* is available at www.vatican.va/content/pius-xi/en/encyclicals/documents/hf_p-xi_enc_29061931_non-abbiamo-bisogno.html. *Mit Brennender Sorge* may be found at www.vatican.va/content/pius-xi/en/encyclicals/documents/hf_p-xi_enc_14031937_mit-brennender-sorge.html. *Divini Redemptoris* is available at www.vatican.va/content/pius-xi/en/encyclicals/documents/hf_p-xi_enc_19370319_divini-redemptoris.html. *Firmissimam Constantiam*, which was also published in Spanish as *Nos es muy conocida*, is available at www.vatican.va/content/pius-xi/en/encyclicals/documents/hf_p-xi_enc_28031937_nos-es-muy-conocida.html. The anti-Nazi, anti-communist, and anti-Mexican-secularist encyclicals were issued within two weeks of each other in March 1937. Pius XI had previously issued two encyclicals on religious persecution in Mexico (*Iniquis Afflictisque* [www.vatican.va/content/pius-xi/en/encyclicals/documents/hf_p-xi_enc_18111926_iniquis-afflictisque.html] in 1926 and *Acerba Animi* [www.vatican.va/content/pius-xi/en/encyclicals/documents/hf_p-xi_enc_29091932_acerba-animi.html] in 1932), and one in Spain (*Dilectissima Nobis* [www.vatican.va/content/pius-xi/en/encyclicals/documents/hf_p-xi_enc_03061933_dilectissima-nobis.html] in 1933).

3. O'Malley, *What Happened at Vatican II*, 92.

4. See George Weigel, "Papacy and Power," *First Things*, February 2001: www.firstthings.com/article/2001/02/papacy-and-power.

5. For a brief analysis of Pius XI's *Quadragesimo Anno*, see Weigel, *The Irony of Modern Catholic History*, 99–101. The text of the encyclical may be found at www.vatican.va/content/pius-xi/en/encyclicals/documents/hf_p-xi_enc_19310515_quadragesimo-anno.html.

6. Eamon Duffy, *Saints and Sinners: A History of the Popes* (New Haven, CT: Yale University Press, in association with S4C, 1997), 231.

7. Cited in Peter Godman, "Graham Greene's Vatican Dossier," *Atlantic*, July/August 2001: www.theatlantic.com/magazine/archive/2001/07/graham-greenes-vatican-dossier/302264.

8. O'Malley, *What Happened at Vatican II*, 85.

7: What Kind of Council? To What Ends?

1. Cited in Seewald, *Benedict XVI*, 338.
2. Balthasar, *Razing the Bastions*, 37, 51.
3. Seewald, *Benedict XVI*, 339.
4. Cited in Robert de Mattei, *The Second Vatican Council: An Untold Story* (Fitzwilliam, NH: Loreto, 2013), 94. Louis Billot would eventually become a victim of the ultramontanism he espoused. Pius XI was determined to put an end to the reactionary movement *Action Française* and condemned it in December 1926, placing its eponymous newspaper on the Index of Forbidden Books, the first newspaper ever so proscribed. Cardinal Billot, whose politics were as conservative as his theology, wrote a letter to the newspaper sympathizing with its plight; the newspaper, understandably, published it; the cardinal was summoned to an audience with an irate Pius XI; and by the time Billot left the papal library he had resigned his cardinalate, presumably at the Pope's insistence.
5. De Mattei, *The Second Vatican Council*, 95–96.
6. De Mattei, *The Second Vatican Council*, 96.
7. Mercifully, the suggestion that the assembly be called the First Ostiensian Council, because the Pope had announced it at the Basilica of St. Paul Outside the Walls on the Via Ostiense, never got any traction.
8. O'Malley, *What Happened at Vatican II*, 18.
9. Cited in O'Malley, *What Happened at Vatican II*, 17.
10. O'Malley, *What Happened at Vatican II*, 19–20. Joseph A. Komonchak examines the American submissions to the Ante-Preparatory Commission in "What They Said Before the Council," *Commonweal*, December 7, 1990, 714–717, and "U.S. Bishops' Suggestions for Vatican II," *Cristianesimo nella Storia* 15 (1994): 313–371. In the latter article, Komonchak notes a striking proposal for the Council's discussion from Bishop George Ahr of Trenton, New Jersey, who asked that "some provision be made for what the Church should do if the enemies of the Church use an atomic bomb to kill the Cardinal-electors of the pope and all the other bishops assembled for the Council" (p. 318).
11. Citations are from "Exc.mi P.D. Caroli Vojtyla, Episcopi tit. Ombitani, Auxiliaris Cracoviensis, Cracoviae, die 30 decembris 1959," in *Acta et Documenta Concilio Oecumenico Vaticano II Apparando*, Series I (Anteprae-paratoria), volume 2, *Consilia et Vota Episcoporum ac Praelatorum*, part 2, *Europa*, 741–748. Translations by Paul V. Mankowski, SJ, and the author.
12. Cited in Kerr, *Twentieth-Century Catholic Theologians*, 126.
13. Cited in Seewald, *Benedict XVI*, 370.
14. Seewald, *Benedict XVI*, 382.

PART II: WHAT VATICAN II TAUGHT

8: The Council's Distinctive Features

1. On this point, see Hittinger, "The Spirit of Vatican I."

2. The ultramontanism of the journal, in abeyance after Vatican II, was notably revived in the pontificate of Pope Francis.

3. Hittinger, "The Spirit of Vatican I."

4. O'Malley, *What Happened at Vatican II*, 26.

5. O'Malley, *What Happened at Vatican II*, 23.

6. O'Malley, *What Happened at Vatican II*, 33. As O'Malley notes, by the Council's fourth period in 1965 there were 182 such ecumenical observers present. Robert McAfee Brown, present at Vatican II's second period in 1963, gives some flavor of the ecumenical guests' experience (and some insider humor) in *Observer in Rome: A Protestant Report on the Vatican Council* (Garden City, NY: Doubleday, 1964).

O'Malley describes the seating arrangements in the conciliar *Aula* in detail:

> The meetings were held in the central nave of St. Peter's basilica. Despite the huge proportions of that space (2,500 square meters), it was barely sufficient to hold all the attendees. The nave was outfitted to provide 2,905 spaces: 102 for cardinals, 7 for patriarchs, 26 for the general secretariat of the Council, 2,440 for the bishops and archbishops, 200 for the *periti*, and 130 for guests and observers from other Churches. The observers and guests sat in a tribune reserved especially for them, right under the statue of St. Longinus, nearer to the presiders' table than even the cardinals—the best seats in the house. Two catering stations or coffee bars (no alcoholic beverages) were set up in the basilica, and lavatories were installed both inside and outside St. Peter's. (O'Malley, *What Happened at Vatican II*, 23)

The coffee bars were quickly dubbed *Bar-Jonah* and *Bar-Abbas*.

The presence of Russian Orthodox observers, a special concern of Pope John XXIII, had the unintended consequence of opening a period during which Soviet bloc secret intelligence services made considerable (and successful) efforts to penetrate the Vatican. See George Weigel, *The End and the Beginning: Pope John Paul II—The Victory of Freedom, the Last Years, the Legacy* (New York: Doubleday, 2010).

7. On the theologians at Vatican II, see O'Malley, *What Happened at Vatican II*, 119–120. Thomas G. Guarino gives Gérard Philips his overdue due in *The Disputed Teachings of Vatican II: Continuity and Reversal in Catholic*

Doctrine (Grand Rapids, MI: Eerdmans, 2018). Philips was such an important figure behind the scenes, especially in the Council's Theological Commission, that Yves Congar, himself quite influential in shaping several conciliar documents, joked in his diary that Vatican II should have been named "Louvain I," after Philips's university. For two of Congar's many testimonies to Philips's contributions to the Council's work, see Yves Congar, OP, *My Journal of the Council* (Collegeville, MN: Liturgical Press, 2012), 793, 835. Philips worked himself into a heart attack during the Council's fourth period.

8. See O'Malley, *What Happened at Vatican II*, 24–25. O'Malley also notes, "During the Council the question of cost was never raised as a reason for curtailing the agenda or speeding up the discussions. Nonetheless, Vatican II was a tremendous strain on the finances of the Holy See, a fact that surely strengthened Paul VI's resolve to close the Council after a fourth period." See also Ralph M. Wiltgen, SVD, *The Inside Story of Vatican II* (Charlotte, NC: TAN Books, 2014), 445. (*The Inside Story of Vatican II* is the slightly revised edition of Father Wiltgen's 1967 book, *The Rhine Flows into the Tiber*.)

9. Before the Council even began, a thousand journalists had been accredited to cover it. See Wiltgen, *The Inside Story of Vatican II*, 29–37, for the early dynamics of conciliar press coverage and the various bodies created to supplement the work of the Vatican-run Council Press Office.

10. Xavier Rynne, *Vatican Council II* (Maryknoll, NY: Orbis Books, 1999), 15–16. This volume is an edited compendium of Rynne's four books on the Council, *Letters from Vatican City*, *The Second Session*, *The Third Session*, and *The Fourth Session*, all of which were edited and expanded versions of his *New Yorker* articles.

11. O'Malley, *What Happened at Vatican II*, 35.

12. See O'Malley, *What Happened at Vatican II*, 36.

13. See Wiltgen, *The Inside Story of Vatican II*, and especially 7–13, 152–156, and 215–219, for a description of the various groups that formed at the Council. Wiltgen is particularly noteworthy for his analysis of the work of the *Coetus Internationalis Patri* (the International Group of Fathers), the best-organized traditionalist bloc at Vatican II.

14. Peter Hebblethwaite, *Paul VI: The First Modern Pope* (New York: Paulist Press, 1993), 284. Cardinal Francis Spellman of New York was even harsher, telling the French consul in New York that he thought the Council "premature, meaningless, and doomed to failure." Cited in Komonchak, "U.S. Bishops' Suggestions for Vatican II," 312.

15. O'Malley, *What Happened at Vatican II*, 97–98.

16. O'Malley, *What Happened at Vatican II*, 116.

17. The specifics of this debate are outlined below in the discussion of the Council's Dogmatic Constitution on Divine Revelation, *Dei Verbum*.

18. See Wiltgen, *The Inside Story of Vatican II*, 56–64, for an account of the drama leading up to this papal intervention. See also Giuseppe Alberigo and Joseph A. Komonchak, eds., *History of Vatican II*, volume 2, *The Formation of the Council's Identity* (Maryknoll, NY: Orbis Books, 1997), 249–266; O'Malley, *What Happened at Vatican II*, 141–152.

19. Seewald, *Benedict XVI*, 403–404. In *My Journal of the Council* (Collegeville, Minnesota: Liturgical Press, 2012), 195, Congar writes that he "would never have believed" that the bishops would vote so overwhelmingly against a text prepared by the Theological Commission.

20. Wiltgen, *The Inside Story of Vatican II*, 362.

21. Xavier Rynne describes the drama of "Black Thursday" in *The Third Session* (New York: Farrar, Straus & Giroux, 1965), 254–263. For other accounts, see O'Malley, *What Happened at Vatican II*, 238–245; de Mattei, *The Second Vatican Council*, 411–423; and Luis Antonio G. Tagle, "The 'Black Week' of Vatican II," in Giuseppe Alberigo and Joseph A. Komonchak, eds., *History of Vatican II*, volume 4, *Church as Communion* (Maryknoll, NY: Orbis Books, 2003), 388–452.

9: John XXIII's Original Intention

1. This and all subsequent quotations from *Humanae Salutis* are taken from John XXIII, "Pope John XXIII Convokes the Second Vatican Council," trans. Joseph A. Komonchak (https://jakomonchak.files .wordpress.com/2011/12/humanae-salutis.pdf), as amended by the author and Daniel B. Gallagher.

2. This and all subsequent quotations from the address are taken from "Address of Pope John XXIII at the Final Meeting of the Central Preparatory Commission for the Ecumenical Council," *The Pope Speaks* 8 (1962–1963): 182–187.

3. This and all other quotations from the radio address are taken from Giuseppe Alberigo and Joseph A. Komonchak, eds., *History of Vatican II*, volume 1, *Announcing and Preparing Vatican Council II: Toward a New Era in Catholicism* (Maryknoll, NY: Orbis Books, 1995), 436–439 (emphasis added).

4. Alberigo and Komonchak, *History of Vatican II*, 1:442.

5. On the diagnosis of Pope John's cancer, see Peter Hebblethwaite, *Pope John XXIII: Shepherd of the Modern World* (Garden City, NY: Doubleday, 1985), 425. The Pope's remark to Cardinal Suenens is cited in Alberigo and Komonchak, *History of Vatican II*, 1:435.

6. This and all subsequent quotations from the opening address are from John XXIII, "*Gaudet Mater Ecclesia*: Pope John's Open-

ing Speech to the Council," trans. Joseph A. Komonchak (https://jakomonchak.files.wordpress.com/2012/10/john-xxiii-opening-speech.pdf) (emphasis added).

7. Here, John XXIII echoes the fifth-century theologian St. Vincent of Lérins, whose teaching the Church remembers every year in the Office of Readings for Friday of the Twenty-Seventh Week of the Year: "The understanding, knowledge, and wisdom of one and all, of individuals as well as the whole Church, ought therefore to make great and vigorous progress with the passing of the ages and the centuries, but only along its own line of development, that is, with the same doctrine, the same meaning, and the same import." For more on St. Vincent, see Thomas G. Guarino, *Vincent of Lérins and the Development of Christian Doctrine* (Grand Rapids, MI: Baker Academic, 2013).

8. On the character and achievements of Counter-Reformation Catholicism, see George Weigel, *Evangelical Catholicism: Deep Reform in the 21st-Century Church* (New York: Basic Books, 2013), especially 54–56.

9. Wiltgen, *The Inside Story of Vatican II*, 47.

10: The Word of God Breaks Through the Silence

1. See Leon R. Kass, *Founding God's Nation: Reading Exodus* (New Haven, CT: Yale University Press, 2021).

2. Augustine, *Confessions* 1.1 (author's translation).

3. Cited in Aidan Nichols, OP, *Conciliar Octet: A Concise Commentary on the Eight Key Texts of the Second Vatican Council* (San Francisco: Ignatius Press, 2019), 119.

4. Cited in Nichols, *Conciliar Octet*, 120. The vote count is given in Matthew L. Lamb and Matthew Levering, eds., *Vatican II: Renewal Within Tradition* (New York: Oxford University Press, 2008), 55.

5. Francis Martin, "Revelation and Its Transmission," in Lamb and Levering, *Vatican II: Renewal Within Tradition*, 57.

6. *Dei Verbum*, 2. Unless otherwise indicated, all translations of conciliar documents are taken from *Vatican Council II*, volume 1, *The Conciliar and Post Conciliar Documents*, new revised edition, general editor Austin Flannery, OP (Northport, NY: Costello, 2004).

7. *Dei Verbum*, 3.

8. *Dei Verbum*, 4.

9. Nichols, *Conciliar Octet*, 121 (emphases in original).

10. *Dei Verbum*, 9–10.

11. *Dei Verbum*, 7–8.

12. *Dei Verbum*, 8. Here, we may note with his biographer, is where John Henry Newman's influence on Vatican II "can be directly felt," as the

Council acknowledged "the fact of doctrinal development." (Ian Ker, *Newman on Vatican II* [Oxford: Oxford University Press, 2014], 2.)

13. *Dei Verbum*, 10.

14. *Dei Verbum*, 24.

15. Cited in *Dei Verbum*, 25.

16. Lindbeck reflected on his years of experience at Vatican II in a lengthy interview with the author, "Re-Viewing Vatican II," published in *First Things*, April 1994: www.firstthings.com/article/1994/12/re-viewing-vatican-iian-interview-with-george-a-lindbeck.

17. *Dei Verbum*, 11.

18. "The books of Scripture firmly, faithfully, and without error, teach that truth which God, for the sake of our salvation, wished to see confided to the sacred Scriptures." (*Dei Verbum*, 11, citing Augustine, Thomas Aquinas, the Council of Trent, Leo XIII, and Pius XII.)

19. *Dei Verbum*, 19.

20. *Dei Verbum*, 12. On the unity of the Scriptures, the Council affirmed an exegetical method that would be developed decades later under the rubric of "Canon Criticism," which did biblical interpretation within the "canon" of the Old and New Testaments understood as interacting with each other. Thus in *Dei Verbum*, 16, the Council declared that "God, the inspirer and author of the books of both Testaments, in his wisdom so brought it about that the New should be hidden in the Old and that the Old should be made manifest in the New. For, although Christ founded the New Covenant in his blood . . . still the books of the Old Testament, all of them caught up into the Gospel message, attain and show forth their full meaning in the New Testament . . . and, in their turn, shed light on it and explain it."

21. *Dei Verbum*, 21, 22, 25.

22. *Dei Verbum*, 1.

23. *Dei Verbum*, 26.

24. John Paul II, *Fides et Ratio*: www.vatican.va/content/john-paul-ii/en/encyclicals/documents/hf_jp-ii_enc_14091998_fides-et-ratio.html, 8–9.

25. John Paul II, *Fides et Ratio*, 1.

26. *Dei Verbum*, 2.

27. *Dei Verbum*, 2.

28. Athanasius, "On the Incarnation of the Word," 54.

29. Seewald, *Benedict XVI*, 462.

30. Robert Imbelli makes a similar point:

The challenge is to appropriate the texts of the Council in a comprehensive way that does justice to all of the documents it bequeathed the Church. Nonetheless, not all the documents of the Council are of equal weight. The Council itself signaled its intent by designating four of its documents as "constitutions," hence as of primary importance. These are, of course, *Sacrosanctum Concilium* (The Constitution on the Sacred Liturgy), *Lumen Gentium* (The Dogmatic Constitution on the Church), *Gaudium et Spes* (The Pastoral Constitution on the Church in the Modern World), and *Dei Verbum* (The Dogmatic Constitution on Divine Revelation). . . .

Among the four, I maintain that *Dei Verbum* deserves to be considered a "first among equals." The reason is simple. Unless God has revealed himself fully through Jesus Christ in the Holy Spirit, then the Church is without foundation and the liturgy a merely human construct. (*Rekindling the Christic Imagination*, xiv–xv)

It is worth noting that the report on the penultimate draft of *Dei Verbum*, given to the Council fathers in November 1964, stressed that "this constitution is, in a way, the first of all the constitutions of the Council, so that its introduction [i.e., paragraph 1] serves, in a sense, as an introduction to all of them." Cited in Giuseppe Alberigo and Joseph A. Komonchak, eds., *History of Vatican II*, volume 5, *The Council and the Transition: The Fourth Period and the End of the Council, September 1965–December 1965* (Maryknoll, NY: Orbis, 2006), 279.

11: Sacrament of Authentic Human Community

1. Jedin, *Ecumenical Councils of the Catholic Church*, 239.

2. *Lumen Gentium*, 1.

3. See Avery Dulles, SJ, *Models of the Church* (Garden City, NY: Doubleday, 1974), 31–42.

4. Cited in Wiltgen, *The Inside Story of Vatican II*, 73.

5. Nichols, *Conciliar Octet*, 43. Father Nichols goes on to note an even more striking element in the draft of *De Ecclesia*: "Indeed, when speaking of the primacy of the pope, the curial draft ventured a statement that, spurned as too daring, failed to survive in any form in the process of subsequent debate—namely, that when the pope teaches *ex cathedra*, from his chair, he does so not only as universal pastor (so much had been defined at Vatican I) but also as *head of the college of bishops*" (emphasis in original).

6. On this, and on the previously discussed points of continuity between the original draft of *De Ecclesia* and *Lumen Gentium*, see Nichols, *Conciliar Octet*, 42–44.

7. See Nichols, *Conciliar Octet*, 45.

8. *Lumen Gentium*, 1.

9. Nichols, *Conciliar Octet*, 47. See Guarino, *The Disputed Teachings of Vatican II*, 91–97, for a detailed defense of *subsistit in* that draws in part on the analysis of one of the dogmatic constitution's theological architects, Gérard Philips.

10. *Lumen Gentium*, 1.

11. See Avery Dulles, SJ, "Nature, Mission, and Structure of the Church," in Lamb and Levering, *Vatican II: Renewal Within Tradition*, 26. Cardinal Dulles also notes that this idea of the Church as an instrument or sign of the unity of humanity was an extension and development of the teaching of Vatican I's dogmatic constitution, *Pastor Aeternus*, which began as follows: "The eternal Shepherd and Guardian of our souls . . . in order to continue for all time the saving work of redemption, determined to build his holy Church so that in it, the house of the living God, all who believe might be united together in the bond of one faith and one love. For this reason, before he was glorified, he prayed to the Father not only for the apostles only but for those who would also believe in him through their testimony, that all might be one as he, the Son, and the Father are one [cf. John 17.20ff]."

12. *Lumen Gentium*, 3, 5.

13. *Lumen Gentium*, 29.

14. Nichols, *Conciliar Octet*, 48–49.

15. *Lumen Gentium*, 13.

16. *Lumen Gentium*, 22. Cardinal Dulles explains the patristic roots of the concept of episcopal collegiality and its modern development, which was a much-controverted subject at Vatican II, in "Nature, Mission, and Structure of the Church," 33. He concludes that there was no contradiction between Vatican I's definition of papal authority and primacy and Vatican II's explication of episcopal collegiality.

17. See Patrick Granfield, OSB, *The Limits of the Papacy: Authority and Autonomy in the Church* (New York: Crossroad, 1987), 62–63.

18. *Lumen Gentium*, 22. The sometimes bruising debate on episcopal "collegiality" was a major factor leading to the formation of the *Coetus Internationalis Patri*, the most influential "opposition" group of conciliar bishops. Their concerns on this topic, at least, seem to have been largely assuaged by the "Preliminary Explanatory Note," which Pope Paul VI insisted be given to the bishops before they voted on the various texts on collegiality in *Lumen Gentium*. The "Note" was then published as an appendix to the official Latin text of the dogmatic constitution. On its origins, see Wiltgen, *The Inside Story of Vatican II*, 345–356. See also Tagle, "The 'Black Week' of Vatican II," 417–445.

19. *Lumen Gentium*, 19–20.

20. *Lumen Gentium*, 25.

21. *Lumen Gentium*, 38.

22. *Lumen Gentium*, 38.

23. *Lumen Gentium*, 33. See Dulles, "Nature, Mission, and Structure of the Church," 32, for more on the Council, "to its great credit," giving "new prominence to the biblical and patristic notion of the baptismal priesthood."

24. See *Lumen Gentium*, 10.

25. *Lumen Gentium*, 35.

26. *Lumen Gentium*, 37

27. See Rodney Stark, *The Rise of Christianity: How the Obscure, Marginal Jesus Movement Became the Dominant Religious Force in the Western World in a Few Centuries* (San Francisco: Harper San Francisco, 1997).

28. *Lumen Gentium*, 39.

29. *Lumen Gentium*, 42.

30. *Lumen Gentium*, 42.

31. Nichols, *Conciliar Octet*, 49–50.

32. *Lumen Gentium*, 54, 53.

33. *Lumen Gentium*, 68.

34. Nichols, *Conciliar Octet*, 51.

35. *Lumen Gentium*, 8. On this point, see also Nichols, *Conciliar Octet*, 51.

36. Dulles, "Nature, Mission, and Structure of the Church," 28. Dulles also indicates how *Lumen Gentium* dealt with other Christian communities through the ecclesiology of sacramentality:

> Vatican II . . . spoke of perfect and imperfect realizations of the sacrament. The sacrament of the Church is fully realized only in the Catholic Church, the visible and grace-filled society in which the bonds of professed faith, ecclesiastical government, and sacramental communion remain fully intact [*Lumen Gentium*, 14]. These bonds belong together insofar as the true Church indefectibly possesses them all. But the bonds are separable in the sense that some may survive in the absence of others. Non–Roman Catholic communities may possess some authentic ecclesial elements and be able to make fruitful use of them as channels of grace [*Lumen Gentium*, 15]. (Dulles, "Nature, Mission, and Structure of the Church," 27–28)

37. Nichols, *Conciliar Octet*, 52. See also Dulles, "Nature, Mission, and Structure of the Church," 28–29.

38. *Lumen Gentium*, 15.

39. Father Robert Imbelli pointed out in a personal communication that "a 'People of God' approach allowed the Council to develop the analogous participation of non-Catholics in a way that 'Mystical Body' did not."

40. *Lumen Gentium*, 16.

41. *Lumen Gentium*, 16.

42. *Lumen Gentium*, 17.

43. *Lumen Gentium*, 16–17. The debate on the relationship between the universality of God's salvific will and evangelization continued decades after Vatican II. For two perspectives, see Hans Urs von Balthasar, *Dare We Hope "That All Men Be Saved"?* (San Francisco: Ignatius Press, 1988), and Ralph Martin, *Will Many Be Saved? What Vatican II Actually Teaches and Its Implications for the New Evangelization* (Grand Rapids, MI: Eerdmans, 2012). The latter is a close examination of *Lumen Gentium*, 16–17.

12: To Worship the One Worthy of Worship

1. Joseph Ratzinger, *The Spirit of the Liturgy* (San Francisco: Ignatius Press, 2000), 22–23.

Leon Kass's commentary on the prohibition of images in the Ten Commandments identifies both the personal and social consequences of false worship:

> To worship things unworthy of worship is demeaning to the worshipper; it is to be oriented falsely in the world, taking one's bearings from merely natural phenomena that, although powerful, are not providential, intelligent, or beneficent. Moreover, such apparently humble submission masks a species of presumption. Human beings will have decided which heavenly bodies or animals are worthy of reverence and how these powers are to be appeased. The same human beings believe that they themselves, through artful representation, can fully capture these natural beings and powers and then, through obeisance, manipulate them. Worse, with increased artistic sophistication comes the danger that people will come to revere not the things idolized but the idols themselves. . . .
>
> Perhaps the most important objection is that neither the worship of dumb nature nor the celebration of human artfulness teaches anything about righteousness, holiness, or basic human decency. (Kass, *Founding God's Nation*, 311–312)

2. Nichols, *Conciliar Octet*, 19.

3. See Wiltgen, *The Inside Story of Vatican II*, 37–45, for some early interventions by missionary bishops, proposing various adaptations of the liturgy.

4. *Sacrosanctum Concilium*, 1.

5. *Sacrosanctum Concilium*, 2.

6. Nichols, *Conciliar Octet*, 29, citing *Sacrosanctum Concilium*, 7.

7. *Sacrosanctum Concilium*, 8.

8. *Sacrosanctum Concilium*, 9.

9. Nichols, *Conciliar Octet*, 26–27.

10. See *Sacrosanctum Concilium*, 5–6. The constitution's emphasis on the Paschal Mystery marked another development beyond *Mediator Dei*. Pius XII's accent was on the Mass as the re-presentation of Christ's saving passion and death. *Sacrosanctum Concilium* extended that understanding to include the salvific character of Christ's resurrection and ascension. See Dominic Langevin, OP, *From Passion to Paschal Mystery: A Recent Magisterial Development Concerning the Christological Foundation of the Sacraments* (Fribourg, Switzerland: Academic Press, 2015).

11. See Robert Jenson, "How the World Lost Its Story," *First Things*, March 2010: www.firstthings.com/article/2010/03/how-the-world-lost-its -story.

12. On salvation history and *Sacrosanctum Concilium*, see Nichols, *Conciliar Octet*, 28–29, and Pamela E. J. Jackson, "Theology of the Liturgy," in Lamb and Levering, *Vatican II: Renewal Within Tradition*, 102–103.

13. *Sacrosanctum Concilium*, 10.

14. *Sacrosanctum Concilium*, 7.

15. *Sacrosanctum Concilium*, 14.

16. *Sacrosanctum Concilium*, 48. On this point, see also Jackson, "Theology of the Liturgy," 109.

17. *Sacrosanctum Concilium*, 48; see also Jackson, "Theology of the Liturgy," 109–110.

18. *Sacrosanctum Concilium*, 106.

19. *Sacrosanctum Concilium*, 24.

20. *Sacrosanctum Concilium*, 51.

21. *Sacrosanctum Concilium*, 52.

22. See *Sacrosanctum Concilium*, 92, 100.

23. Jackson, "Theology of the Liturgy," 105.

24. *Sacrosanctum Concilium*, 111.

25. *Sacrosanctum Concilium*, 102.

26. On this point, see Jackson, "Theology of the Liturgy," 102–103.

27. Cited in Jackson, "Theology of the Liturgy," 114.

28. Jackson, "Theology of the Liturgy," 113.

29. *Sacrosanctum Concilium* envisioned the organic development of the Church's liturgy. As described by its chief architect, the Italian liturgist Annibale Bugnini, in a posthumously published and massive book, the implementation of the Constitution on the Sacred Liturgy was quite different. (See Annibale Bugnini, *The Reform of the Liturgy, 1948–1975* [Collegeville, MN:

Liturgical Press, 1990].) The implementation was characterized by peremptory changes, not organic development, because it was driven by academic abstractions and shibboleths, among them a fideistic conviction that what was more primitive was necessarily more authentic. So more often than not, the post-conciliar liturgical reform led to a stripped-down, bare-bones Mass rather than the liturgy of "noble simplicity" mandated by *Sacrosanctum Concilium*. This was an impoverished response to modernity's loss of a sense of the sacred.

The desacralization of Catholic worship was compounded by inaccurate or puerile translations into vernacular languages of the prayers of the Mass; by the change in the orientation of prayer during the central part of the Mass; and by a massive breakdown of liturgical discipline that resulted in priests essentially making up their own Mass to suit their personal tastes. In the immediate post-conciliar years, Pope Paul VI tried to stop this improvisational chaos by agreeing to a specific number of new Eucharistic Prayers that could licitly be used in addition to the traditional Roman Canon. (See Cassian Folsom, OSB, "From One Eucharistic Prayer to Many: How It Happened and Why," *Adoremus*, September 15, 1996: http://adoremus.org/1996/09'from-one-eusharistic-prayer-to-many-how-it-happened-and-why.) Those new Eucharistic Prayers, which are the crux of the Mass, were often written under extreme time pressure; nonetheless, as the French theologian and liturgical scholar Louis Bouyer noted, they did "retrieve pieces of great antiquity and unrivalled theological and euchological richness" from both the Western and Eastern liturgical traditions. The same Bouyer, however, bitterly lamented "the new [liturgical] calendar, the work of a trio of maniacs" who stripped entire seasons and octaves out of the liturgical year, but eventually got their way because "the Pope wanted to finish [the new Roman Missal and liturgical calendar] quickly so as not to let chaos spread." (See Louis Bouyer, *Memoirs* [San Francisco: Ignatius Press, 2015], 257, 259.)

It was all done far too quickly. A certain sympathy is owed Paul VI for trying to use an accelerated reform process to halt the post-conciliar degradation of the liturgy through bizarre improvisations and other unauthorized experiments. Yet the fact remains that, as Bouyer (who was involved in the process, often to his distress) put it, there was "no hope" of creating a reformed liturgy that would be an organic development from the past when "one was claiming to remake comprehensively in a few months an entire liturgy that took twenty centuries to develop gradually." (See Bouyer, *Memoirs*, 256.) The "remake" in fact took a few years, but the point remains, and remains sound. (Bugnini seems not to have been averse to deceiving Paul VI during the entire process, including on the accuracy of vernacular translations; one such deception may have led to Bugnini being de facto exiled to the Vatican nunciature in Tehran. See Bouyer, *Memoirs*, 264–265.)

The teaching of *Sacrosanctum Concilium* remains to be properly implemented in full. That process of "reforming the reform" must begin with an honest reading of the constitution itself, which would seek to recover one of the great accomplishments of *Sacrosanctum Concilium*: its retrieval of the Eastern Catholic insight that the liturgy is a celebration of the presence of the living Christ among his people and is therefore an anticipation of Christ's return in glory. The Constitution on the Liturgy emphasized the future-oriented dimension of the liturgy and its capacity to link the sanctification of the Church and the world, here and now, to the Church's eschatological hope for the coming of God's Kingdom in full—the Wedding Feast of the Lamb described in the Book of Revelation. When that eschatological dimension of the Church's worship is diminished or lost, the liturgy's transformative power is blunted, as the Church forgets the remarkable fact that, as patristics scholar Robert Louis Wilken put it, "liturgy is always in the present tense," but a different kind of "present": a present in which "the past becomes a present presence that opens a new future." (Robert Louis Wilken, *The Spirit of Early Christian Thought: Seeking the Face of God* [New Haven, CT: Yale University Press, 2003], 35.)

The "eschatological deficit" in post-conciliar Catholic worship has been paralleled by a deficit of adoration, a loss of the sense of the Mass being celebrated as a communal act of adoration of the Triune God. Both deficits, unanticipated by *Sacrosanctum Concilium*, were influenced by the change in the orientation of priest and people during Mass, with celebrant and congregation facing each other over the altar: a change that often resulted in the priest-celebrant's personality becoming the dominant factor in the congregation's experience of the Mass. This radical change in orientation, which was not mandated by the Constitution on the Sacred Liturgy, immediately became one of the most notable features of the post-conciliar liturgy, with important consequences. For it is difficult to pray the liturgy as an anticipation of the Kingdom of God in its fullness when celebrant and congregation are facing each other rather than reaching out together, as a pilgrim Church in history, for the consummation of history in the return of the Lord in glory. Thus "reforming the reform" of the liturgy according to the mind of *Sacrosanctum Concilium* would involve a restoration of the traditional orientation of prayer during Mass, with priest-celebrant and congregation facing each other during the Liturgy of the Word, and both priest-celebrant and congregation turning together toward the Lord for the Liturgy of the Eucharist, facing the altar as the Eucharistic Prayer is prayed. This is the Church's ancient practice and its wisdom has been demonstrated, if negatively, by the eschatology deficit and the adoration deficit of the post-conciliar years. (See U. M. Lang, *Turning Toward the Lord: Orientation in Liturgical Prayer* [San Francisco: Ignatius Press, 2004].)

The trend in the Church since the pontificates of John Paul II and Benedict XVI has been toward a re-sacralization of the liturgy, influenced in part by the receptivity of many young Catholics to the pre-conciliar liturgy, whose more widespread use was authorized by Benedict XVI, one of the most liturgically knowledgeable of popes. This fact of mid-twenty-first-century Catholic life seems not to have been recognized in the preparation of Pope Francis's 2021 *motu proprio, Traditionis Custodes*, which placed severe restrictions on the celebration of Mass according to the pre-conciliar Roman Missal. Whatever its intention, this papal intervention intensified the liturgical controversies within the Church and further fractured Catholic unity. (See *Traditionis Custodes*: www.vatican.va/content/francesco/en/motu _proprio/documents/20210716-motu-proprio-traditionis-custodes.html. For its accompanying letter to the world episcopate, see www.vatican.va /content/francesco/en/letters/2021/documents/20210716-lettera-vescovi -liturgia.html.)

The organic development of the Church's liturgy will continue. The effect of that development anticipated by *Sacrosanctum Concilium*—the deepening of Catholic faith and a consequent empowerment of the Church for mission—depends on a recovery of the actual teaching of the liturgical constitution on the Christocentric and eschatological nature of the Church's public worship.

13: Design for a Christocentric Humanism

1. Part Two of *Gaudium et Spes* was originally a "supplement," rather than an integral part of the text; even this supplement was criticized by the archbishop of Westminster, John Carmel Heenan, who warned that the Council would become a "laughingstock in the eyes of the world" if, after spending so much time on serious theological matters, it "now rushed breathlessly through a debate on world hunger, nuclear war, and family life." After the supplement was incorporated into the text, Cardinal Bea criticized its shoddy ("frequently unintelligible") Latin. Cardinals Franz König and Giuseppe Siri (two men at opposite poles of Catholic opinion) thought that the draft prepared during the 1965 intersession was deficient for omitting references to "sin, the truth of the Cross, the need for repentance, and the hope of resurrection with Christ." The lack of these themes, they said, could suggest that the Church was "promising a paradise on earth and a solution to all problems, something that cannot be realized save in the world to come." (Wiltgen, *The Inside Story of Vatican II*, 316–317, 384–385.) As will be seen, many of these concerns were addressed in Part One of *Gaudium et Spes* before the pastoral constitution was adopted.

Nonetheless, the question of the prudence of a conciliar text dealing with immediate issues of public policy remained.

2. See Nichols, *Conciliar Octet*, 147–158, for a concise summary of a very complicated process; much more detail is available in Gilles Routhier, "Schema XIII," in Alberigo and Komonchak, *History of Vatican II*, 5:122–176, and Peter Hünermann, "Final Work on *Gaudium et Spes*," in the same work, 386–426. See also George Weigel, "Rescuing *Gaudium et Spes*: The New Humanism of John Paul II," *Nova et Vetera* (English edition) 8, no. 2 (2019): 251–267.

3. Nichols, *Conciliar Octet*, 152–153.

4. J. Brian Benestad, "Doctrinal Perspectives on the Church in the Modern World," in Lamb and Levering, *Vatican II: Renewal Within Tradition*, 148 (emphasis in original).

5. On these points, see *Gaudium et Spes*, 12–18.

6. *Gaudium et Spes*, 19, 18.

7. *Gaudium et Spes*, 22 (emphasis added).

8. *Gaudium et Spes*, 24 (emphasis added).

9. See *Gaudium et Spes*, 32.

10. *Gaudium et Spes*, 36.

11. *Gaudium et Spes*, 34.

12. See *Gaudium et Spes*, 37.

13. *Gaudium et Spes*, 29.

14. *Gaudium et Spes*, 29.

15. Benestad, "Doctrinal Perspectives on the Church in the Modern World," 156, citing *Gaudium et Spes*, 25; *Gaudium et Spes*, 26.

16. Benestad, "Doctrinal Perspectives on the Church in the Modern World," 157.

17. *Gaudium et Spes*, 27.

18. *Gaudium et Spes*, 43.

19. *Gaudium et Spes*, 42.

20. *Gaudium et Spes*, 45.

21. On these points, see Matthew Levering, "Pastoral Perspectives on the Church in the Modern World," in Lamb and Levering, *Vatican II: Renewal Within Tradition*, 176. Catholic pacifist organizations and individuals lobbied heavily for a conciliar endorsement of the pacifist moral option and its corollary of nonviolent methods of self-defense; on this point and others in Vatican II's discussion of war and peace, see George Weigel, Tranquillitas Ordinis: *The Present Failure and Future Promise of U.S. Catholic Thought on War and Peace* (New York: Oxford University Press, 1987), 74–106.

22. See Nicholas Eberstadt, "Five Myths About the World's Population," *Washington Post*, November 4, 2011: www.washingtonpost.com/opinions

/five-myths-about-the-worlds-population/2011/10/26/gIQArjSWmM_story
.html.

23. See Paul Collier, *The Bottom Billion: Why the Poorest Countries Are Failing and What Can Be Done About It* (New York: Oxford University Press, 2008).

24. See George Weigel, *Practicing Catholic: Essays Historical, Literary, Sporting, and Elegiac* (New York: Crossroad, 2012), 21–23; Weigel, "Gaia, False Gods, and Public Policy," *First Things*, May 5, 2021: www.firstthings.com/web-exclusives/2021/05/gaia-false-gods-and-public-policy.

25. On the origin of this now familiar phrase, see Richard John Neuhaus, *The Naked Public Square: Religion and Democracy in America* (Grand Rapids, MI: Eerdmans, 1984).

26. For more on the lacunae in *Gaudium et Spes*, see Weigel, "Rescuing *Gaudium et Spes*," and Weigel, *The Irony of Modern Catholic History*, 155–166.

27. *Gaudium et Spes*, 55, as translated in Levering, "Pastoral Perspectives on the Church in the Modern World," 169.

28. See Nichols, *Conciliar Octet*, 154–156.

14: Truth, Liberty, and the Limits of State Power

1. For more on Archbishop Lefebvre's dissent, see Weigel, *Witness to Hope*, 562–564. See also Brian W. Harrison, OS, "Marcel Lefebvre: Signatory to *Dignitatis Humanae*," *Catholic Culture*, n.d.: www.catholicculture.org/culture/library/view.cfm?recnum=857.

2. F. Russell Hittinger, "The Declaration on Religious Liberty, *Dignitatis Humanae*," in Lamb and Levering, *Vatican II: Renewal Within Tradition*, 359–360.

3. Hittinger, "The Declaration on Religious Liberty," 360.

4. See Hittinger, "The Declaration on Religious Liberty," 360–361.

5. See Anthony Rhodes, *The Vatican in the Age of the Dictators, 1922–1945* (New York: Holt, Rinehart and Winston, 1973), and Frank J. Coppa, ed., *Controversial Concordats: The Vatican's Relations with Napoleon, Mussolini, and Hitler* (Washington, DC: Catholic University of America Press, 1999).

6. Hittinger, "The Declaration on Religious Liberty," 361–362.

7. See George Weigel, *The Final Revolution: The Resistance Church and the Collapse of Communism* (New York: Oxford University Press, 1992), and Alexander Grúňová, ed., *NKVD/KGB Activities and Its Cooperation with Other Secret Services in Central and Eastern Europe, 1945–1989* (Bratislava, Slovakia: Nation's Memory Institute, 2008).

8. See Pius XI, *Quadragesimo Anno*.

9. Nichols, *Conciliar Octet*, 131.

10. On Blondel, Maritain, and Murray, see Weigel, *The Irony of Modern Catholic History*, 118–119, 123, 126–127.

11. On this point, see Nichols, *Conciliar Octet*, 135.

12. See Nichols, *Conciliar Octet*, 131–132.

13. See Leo XIII, *Longinqua Oceani*: www.vatican.va/content/leo-xiii/en/encyclicals/documents/hf_l-xiii_enc_06011895_longinqua.html.

14. On this history, see Nichols, *Conciliar Octet*, 129–135. The struggle to finalize the text during the Council's fourth period is summarized in Gilles Routhier, "Finishing the Work Begun: The Trying Experience of the Fourth Period," in Alberigo and Komonchak, *History of Vatican II*, 5:63–122. Routhier cites 249 negative votes against 1,967 in favor at the end of the debate on *Dignitatis Humanae*. In *The Fourth Session* (New York: Farrar, Straus & Giroux, 1966), "Xavier Rynne" gives the final vote on *Dignitatis Humanae* at the Council's concluding public session on December 7, 1965, as 2,308 in favor and 70 opposed (p. 250). The discrepancy between these two vote counts likely has to do with the number of bishops attending the two sessions.

15. *Dignitatis Humanae*, 1.

16. *Dignitatis Humanae*, 1.

17. *Dignitatis Humanae*, 2.

18. *Dignitatis Humanae*, 6. Similar strictures would apply, of course, to twenty-first-century Islamist regimes.

19. *Dignitatis Humanae*, 2.

20. *Gaudium et Spes*, 16.

21. *Dignitatis Humanae*, 13. The most important practical consequence of the declaration's teaching on the *libertas ecclesiae* would be drawn out in the Council's decree on the episcopate in the life of the Church, where Vatican II declared that, in the future, no concessions were to be made to state authorities in the nomination of bishops—a teaching later embodied in the Church's Code of Canon Law. More will be said on this later.

22. Pius XI, *Quas Primas*: www.vatican.va/content/pius-xi/en/encyclicals/documents/hf_p-xi_enc_11121925_quas-primas.html.

23. On these points, see Hittinger, "The Declaration on Religious Liberty," 366. Hittinger also notes that the *Catechism*, in teaching that the social kingship of Christ is advanced through the lay mission to evangelize culture and society, cited not only *Dignitatis Humanae*, but also Leo XIII's *Immortale Dei* and Pius XI's *Quas Primas*, thereby underscoring the continuities between the Council's teaching and Catholic tradition.

24. Edmund Waldstein, OCist, a prominent exponent of the new Catholic integralism, defines it succinctly in the movement's online

journal. See his "Integralism in Three Sentences," *The Josias*, October 17, 2016: http://thejosias.com/2016/10/17/integralism-in-three-sentences. For a more extensive explication of the integralist position, see Thomas Crean, OP, and Alan Fimister, *Integralism: A Manual of Political Philosophy* (Neunkirchen-Seelscheid, Germany: Editiones Scholasticae, 2020). Many integralists reject the Second Vatican Council as ill conceived (at least), and all find *Dignitatis Humanae* deplorable (at best). In *Conciliar Octet*, 129, Aidan Nichols usefully points out that twenty-first-century appeals to the "social kingship of Christ" in defense of a new Catholic integralism echo the schismatic Archbishop Marcel Lefebvre's critique of *Dignitatis Humanae*.

15: Witnesses and Missionaries

1. *Christus Dominus*, 1.
2. *Christus Dominus*, 11.
3. *Christus Dominus*, 15.
4. *Christus Dominus*, 17.
5. Brian Ferme, "The Decree on the Bishops' Pastoral Office in the Church, *Christus Dominus*," in Lamb and Levering, *Vatican II: Renewal Within Tradition*, 199, with reference to *Christus Dominus*, 38.
6. Neither *Lumen Gentium* nor *Christus Dominus* anticipated the vast expansion of ecclesiastical bureaucracy that followed the Second Vatican Council in the developed world, at both the national and diocesan levels. In too many cases, post–Vatican II ecclesiastical bureaucracy became an obstacle to the clarity of Catholic teaching, to the recovery of the Catholic identity of Catholic institutions in which that identity had become attenuated (or worse), and to the effectiveness of the Church's public witness. Local Catholic bureaucracies also tend to absorb far more of the time and energy of the Church's bishops than is appropriate. National conferences of bishops seem to have smothered the instinct for "fraternal correction" among bishops that was a feature of patristic Christianity—a diminishment of mutual responsibility that is not what the Council's teaching on episcopal collegiality intended. A reassessment of this phenomenon of ecclesiastical bureaucratization, the evangelically enervating effects of which are most apparent in Germany, is long overdue.
7. *Christus Dominus*, 21. The mandate that a bishop must offer the pope his resignation at age seventy-five would come later, in Pope Paul VI's 1966 apostolic letter *Ecclesiae Sanctae*. Canon 401 of the 1983 Code of Canon Law puts the matter somewhat more gently, stating that a bishop, on reaching his seventy-fifth birthday, "is requested to offer" his resignation to the pope. Irrespective of the language, the "new normal" is episcopal

resignation at seventy-five, although the pope can decline to accept the resignation for whatever period of time he chooses.

8. *Christus Dominus*, 20. This "desire" was then given legal form by Canon 377.5 of the 1983 Code of Canon Law—which would seem to make the arrangements the Vatican reached with the People's Republic of China in 2018 (and reaffirmed in 2020) illegal under Church law.

9. Guy Mansini, OSB, and Lawrence J. Welch, "The Decree on the Ministry and Life of Priests, *Presbyterorum Ordinis*," in Lamb and Levering, *Vatican II: Renewal Within Tradition*, 205.

10. Mansini and Welch, "The Decree on the Ministry and Life of Priests," 207.

11. Cited in Mansini and Welch, "The Decree on the Ministry and Life of Priests," 208.

12. See *Presbyterorum Ordinis*, 2.

13. *Presbyterorum Ordinis*, 5.

14. *Presbyterorum Ordinis*, 2.

15. *Presbyterorum Ordinis*, 12.

16. On this point, see Mansini and Welch, "The Decree on the Ministry and Life of Priests," 221. See also Robert P. Imbelli, "The Identity and Ministry of the Priest in Light of Vatican II: The Promise and Challenge of *Presbyterorum Ordinis*," *Josephinum Journal of Theology* 22 (2015): 23–43.

17. Anthony A. Akinwale, OP, "The Decree on Priestly Formation, *Optatam Totius*," in Lamb and Levering, *Vatican II: Renewal Within Tradition*, 246.

18. Cited in Akinwale, "The Decree on Priestly Formation," 234.

19. *Optatam Totius*, 4.

20. Akinwale, "The Decree on Priestly Formation," 237.

21. *Optatam Totius*, 8.

22. Akinwale, "The Decree on Priestly Formation," 239.

23. *Optatam Totius*, 8.

24. *Optatam Totius*, 16.

25. *Optatam Totius*, 14–15.

26. *Optatam Totius*, 15.

27. *Optatam Totius*, 16.

28. *Optatam Totius*, 16.

29. *Optatam Totius*, 9–21.

30. Akinwale, "The Decree on Priestly Formation," 247.

31. M. Prudence Allen, RSM, and M. Judith O'Brien, RSM, "The Decree on the Appropriate Renewal of Religious Life, *Perfectae Caritatis*," in Lamb and Levering, *Vatican II: Renewal Within Tradition*, 251, citing *Lumen Gentium*, 47 (emphasis added).

32. *Perfectae Caritatis*, 2.

33. *Perfectae Caritatis*, 1.

34. See *Perfectae Caritatis*, 8.

35. *Lumen Gentium*, 44.

36. *Perfectae Caritatis*, 17.

37. *Perfectae Caritatis*, 1.

38. Allen and O'Brien, "The Decree on the Appropriate Renewal of Religious Life," 258; *Perfectae Caritatis*, 12.

39. *Perfectae Caritatis*, 12.

40. Allen and O'Brien, "The Decree on the Appropriate Renewal of Religious Life," 261; *Perfectae Caritatis*, 13.

41. *Perfectae Caritatis*, 14.

42. See *Perfectae Caritatis*, 15.

43. *Perfectae Caritatis*, 15.

44. *Perfectae Caritatis*, 25.

45. *Apostolicam Actuositatem*, 1.

46. *Apostolican Actuositatem*, 3.

47. Robert W. Oliver, BH, "The Decree on the Apostolate of the Laity, *Apostolicam Actuositatem*," in Lamb and Levering, *Vatican II: Renewal Within Tradition*, 276.

48. Oliver, "The Decree on the Apostolate of the Laity," 273, citing *Apostolicam Actuositatem*, 3–4.

49. *Apostolicam Actuositatem*, 5.

50. *Apostolicam Actuositatem*, 33.

51. Joseph Ratzinger, *Theological Highlights of Vatican II* (New York: Paulist Press, 1966), 179.

52. See Don J. Briel, "The Declaration on Christian Education, *Gravissimum Educationis*," in Lamb and Levering, *Vatican II: Renewal Within Tradition*, 386.

53. See Briel, "The Declaration on Christian Education," 393. This distinction was, of course, foundational in Newman's classic, *The Idea of a University*.

54. Briel, "The Declaration on Christian Education," 387, summarizing *Gravissimum Educationis*, 8.

55. *Gravissimum Educationis*, 3.

56. *Gravissimum Educationis*, 8.

57. On this point, see Briel, "The Declaration on Christian Education," 391, drawing on Ratzinger, *Theological Highlights of Vatican II*.

58. Briel, "The Declaration on Christian Education," 395.

59. *Gravissimum Educationis*, 10.

60. Stanley I. Stuber, "A Response," in Walter M. Abbott, SJ, ed., *The Documents of Vatican II* (New York: Guild Press, 1966), 333.

61. Richard John Neuhaus, "The Decree on the Instruments of Social Communication, *Inter Mirifica*," in Lamb and Levering, *Vatican II: Renewal Within Tradition*, 353.

62. Neuhaus, "The Decree on the Instruments of Social Communication," 353.

63. *Inter Mirifica*, 3.

64. *Inter Mirifica*, 5.

65. *Inter Mirifica*, 5.

66. *Inter Mirifica*, 9.

67. *Inter Mirifica*, 10.

68. *Inter Mirifica*, 3.

69. *Inter Mirifica*, 12.

70. See Irving Kristol, "Pornography, Obscenity, and the Case for Censorship," in *Reflections of a Neoconservative: Looking Back, Looking Ahead* (New York: Basic Books, 1983), 43–54.

71. On these points, see Francis Cardinal George, OMI, "The Decree on the Church's Missionary Activity, *Ad Gentes*," in Lamb and Levering, *Vatican II: Renewal Within Tradition*, 277–289. The quote from Guardini is taken from his book *The Church of the Lord* (Chicago: Regnery, 1966), 73.

72. On this point, see George, "The Decree on the Church's Missionary Activity," 292.

73. *Ad Gentes*, 8.

74. George, "The Decree on the Church's Missionary Activity," 286.

75. *Ad Gentes*, 6, 5.

76. *Ad Gentes*, 8.

77. George, "The Decree on the Church's Missionary Activity," 295.

78. George, "The Decree on the Church's Missionary Activity," 299.

79. *Ad Gentes*, 11.

80. *Ad Gentes*, 13.

16: From Plurality to Pluralism

1. Berger describes modernity in these terms in an unpublished paper, "The Two Pluralisms: Toward a New Paradigm on Modernity and Religion," which set the framework for an academic conference held at Boston University on April 10–12, 2015.

2. Murray was writing about the situation in the United States, but his distinction between "plurality" and "pluralism" has a far wider application. See John Courtney Murray, SJ, *We Hold These Truths: Catholic Reflections on the American Proposition* (Garden City, NY: Image Books, 1964).

3. For an overview of this complex ecclesiastical tapestry, see Ronald G. Roberson, CSP, *The Eastern Christian Churches: A Brief Survey*, fifth edition (Rome: Edizioni Orientalia Christiana, 1995). See also Khaled Anatolios, "The Decree on the Eastern Catholic Churches, *Orientalium Ecclesiarum*," in Lamb and Levering, *Vatican II: Renewal Within Tradition*, 349n1.

4. See Nichols, *Conciliar Octet*, 63.

5. *Orientalium Ecclesiarum*, 5.

6. On December 7, 1965, the day before Vatican II solemnly closed, Pope Paul VI and Ecumenical Patriarch Athenagoras of Constantinople mutually lifted the excommunications that had marked a decisive moment in 1054 in the breach between Latin and Byzantine Christianity.

7. *Orientalium Ecclesiarum*, 7–11.

8. On this point, see Nichols, *Conciliar Octet*, 69–71. See Wiltgen, *The Inside Story of Vatican II*, 297–303, for the controversy over how the Eastern patriarchs were to be seated at the Council.

9. Khaled Anatolios, "The Decree on the Eastern Catholic Churches," 348.

10. On these points, see Nichols, *Conciliar Octet*, 77.

11. For an overview of Bea's work, see Jerome-Michael Vereb, *"Because He Was a German!" Cardinal Bea and the Origins of Roman Catholic Engagement in the Ecumenical Movement* (Grand Rapids, MI: Eerdmans, 2006).

12. *Unitatis Redintegratio*, 1.

13. See *Unitatis Redintegratio*, 2; see also Nichols, *Conciliar Octet*, 82.

14. *Unitatis Redintegratio*, 3.

15. On this point, see Nichols, *Conciliar Octet*, 85.

16. *Unitatis Redintegratio*, 11.

17. Misinterpretations of this teaching about the hierarchy of truths within the deposit of faith have played a significant role in the evolution of Liquid Catholicism in the post-conciliar Church. As Aidan Nichols writes, "The claim [in article 11 of *Unitatis Redintegratio*] that in Catholic teaching there is a 'hierarchy of truths' was sadly abused in the post-conciliar period by those who believed it licensed the marginalization of a number of doctrines," often in response to cultural pressures. (Nichols, *Conciliar Octet*, 88–89.) Thus the Church must always be reminded that the truths the Church teaches are true, although some are more fundamental to the deposit of faith than others. As Cardinal Franz König of Vienna put it during the Council, "Without any doubt all revealed truths must be held with the same divine faith, but their importance and 'weight' differ in reason of their link with the history of salvation and the mystery of Christ." (For more on the "hierarchy of truths" and how it can be misunderstood, see Charles Morerod, OP, "The Decree on Ecumenism, *Unitatis Redintegratio*," in Lamb

and Levering, *Vatican II: Renewal Within Tradition*, 322–324, from which the König quote is taken.)

18. *Unitatis Redintegratio*, 17. It is hard to imagine a similarly generous statement issuing in the twenty-first century from the monks of Mt. Athos or the Russian Orthodox patriarchate of Moscow.

19. *Unitatis Redintegratio*, 21, 22.

20. On the tortured history of the declaration, see Nichols, *Conciliar Octet*, 96–106; Arthur Kennedy, "The Declaration on the Relationship of the Church to Non-Christian Religions, *Nostra Aetate*," in Lamb and Levering, *Vatican II: Renewal Within Tradition*, 398–399; and Mauro Velati, "Completing the Conciliar Agenda," in Alberigo and Komonchak, *History of Vatican II*, 5:211–221.

21. *Nostra Aetate*, 2.

22. Kennedy, "The Declaration on the Relationship of the Church to Non-Christian Religions," 398.

23. Nichols, *Conciliar Octet*, 108. On the theological infelicity of the notion of "three Abrahamic faiths," see also George Weigel, *Faith, Reason, and the War Against Jihadism: A Call to Action* (New York: Doubleday, 2007), 17–34. Nichols also notes that *Nostra Aetate* deliberately and strikingly declined to affirm a link between Abraham and Islam (pp. 108–109).

24. *Nostra Aetate*, 4.

25. See Nichols, *Conciliar Octet*, 110. For more on the declaration's development of a theology of Jewish-Catholic relations, see Kennedy, "The Declaration on the Relationship of the Church to Non-Christian Religions," 400–404.

PART III: THE KEYS TO VATICAN II

17: Jacques Maritain's Lament

1. Cited in Jean-Luc Barré, *Jacques and Raïssa Maritain: Beggars for Heaven* (Notre Dame, IN: University of Notre Dame Press, 2005), 426.

2. See Barré, *Jacques and Raïssa Maritain*, 419ff.

3. See "Address of Pope Paul VI During the Last General Meeting of the Second Vatican Council," December 7, 1965: www.vatican.va/content /paul-vi/en/speeches/1965/documents/hf_p-vi_spe_19651207_epilogo -concilio.html.

4. Jacques Maritain, *The Peasant of the Garonne: An Old Layman Questions Himself About the Present Time* (New York: Holt, Rinehart and Winston, 1968), 1–7, 53–56 (emphases in original).

5. Cited in Barré, *Jacques and Raïssa Maritain*, 434.

18: The Council Without Keys

1. St. Basil, "On the Holy Spirit," chapter 30, available at New Advent: www.newadvent.org/fathers/3203.htm.

2. Joseph Carola, SJ, "*Aggiornamento* Rooted in *Ressourcement*: Concluding Remarks for a Patristic Synthesis of Theology," May 5, 2021, author's personal copy.

3. See Weigel, *The Irony of Modern Catholic History*, 186–190.

4. On this point, see Nichols, *Conciliar Octet*, 151–156.

5. As suggested below, this fruitful interaction is particularly evident in John Paul II's 1993 encyclical *Veritatis Splendor*. A similar disagreement between those promoting a biblical- and patristics-based renewal of theology and the Church and those defending a form of Scholasticism took place during the turbulent decades before the Council of Trent. See Jedin, *A History of the Council of Trent*, 1:158–159.

6. For the precise notion of a "paradigm shift," a term often misused in twenty-first-century Catholicism, see Thomas S. Kuhn, *The Structure of Scientific Revolutions*, second edition, enlarged (Chicago: University of Chicago Press, 1970).

7. Cited in Matthew Levering, *An Introduction to Vatican II as an Ongoing Theological Event* (Washington, DC: Catholic University of America Press, 2017), 1.

8. On these procedural changes, see Wiltgen, *The Inside Story of Vatican II*, 111–115.

9. Author's interview with Cardinal Franz König, December 11, 1997.

10. On this point, and with specific reference to the exodus from consecrated religious life among women, see Ann Carey, *Sisters in Crisis: The Tragic Unraveling of Women's Religious Communities* (Huntington, IN: Our Sunday Visitor Press, 1997).

11. Nichols, *Conciliar Octet*, 163. In the documents of Vatican II, the teaching of Pope Pius XII is cited more frequently than any other source except for the Bible, an important statistical refutation of the claim that the Council represented a break with Catholic tradition.

12. Cited in Seewald, *Benedict XVI*, 450–451.

13. See Paul VI, *Evangelii Nuntiandi*: www.vatican.va/content/paul-vi/en/apost_exhortations/documents/hf_p-vi_exh_19751208_evangelii-nuntiandi.html.

14. Lucas Moreira Neves, OP, in *L'Osservatore Romano*, January 17, 2001.

15. See Paul VI, *Evangelii Nuntiandi*, 2. The Pope finished his apostolic exhortation with this striking call to the Church of the future: "Let us therefore preserve our fervor of spirit. Let us preserve the delightful and comfort-

ing joy of evangelizing, even when it is in tears that we must sow. May it mean for us—as it did for John the Baptist, for Peter and Paul, for the other apostles and for a multitude of splendid evangelizers all through the Church's history—an interior enthusiasm that nobody and nothing can quench. May it be the great joy of our consecrated lives. And may the world of our time, which is searching, sometimes with anguish, sometimes with hope, be enabled to receive the Good News not from evangelizers who are dejected, discouraged, impatient or anxious, but from ministers of the Gospel whose lives glow with fervor, who have first received the joy of Christ, and who are willing to risk their lives so that the kingdom may be proclaimed and the Church established in the midst of the world" (*Evangelii Nuntiandi*, 80).

16. For an instructive interview with Cardinal Siri, which took place between the Council's first and second periods and in which the cardinal said that his hope for the Council was that it would quickly "come to the completion of its work," see Walter M. Abbott, SJ, *Twelve Council Fathers* (New York: Macmillan, 1963), 55–60, especially 59. Louis Bouyer comments on Cardinal Lercaro's susceptibility to progressive Catholic manipulations in *Memoirs*, 255–256.

17. See Weigel, *The Irony of Modern Catholic History*, 177. See also Weigel, *The Courage To Be Catholic* (New York: Basic Books, 2002), 68–72, on the "Truce of 1968" and its effects on doctrinal, moral, and disciplinary disorder in the Church in the United States—and likely elsewhere.

18. Avery Cardinal Dulles, SJ, "Pope Benedict XVI: Interpreter of Vatican II," in *Church and Society: The Lawrence J. McGinley Lectures, 1988–2007* (New York: Fordham University Press, 2008), 472.

19: Keys to the Council: John Paul II

1. On Wojtyła and Ratzinger at the first conclave of 1978, see Weigel, *Witness to Hope*, 243–244.

2. Taylor Marshall's *Infiltration*, previously referenced, is a prime example of such fevered conspiracy-theorizing.

3. See Karol Wojtyła, *Sources of Renewal: The Implementation of Vatican II* (San Francisco: Harper & Row, 1979). Wojtyła's conciliar *vademecum* was first published in Poland in 1972. The entire process of conciliar implementation in Kraków is described in *Il Sinodo Pastorale dell'Archidiocesi di Cracovia* (Rome: Libreria Editrice Vaticana, 1985), a translation of the original Polish record of the process, *Duszpasterski Synod Archidiecezji Krakowskiej*, published in two volumes in 1985. Wojtyła's "synodal process" for the implementation of Vatican II thus antedated the twenty-first-century debate over synodality in the Church by four decades.

4. Weigel, *Witness to Hope*, 266–267.

5. "Editor's Introduction" to *Redemptor Hominis*, in John Paul II, *The Encyclicals of John Paul II*, ed. J. Michael Miller, CSB (Huntington, IN: Our Sunday Visitor, 2001), 35.

6. For a summary of *Redemptor Hominis*, see Weigel, *Witness to Hope*, 287–290; for a summary of *Dives in Misericordia*, see *Witness to Hope*, 386–388; for a summary of *Dominum et Vivificantem*, see *Witness to Hope*, 516–518. The full texts of the encyclicals and more extended summaries of their teaching may be found in John Paul II, *The Encyclicals of John Paul II*.

7. The first sixteen of these letters are anthologized in John Paul II, *Letters to My Brother Priests (Holy Thursday 1979–1994)*, second edition, ed. James P. Socias (Princeton, NJ: Scepter Publishers, 1994).

Breakdowns of ecclesiastical discipline always have grave effects on the Church's evangelical and missionary vitality. This lesson was driven home in the most shocking and painful way by revelations of the clerical sexual abuse that peaked in the years that immediately followed the Council.

The clerical sexual abuse crisis that came to light in the first years of the twenty-first century cannot be blamed on the Second Vatican Council. Revelations of clerical sexual abuse in Ireland, Québec, and the United States that antedated the Council by decades suggest that a serious analysis of this crisis cannot be driven by the fallacy of *post Concilium ergo propter Concilium*. The abuse crisis began before the Council.

Nonetheless, the breakdown of discipline in the post-conciliar Church accelerated and intensified the crisis. This was particularly true of the breakdown of doctrinal clarity and behavioral discipline in seminaries. There, a culture of dissent created by theologians in the wake of the Council (and especially after the 1968 encyclical *Humanae Vitae*) contributed to an atmosphere in which a rejection of Church teaching facilitated a rejection of Catholic behavioral standards, creating situations in which it was the orthodox and the well behaved who were often considered dubious candidates for the priesthood. The failures of bishops to get to grips with dissenting clergy who rejected Church teaching, liturgical norms, and Christian moral standards, coupled with a tendency on the part of post-conciliar bishops to perceive deviant behavior through the therapeutic prism of psychology rather than the theological prism of right and wrong, were major contributing factors in the evolution of a clerical subculture that protected abusers. Vatican laxity in disciplining dissenting theologians and clergy in the aftermath of *Humanae Vitae* also played a role in weakening bishops' resolve and reducing bishops' disciplinary options. In the U.S. case, the spike in incidences of clerical sexual abuse that followed the Council only began to abate when John Paul II's decades-long efforts to reform the priesthood and seminary formation according to the teaching of Vatican II began to take hold. (On these points, see Weigel, *The Courage To Be Catholic*, 57–87.)

8. *Ecclesia in Europa* can also be read as a kind of report card on the progress (or lack thereof) in building the free and virtuous society throughout the post–Cold War West, measured by the criteria of authentic social, cultural, political, and economic development identified in the 1991 encyclical *Centesimus Annus*.

9. For summaries of the key themes in these encyclicals and many of the apostolic exhortations, see Weigel, *Witness to Hope* and *The End and the Beginning*; John Paul II, *The Encyclicals of John Paul II*; and John Paul II, *The Post-Synodal Apostolic Exhortations of John Paul II*, ed. J. Michael Miller, CSB (Huntington, IN: Our Sunday Visitor, 1998). The apostolic exhortations concluding the pre–Great Jubilee continental synods may be found at www.vatican.va.

10. *Sacrosanctum Concilium*, 23.

11. Citations are from John Paul II, *Ecclesia de Eucharistia*: www.vatican
.va/content/john-paul-ii/en/encyclicals/documents/hf_jp-ii_enc_20030417_
eccl-de-euch.html, 1–10.

12. See Congregation for Divine Worship and the Discipline of the Sacraments, *Liturgiam Authenticam*: www.vatican.va/roman_curia
/congregations/ccdds/documents/rc_con_ccdds_doc_20010507_liturgiam
-authenticam_en.html; *Redemptionis Sacramentum*: www.vatican.va/roman
_curia/congregations/ccdds/documents/rc_con_ccdds_doc_20040423
_redemptionis-sacramentum_en.html.

13. See Weigel, *The End and the Beginning*, 308–309.

14. For text, summary, and commentary on *Reconciliatio et Paenitentia*, see John Paul II, *The Post-Synodal Apostolic Exhortations of John Paul II*, 234–330.

15. See Weigel, *Witness to Hope*, 419–421. See also Deborah Savage, *The Subjective Dimension of Human Work: The Conversion of the Acting Person According to Karol Wojtyła / John Paul II and Bernard Lonergan* (New York: Peter Lang Publishing, 2008).

16. See Weigel, *Witness to Hope*, 577–561.

17. See Weigel, *Witness to Hope*, 612–619. For further commentary on the encyclical, see George Weigel, ed., *A New Worldly Order: John Paul II and Human Freedom* (Washington, DC: Ethics and Public Policy Center, 1992).

18. See Weigel, *Witness to Hope*, 756–760.

19. The texts of *Salvifici Doloris* (February 11, 1984), *Familiaris Consortio* (November 22, 1981), and *Mulieris Dignitatem* (August 15, 1988) are available at the Vatican website and also discussed in Weigel, *Witness to Hope*, 475, 385–386, and 577–581. (See www.vatican.va/content/john
-paul-ii/en/apost_letters/1984/documents/hf_jp-ii_apl_11021984_salvifici
-doloris.html; www.vatican.va/content/john-paul-ii/en/apost_exhortations
/documents/hf_jp-ii_exh_19811122_familiaris-consortio.html; and www
.vatican.va/content/john-paul-ii/en/apost_letters/1988/documents/hf

_jp-ii_apl_19880815_mulieris-dignitatem.html.) See John Paul II, *Man and Woman He Created Them: A Theology of the Body*, translation, introduction, and index by Michael Waldstein (Boston: Pauline Books and Media, 2006), for the texts of the Theology of the Body and a fine introduction to John Paul II's thought by Waldstein. Jarosław Kupczak, OP, provides an excellent commentary on the entirety of the Theology of the Body in *Gift & Communion: John Paul II's Theology of the Body* (Washington, DC: Catholic University of America Press, 2014). The Theology of the Body texts are summarized in Weigel, *Witness to Hope*, 333–343.

20. On the 1979 papal U.N. address, see Weigel, *Witness to Hope*, 327–328, 346–350. On the 1995 U.N. address, see Weigel, *Witness to Hope*, 774–781.

21. For the text and a summary of *Veritatis Splendor*, see John Paul II, *The Encyclicals of John Paul II*, 563–662. See also Reinhard Hütter and Theodore Dieter, eds., *Ecumenical Ventures in Ethics: Protestants Engage Pope John Paul II's Moral Encyclicals* (Grand Rapids, MI: Eerdmans, 1998), and J. A. DiNoia, OP, and Romanus Cessario, OP, eds., *Veritatis Splendor and the Renewal of Moral Theology* (Princeton, NJ: Scepter Publishers, 1999).

22. On *Ut Unum Sint*, see John Paul II, *The Encyclicals of John Paul II*, 763–780; Weigel, *Witness to Hope*, 760–766.

23. The text of *Catechesi Tradendae* is available at www.vatican.va /content/john-paul-ii/en/apost_exhortations/documents/hf_jp-ii_exh _16101979_catechesi-tradendae.html.

24. See Weigel, *Witness to Hope*, 625–627.

25. On *Redemptoris Missio*, see John Paul II, *The Encyclicals of John Paul II*, 421–434; see also Weigel, *Witness to Hope*, 633–635.

26. John Paul II, *Incarnationis Mysterium*: www.vatican.va/jubilee _2000/docs/documents/hf_jp-ii_doc_30111998_bolla-jubilee_en.html, 2 (emphasis in original).

27. On John Paul II's pilgrimage to the Holy Land, see Weigel, *The End and the Beginning*, 218–225. On *Novo Millennio Ineunte*, see Weigel, *The End and the Beginning*, 252–260. Emphases in citations from the apostolic letter are in the original.

20: Keys to the Council: Benedict XVI

1. On the Genoa speech, see Seewald, *Benedict XVI*, 356ff.

2. Seewald, *Benedict XVI*, 462.

3. Henri de Lubac, SJ, *Vatican Council Notebooks*, volume two (San Francisco: Ignatius Press, 2016), 195.

4. De Lubac, *Vatican Council Notebooks*, 2:354–355.

5. See Weigel, *Witness to Hope*, 284–286.

6. Congregation for the Doctrine of the Faith, *Instruction on Christian Freedom and Liberation*: www.vatican.va/roman_curia/congregations/cfaith /documents/rc_con_cfaith_doc_19860322_freedom-liberation_en.html, 3.

7. On the two Instructions on Christian liberation, see Weigel, *Witness to Hope*, 457–459.

8. Congregation for the Doctrine of the Faith, *Dominus Iesus*: www .vatican.va/roman_curia/congregations/cfaith/documents/rc_con_cfaith _doc_20000806_dominus-iesus_en.html.

9. On these points, see Richard John Neuhaus, "To Say Jesus Is Lord," *First Things*, November 2000: www.firstthings.com/article/2000/11/to-say -jesus-is-lord.

10. The deficient Christologies of Jacques Dupuis, SJ; Roger Haight, SJ; and Anthony DeMello, SJ, each of which seemed (if in different ways) to diminish the unique salvific role of Jesus Christ, were among the post-conciliar theological distortions that *Dominus Iesus* sought to correct. That all three men were Jesuits highlighted a continuing problem in the post-conciliar Church: the transformation of the prestigious Society of Jesus from a bulwark of orthodoxy to a community notable for its number of prominent theological dissidents. For an analysis of John Paul II's failed attempt to address this issue, see Weigel, *Witness to Hope*, 425–430, 468–470.

11. Joseph Ratzinger, *Jesus of Nazareth: From the Baptism in the Jordan to the Transfiguration* (New York: Doubleday, 2007), xv–xviii. See also Ratzinger, *Jesus of Nazareth: Holy Week—From the Entrance into Jerusalem to the Resurrection* (San Francisco: Ignatius Press, 2011), and Ratzinger, *Jesus of Nazareth: The Infancy Narratives* (New York: Image, 2012).

12. Benedict XVI, *Sacramentum Caritatis*: www.vatican.va/content /benedict-xvi/en/apost_exhortations/documents/hf_ben-xvi_exh_20070222 _sacramentum-caritatis.html.

13. This and all subsequent quotations from Benedict XVI's address are from "Address of His Holiness Benedict XVI to the Roman Curia Offering Them His Christmas Greetings": www.vatican.va/content/benedict-xvi/en/speeches /2005/december/documents/hf_ben_xvi_spe_20051222_roman-curia.html.

21: The Master Key

1. Joseph Cardinal Ratzinger and Vittorio Messori, *The Ratzinger Report: An Exclusive Interview on the State of the Church* (San Francisco: Ignatius Press, 1985).

2. In this, the Synod was reaffirming the teaching of *Dei Verbum*, 2: "It pleased God, in his goodness and wisdom, to reveal himself and to make

known the mystery of his will. . . . His will was that men should have access to the Father, through Christ, the Word made flesh, in the Holy Spirit, and thus become sharers in the divine nature."

3. All quotations from Synod-1985's Final Report are from EWTN Global Catholic Network: www.ewtn.com/catholicism/library/final-report -of-the-1985-extraordinary-synod-2561.

4. John Paul II, *Fidei Depositum*, in *Catechism of the Catholic Church*, second edition (Vatican City: Libreria Editrice Vaticana, 1997), 2.

5. *Fidei Depositum*, 5.

6. On the development, content, and significance of the *Catechism of the Catholic Church*, see Weigel, *Witness to Hope*, 661–665.

22: Christ at the Center

1. Paul VI, *Perché la reforma non è una rottura*, cited in *L'Osservatore Romano: Vaticano II*, October 11, 2012, 80 (author's translation).

2. Jean Guitton, *Perché non possiamo non dirci filosofi*, cited in *L'Osservatore Romano: Vaticano II*, October 11, 2012, 34 (author's translation).

3. *Dei Verbum*, 19.

4. Ratzinger, *Principles of Catholic Theology*, 370.

5. Ratzinger, *Principles of Catholic Theology*, 370.

6. Ratzinger, *Principles of Catholic Theology*, 372.

7. Ratzinger, *Principles of Catholic Theology*, 373.

8. See "An Anthropological Solution," in O. Carter Snead, *What It Means to Be Human: The Case for the Body in Public Bioethics* (Cambridge, MA: Harvard University Press, 2020), for a brilliant summary of the new Gnosticism's deconstruction of the givens in the human condition. See also Carl E. Trueman, *The Rise and Triumph of the Modern Self: Cultural Amnesia, Expressive Individualism, and the Road to the Sexual Revolution* (Wheaton, IL: Crossway, 2020).

In addition to its effects on democratic civil society and politics, the new Gnosticism, expressed in the ideology of gender and the transgender movement, poses severe challenges to biblical religion. If a biological man can, by an act of will, "become" a woman, or vice versa, then both Judaism and Christianity teach destructive falsehoods about the human person.

9. Ratzinger, *Principles of Catholic Theology*, 391.

Index

Index

347

Index

Index

© PICTUREBILLY

GEORGE WEIGEL, one of the world's premier Catholic authors, is Distinguished Senior Fellow of Washington's Ethics and Public Policy Center, where he holds the William E. Simon Chair in Catholic Studies. The first volume of his biography of Pope John Paul II, *Witness to Hope*, was a *New York Times* bestseller, and his writing appears regularly in a variety of publications, including the *Wall Street Journal*. His weekly column, "The Catholic Difference," is syndicated to eighty-five newspapers and magazines in seven countries. A frequent guest on television and radio, he is also senior Vatican analyst for NBC News. He lives in North Bethesda, Maryland.